Re-Making Sound

Re-Making Sound

An Experiential Approach
to Sound Studies

**THOMAS PORCELLO AND
JUSTIN PATCH**

BLOOMSBURY ACADEMIC
NEW YORK · LONDON · OXFORD · NEW DELHI · SYDNEY

BLOOMSBURY ACADEMIC
Bloomsbury Publishing Inc
1385 Broadway, New York, NY 10018, USA
50 Bedford Square, London, WC1B 3DP, UK
29 Earlsfort Terrace, Dublin 2, Ireland

BLOOMSBURY, BLOOMSBURY ACADEMIC and the Diana logo are trademarks of
Bloomsbury Publishing Plc

First published in the United States of America 2022

Copyright © Thomas Porcello and Justin Patch, 2022

For legal purposes the Acknowledgments on p. xi constitute an extension
of this copyright page.

Cover design by Louise Dugdale
Cover image © Pablo Andrs Carvajal / EyeEm / Getty Images.

All rights reserved. No part of this publication may be reproduced or transmitted
in any form or by any means, electronic or mechanical, including photocopying,
recording, or any information storage or retrieval system, without prior permission
in writing from the publishers.

Bloomsbury Publishing Inc does not have any control over, or responsibility for,
any third-party websites referred to or in this book. All internet addresses given in this
book were correct at the time of going to press. The author and publisher regret any
inconvenience caused if addresses have changed or sites have ceased to exist,
but can accept no responsibility for any such changes.

Library of Congress Cataloging-in-Publication Data
Names: Porcello, Thomas, author. | Patch, Justin, author.
Title: Re-making sound : an experiential approach to sound studies / Thomas Porcello and
Justin Patch. Description: New York : Bloomsbury Academic, 2022. |
Includes bibliographical references and index. |
Summary: "The first authored textbook on sound studies; teaches students about sound
in society through readings about and exercises in media making
and sound editing"– Provided by publisher.
Identifiers: LCCN 2021046652 (print) | LCCN 2021046653 (ebook) |
ISBN 9781501354748 (hardback) | ISBN 9781501354731 (paperback) |
ISBN 9781501354755 (epub) | ISBN 9781501354762 (pdf) |
ISBN 9781501354779 (ebook other)
Subjects: LCSH: Sounds–Social aspects–Textbooks. |
Sound–Recording and reproducing–Textbooks.
Classification: LCC CB472 .P67 2022 (print) | LCC CB472 (ebook) |
DDC 909.82/5–dc23/eng/20211029
LC record available at https://lccn.loc.gov/2021046652
LC ebook record available at https://lccn.loc.gov/2021046653

ISBN: HB: 978-1-5013-5474-8
PB: 978-1-5013-5473-1
ePDF: 978-1-5013-5476-2
eBook: 978-1-5013-5475-5

Typeset by Newgen KnowledgeWorks Pvt. Ltd., Chennai, India
Printed and bound in the United States of America

To find out more about our authors and books visit www.bloomsbury.com
and sign up for our newsletters.

Contents

List of Figures vii
Preface ix
Acknowledgments xi

Introduction 1

1 Soundscape: Sound, Space, and Listening 19

2 Noise: From the Everyday to the Exceptional 41

3 Voice: Hearing and Ascribing Individual and Social Identity 65

4 Sound on the Page: Echoes and Resonances in Writing 91

5 Sound Design/Designing Sounds: Intentionally Crafted Sonic Worlds 121

6 Sound Art: What Is Sound Art? Debates and Examples 145

Concluding Project: Putting the Pieces Together through Audio Narratives 171

Author Biographies 179
Index 181

Figures

1   From David Weisner, *Mr. Wuffles.* 93
    Used by permission of the author
2   From David Weisner, *Mr. Wuffles.* 94
    Used by permission of the author
3   Screenshot from the ACLEW project 101
    Used by permission from Max Planck Institute
4   From Gareth Hinds, *Poe: Stories and Poems.* 114
    Used by permission of the author

Preface

Re-Making Sound provides six ways of conceptualizing sound and its connections to other social phenomena: soundscapes; noise; sound and semiotics of the voice; sound and/through/in text; sound design; and sound art. Concise presentations of research and theory from these different scholarly bodies lead to an accompanying exercise for each. These sound collection, editing, curating, and manipulation projects are meant to be a part of classroom activities, to foster experiential leaning, and to act as a tool for discussion and reflection. The choice to format the book in this way was made because we believe that experiential learning is essential for understanding the character, power, and potential of sound in social life. The assignments are designed to allow students to make and share digital sound projects, to learn basic digital audio manipulation, and to have the opportunity to apply theories and concepts about sound that deepen their knowledge beyond what reading alone provides.

The substantive chapters are designed to be modular and nonsequential so that instructors can use them in any order, or distribute them throughout a semester, in whatever sequence works best for their particular course design. The conclusion consists of a podcast exercise, which is cumulative of all six areas the book covers. The chapters contain multiple footnotes: some are simply citational or provide clarification, but many are designed to be used by the instructor (and students) as springboards into further reading and research, or into discussions of related areas of study, theory, or methods.

As we discuss in the introduction, this book is not an exhaustive overview of all areas of inquiry, methods of investigation, or disciplinary approaches to sound studies. We foreground topics and approaches from the humanistic social sciences, with examples that focus on music, language, voice, sound art, text, and soundscape. We do so because, in our opinion, these topics and approaches best open the doors to experiential learning without imposing a burden on students or instructors. And we do not dwell on methodological differences, as they might cloud the presentation of substantive issues. At the end of the introduction, however, we provide pointers to literature from science and technology studies, history, communications, and media studies that are integral to sound studies and that complement the literature and topics that we survey.

Sound studies is trans/multidisciplinary, and each instructor likely has a particular background, disciplinary approach (from within the humanities, arts, social sciences, or sciences), and goals for the specific course the book is assigned to. Thus, *Re-Making Sound* offers multiple points of entry, leaves space to integrate the experiential approach into instructors' own specific interests and specializations, and is easily supplemented by more in-depth excursions into either the subjects in the book or the readings on additional sound studies topics.

Acknowledgments

Thomas Porcello

I am deeply indebted to dialogues with students in multiple classes I've led since 2017: several iterations of Approaches to Media Studies at Vassar College; two sections of UC Berkeley's Music in American Culture and the University of San Francisco's Anthropology of Music, in which I guest-lectured on much of the material in the Sound Design chapter; and Vassar's advanced Anthropology/Media Studies Sound seminar. In Spring 2019, I taught a graduate seminar in UC Berkeley's Music Department entitled Sound Studies: Interdisciplinary Approaches to the Acoustic and Auditory. Its students—Jon Turner, Annie Greenwood, Cameron Johnson, Sarah Plovnick, Ryan Gourley, Andrew Harlan, and Andrew Snyder—were amazing conversational partners who pushed me to refine both my thinking about and my ways of framing the significance of sound studies.

I thank multiple interlocutors for honing, developing, probing, and contesting my thinking over the years: Steven Feld, Jocelyne Guilbault, David W. Samuels, Louise Meintjes, Ana Maria Ochoa Gautier, Aaron A. Fox, David Novak, Matt Sakakeeny, Joshua Pilzer, Carla Brunet, Kathleen Stewart, Greg Urban, and, of course, my co-author Justin Patch. Thanks to Niccolo Dante, who sat through long-winded musings about language, music, voice, and sound; to Nathaniel David and Maria Konovalenko for hours of spirited conversation during the Covid-19 lockdown; and, especially, to Carla Brunet for listening, pushing, believing, supporting, and always bringing out my best.

Justin Patch

There are many who deserve thanks and acknowledgment for their role in making this possible. A deep and heartfelt thank-you to my students and colleagues in Vassar's Media Studies program and Music department for indulging my curiosity and supporting my experiments. The content and exercises at the end of the chapters owe a great deal to their feedback, innovation, and encouragement. For everyone who endured my perseverations about this project I owe a debt of gratitude. I cannot replace the time lost, but I am grateful for your generosity and grace. Thank you to the numerous people in my life without whose love, encouragement, and support this would not have been thinkable.

A few special mentions are due. First to my co-author Tom Porcello, Tarik Elseewi, Eva Woods-Peiró, and Giovanna Borradori for getting me involved with the media studies program. Gratitude to Veit Erlmann who introduced me to sound studies, Katie Stewart who introduced me to experiential writing and research, and my UT cohort for being on-call sounding boards, readers, editors, and peer reviewers. And, as always, thank you to the Patch, Lee, Notch, and Tang clans for their love and support.

Introduction

In March 2020, across much of the world, the sounds of daily life—especially in urban areas—underwent a dramatic change as local, state, provincial, and national governments issued shelter-in-place orders in response to the Covid-19 outbreak. Nonessential businesses were required to close, affecting everything from the restaurant and bar industries, to retailers, cinemas, schools, and personal services such as hairdressers and nail salons, to how one shopped at a grocery store. Throughout much of Europe, North America, East Asia, Australia, and New Zealand, and somewhat later in Central and South America, India, and urban locales in Africa, people were allowed to leave home only for essential purposes such as buying groceries or seeking medical attention. Public transportation was drastically scaled back or closed altogether; airlines nearly shut down, leaving airports virtually empty; highways normally clogged with daily commuters were all but deserted, while gas prices plummeted; entertainment and sporting venues were shuttered; and social and religious services, along with arts performances such as concerts and Broadway shows, were canceled.

The acoustic footprint humans exert upon the world was dramatically and measurably changed due to the lockdowns, especially in the most aggressive locales. Seismometers don't only measure earthquakes; they also detect human activity as a source of seismic signaling (referred to as "anthropogenic noise"). This might be obvious when imagining bomb detonations, strip-mining, and fracking but may be less so for more routine activities such as train and truck traffic, subways, rock concerts, and even crowd reactions at large sporting events. Seismologists have long recognized that, especially in more densely populated areas, human activity is capable of producing enough seismic signal to mask lower-level geological seismic motions associated with earthquakes or volcanic pre-eruptions, potentially interfering with the development of "early warning" systems for such catastrophic geological events. Predictably, given the rhythms of urban life in much of the world, such masking is most prominent on weekdays, during daytime hours, and subsides during holidays and at night. Thomas Lecocq spearheaded a group of researchers in 2020 who conducted a study of the prevalence of humanly produced high-frequency seismic ambient noise (hiFSAN, defined as 4 to 14 Hertz, below the lowest frequencies that the human ear can hear) during Covid-19 lockdowns, as compared to other times that hiFSAN was known to be at its lower levels.[1] A permanent reporting station in Sri Lanka reported a 50 percent decrease after lockdown; a surface station in Belgium reported a 33 percent reduction; Sunday night readings at a station in New York's Central Park were 10 percent lower. Reductions were noted at ski resorts in Europe and the United States and in tourist destinations in the Caribbean. Global median hiFSAN dropped by 50 percent in the period spanning March–May 2020. These researchers were using the pandemic to better understand how human activity covers up geologically based seismic activity, not to study human behavior per se, but they made demonstrably clear that human activity was significantly quieter during Covid-19 lockdowns.

Another scientific study developed in partnership between the University of Michigan's Department of Environmental Health Sciences and Apple also sought to examine how human exposure to noise—in this case acoustic rather than seismic—changed during Covid-19 lockdowns in the United States.[2] Study participants in California, Florida, New York, and Texas agreed to share sound data from their iPhones and/or Apple Watches with the researchers to provide information about their exposure to sound intensities as compared to their pre-lockdown exposure levels.[3] In the end, there were nearly 6,000 participants in the study. The results showed significant decreases in exposure to sound during lockdown. Sound intensity is measured on a logarithmic scale (in units referred to as decibels, or dB for short); every drop of 3 decibels represents a halving of sound energy level. Across all four states, the mean reduction was 2.6 dB; New York data showed the largest decrease (3.1 dB) and Florida the smallest (2.4 dB). Younger participants showed greater reductions than older participants, and the overall range of differences between weekdays and weekends was greatly reduced. The authors note that significant reductions in the range of 65–70 dB and 70–75 dB were observed in all four states. Given that noise-induced hearing loss correlates highly to regular eight-hour exposures to sounds above 70 dB, and that there is growing evidence that repeated exposure to loud sounds is also linked to heart disease, hypertension, and losses in cognitive performance, these findings suggest that the lockdowns likely reduced Americans' overall risk of sound-induced negative health effects.

INTRODUCTION 3

These studies foreground scientific questions that the pandemic raised about sound. But what might a humanities-based or social scientific approach to Covid-19 and the world of sound look like? One might start by examining media coverage of how lockdowns changed the world's soundscape. To believe media accounts, people living in urban areas missed the sounds of city life—even sounds that might have previously been thought of as unwanted noise. All but gone were the sounds of mechanized transport, of nightlife, and of crowded public spaces. Particularly to those accustomed to living within or amid the noise of cities, the change was so dramatic as to elicit news coverage and sound documentation efforts, many overtly referencing a sense of loss. "In India, the incessant beep-beep of cars has disappeared. In New York, Harlem's heart has stopped beating. In Toronto, the trains no longer whistle, and in Marseille, every day sounds like a holiday. All around the world, the silence rolls in and out like a fog," Robin Givhan wrote in late April 2020 in the *Washington Post*.[4] A month later, the *New York Times* asked a researcher at New York University (NYU) to weigh in on what it meant that the city had become quieter than on the coldest of winter days: Juan Pablo Bello replied, "It's the sound of the city aching ... It's not a healthy sound in my mind."[5] Also in May 2020, the New York Public Library released an album entitled *Missing Sounds of New York: An Auditory Love Letter to New Yorkers*, as a reminder of what "makes New York special for so many people."[6]

When New York (and many other locations) briefly relaxed lockdown rules in June and July 2020, *New York* magazine celebrated a longed-for return of the densely layered sonic city:

> I once spent days traipsing around the streets with a recorder to assemble a sonic portrait, not just of New York but of New Yorkers. We'll know that the city is healing when we start to hear something like it again, a collage of multilingual invectives, street-corner negotiations, one-sided phone calls, doomsday harangues, philosophical dialogues, parental lectures, playground squeals, public courtships, shouted breakfast orders, political come-ons, parking-spot disputes, snatches of song—the whole chaotic choir of urban life lived to the loudest.[7]

And by mid-August, the *New York Times* ran another feature comparing the pre-pandemic sounds of the city to those during the lockdown:

> Had we ever considered the reassurance behind a full-throated morning rush hour? How its harried mornings suggest the hum of a sound economy; the pursuit of knowledge; the commitment to provide and be self-sustaining?

... Lately, though, our muted rush hours are cacophonous in the wholesale disruption of earning and learning. The effect of this quiet is the opposite of calming. We find ourselves missing what we once loathed. Those car-horn bleats of annoyance. Those corner clusters of impatience, waiting for a green light. Those barks of "Excuse me!" that sound like the opposite of an apology.[8]

In their focus on what had been sonically lost during lockdowns, such accounts simultaneously evoke and assert a strong nostalgic linkage between sound and sociability and the role that sound plays in the creation of what political scientist Benedict Anderson called an "imagined community": an ideologically created sense of togetherness that binds members of complex societies into feeling that they share an identity with others who they do not know and will never meet.[9] Anderson was writing specifically about national identity, and, given that he wrote his thesis originally in the 1980s, he positioned print and televisual media as key to building such senses of community and belonging. Political polarization since the 2010s as exacerbated by digital and social media—certainly in the United States but also throughout much of Europe and parts of South America—may make the notion of a collective national identity seem outdated, naïve, or quaint. But perhaps shared experiences offer a bridge or a frame of reference in which we can find some measure of recognition of and common ground with others. Is the acoustic world a location in which this might occur?

Overview

Humans live in a sensorial world, defined by what we see with our eyes, hear with our ears, feel via touch, and taste and smell (as complexly linked through oral and nasal sensorial neuroreceptors). This book examines the ways in which sound—as an auditory phenomenon and as perceived through listening practices—shapes how people understand the world they inhabit. How does sound craft and create experiences and identities? How does sound shape what one lives, feels, and projects into the world on a daily basis? If sound impacts us individually, how do we make it meaningful collectively? And how is the idea of a collective "we" challenged by the ways in which people hearing a sound lend it different meanings? These are the questions of the field of "sound studies," an interdisciplinary confluence straddling the humanities and the humanistic social sciences, drawing from academic disciplines including history, literary criticism, film studies, media studies, communications, architectural acoustics, sociology, anthropology, science and technology

INTRODUCTION

studies, geography, ethnomusicology, and linguistics. Spanning multiple areas of inquiry and diverse methodological approaches, sound studies engages in sustained inquiry into the nature of sound and how sound defines, delineates, and demarcates humans' experiences in and of the world.[10]

This book offers a broad introduction to "sound studies" as a field of academic inquiry. It focuses on how sound engages with people's everyday lives: how sound creates the auditory "soundscapes" we live in, how it crafts our perceptions of visual worlds depicted in film and television, how our voices define us as individuals and as social actors in the world we inhabit, and how it manifests in expressive activities such as writing, singing, and sonic artistry. It is therefore selective, in that not all areas of academic research on sound are covered: we do not delve deeply, for example, into scientific discussions of the physics of sound or work on deafness and deaf studies, nor do we chart historical studies that seek to describe and explain changes in the sonic world over time, or focus on the history of sound recording and reproduction technologies, all of which are significant and important dimensions of the larger "sound studies" corpus.

Instead, we have chosen to limit this book to six areas of inquiry—soundscapes, noise, the voice, sound and the written word, sound design, and sound art—that provide fertile entry points into the broader concerns of sound studies. The chapters begin with anecdotes that lead into concise presentations of theory and examples of research by scholars working in these areas of study. The anecdotes and examples are drawn from real-life phenomena, as well as media objects such as movies, sound recordings, and artworks. At times, the media objects are analyzed for their sonic properties, and at other times, they are used as illustrative examples of sonic phenomena (such as when a character in a movie utilizes voice in a way that voices are utilized in day-to-day life). Relationships between real-world sounds and mediated representations of real sounds are one that we seek to foreground and that we hope readers will take care to attend to. Each chapter culminates with an project; five of them involve making or manipulating sound, and one is designed to be a brief sociological "experiment" about sound and identity. The words "Re-Making" and "Experiential" that appear in the book's title foreground our belief that experiential learning is essential for understanding the character, power, and potential of sound in social life. Assignments that allow students to make and share digital sound projects—and that can be springboards for classroom discussion and reflection—provide opportunities to apply theories and concepts about sound, develop some familiarity with basic digital audio tools and techniques, and deepen knowledge beyond what reading alone can provide. The book culminates with an "audio narrative" project that employs all the different dimensions of sound that the book investigates.

What Is "Sound Studies"?

If you are a college or university student, chances are there is no degree offered in, nor department of, sound studies at your institution. There are, of course, many departments and degrees for which sound is a central concern. Communications, music, linguistics, film, drama, media studies, psychology, audiology, languages, and physics, for example (though certainly not intended to be an exhaustive list), all by definition touch on the world of sound in whole or in part. But searching through your institution's faculty profiles won't yield a list of people holding a PhD or an MFA in "sound studies"; one of this book's authors holds a PhD in linguistic anthropology and the other in musicology with a specialization in ethnomusicology, but both are active researchers in and teachers of sound studies. If there are no degrees or departments, how does "sound studies" constitute a field of study or an academic discipline?

Writing in an edited volume published in 2012, Jonathan Sterne offers one possible answer: that it describes scholarship (or artistic creation) that "takes sound as its analytic point of departure or arrival."[11] Sterne suggests that since sometime in the 1990s, a generation of researchers working on sonic questions in many different fields in the humanities and social sciences became self-consciously aware that they were at least indirectly—and increasingly quite directly—part of a group of scholars interested in sonic issues. In many cases, they would discover more common ground, and more productive scholarly engagement, with others outside their own academic disciplines, or at the least, they realized that they were working on related problems, that they would benefit from talking to one another, and that sound was a big enough phenomenon that no single field's approach to studying it could be sufficient. "Sound studies' challenge is to think across sounds, to consider sonic phenomena in relationship to one another—*as types of sonic phenomena rather than as things-in-themselves*—whether they be music, voices, listening, media, buildings, performances or another path into sonic life," Sterne suggested (emphasis in the original).[12]

By the 2010s, there was an increasing recognition that sound studies was no longer an emergent field but an institutionalized one. A "discipline" can be certified and institutionalized in many ways, including special issues of existing journals,[13] disciplinary "readers" and "handbooks,"[14] the creation of new journals,[15] the formation of "interest groups" related to the field within existing professional societies,[16] or academic presses developing book series or distinguishing themselves by committing to publish works in the emergent discipline.[17] As Colombian scholar Ana Maria Ochoa Gautier puts it, sound studies is named as a field through institutional investment in supporting the academic labor of those who identify as sound studies researchers.[18]

In the introduction to their edited volume, *Keywords in Sound*, David Novak and Matt Sakakeeny note how this kind of institutional investment sets agendas for disciplines, draws boundaries around what they include, and is therefore implicated in what counts and does not count as scholarship in the field.

Despite the interdisciplinary breadth of sound studies, the field as a whole has remained deeply committed to Western intellectual lineages and histories. As one example, of the dozens of books about sound published by MIT Press—a leader in science and technology studies, philosophies of aesthetics, and cognition—none is principally invested in non-Western perspectives or subjects. Sound studies has often reinforced Western ideals of a normative subject placed within a common context of hearing and listening. Presumptions of universality have also led scholars to treat sounds as stable objects that have predictable, often technologically determined, effects on a generalized perceptual consciousness which might even be reduced to an entire "human condition."[19]

Ochoa Gautier goes one step further, arguing that it is not just that the intellectual lineages are Western, but so too are the institutional support structures undergirding the field: "Even though they have been working in fields akin to sound studies for decades, colleagues working in Latin America and the Caribbean are forced, through the global intellectual politics of citation and recognition, to speak of sound studies as an a priori *named by* and *emerging from* the North" (emphasis in the original).[20]

Critiques of the Western-centrism of sound studies are increasingly, but also only fairly recently, emerging and leading to scholarship that enacts those critiques. Recent edited collections, such as Guilbault and Rommen's *Sounds of Vacation: Political Economies of Caribbean Tourism* and Steingo and Syke's *Remapping Sound Studies*, as well as several monographs such as Robinson's *Hungry Listening: Resonant Theory for Indigenous Sound Studies*, Ochoa Gautier's *Aurality: Listening and Knowledge in Nineteenth-Century Colombia*, Cardoso's *Sound Politics in São Paulo*, Friedner's *Valuing Deaf Worlds in Urban India*, Tausig's *Bangkok is Ringing: Sound, Protest, and Constraint*, and Bronfman's *Isles of Noise: Sonic Media in the Caribbean* (to name but a few), seek to open up sound studies' borders to a more nuanced and decolonized understanding of sound from beyond the North. This book's authors' primary research areas are in North America, and many of the examples and case studies in this book are pulled from the West, in part because we feel that they are good examples and case studies and in part due to how the majority of sound studies research remains focused on the West. However, we have sought consciously to weave examples from South America, the Caribbean, and Asia into several of the book's chapters.

The Chapters

The six substantive chapters of the book address key concepts and terms in sound studies. These six areas were chosen in part to be a broad representation of some core areas of research in sound studies, but our selection was also guided by our commitment to foregrounding learning through engaging with sound via the creation of sonic media. Each of these topics lends itself well to *making* sound; our hope is that the act of making simultaneously provides a mechanism for reflecting on and analyzing sound objects and the auditory world.

The first substantive chapter of the book addresses a broad conceptualization of the term "soundscape." The term is commonly attributed to Canadian composer R. Murray Schafer, writing in the early 1970s (and onwards) about urban noise pollution. Schafer argues that human intervention in the sonic world since the advent of the Industrial Revolution has altered the soundscape from a hi-fi state (having a very strong signal-to-noise ratio) to an increasingly lo-fi one (having a weak signal-to-noise ratio).[21] Thus, he argues, the modern world is characterized by a growing sonic density that makes it hard to know what one is listening to. Schafer's work in many ways has been moved on from in sound studies, but this key concept, and other vocabulary he offered to define elements within a given soundscape, has remained useful terminological touchstones. Much scholarship subsequent to Schafer has sought to bring listening more fully into the concept of soundscape. In particular, the work of Steven Feld in Papua New Guinea has stressed the relationship among sound, listening, environment, and culture. Feld coined the term "acoustemology" (a blend of acoustics and epistemology) to investigate sound and listening as forms of coming to know through the audible world, especially as deeply shaped by culture and language.[22] The chapter uses this conceptual background to frame Jonathan Sterne's examination of how soundscape is linked to capital and consumer culture in the Minnesota mega-mall, the Mall of America, with a special focus on 1990s lingerie powerhouse Victoria's Secret.[23] The chapter argues that a broad definition of soundscape allows for the examination not just of how soundscapes may act upon individuals or groups but also of how individuals or groups can actively construct, utilize, and resist or refine the sonic world they inhabit.

The subsequent chapter is built around the concept of *noise*, focusing on its role as a power broker, creator, and maintainer of difference and its role in musical and social aesthetics. Social scientists have long noted that it is not sufficient to define noise solely as unwanted or too-loud sound (though those may be factors). Noise is equally deeply implicated in power, labor, aesthetics, and creativity and is often tied to social relations of class, race and ethnicity, and other identity categories. In Victorian England, for example, wealthy white British households began to build quiet interior studies to shield residents from urban noise, much of which was the music and speech of new immigrants using different languages. During the rise of industrial manufacturing and mechanized transport ranging from trains to cars to airplanes, noise was considered both a potential negative influence on human health (ranging from hearing loss to the development of heart conditions) *and* a sign of desirable economic progress and growth. Beginning during the Second World War, the use of sound as a psychological or physical weapon was added to the arsenals of warfare, and via the LRAD ("long range audio device," referred to colloquially as a "sound canon"), it has more recently entered mainstream police tactics of crowd control. But it is important to keep in mind that sometimes noise has pleasurable and desirable connotations, examined here through musics that have incorporated noise deliberately into compositions and performances. The Italian Futurist movement of the early twentieth century valued finding ways to take the cacophony of the factory and of cars and planes and incorporate it as an aesthetic element of musical composition. In postwar Jamaica, portable sound systems capable of cranking out hundreds of thousands of watts turned housing courtyards and beaches into impromptu dance halls, in which music became quite literally a physical force acting upon the body. Noise, then, is not an absolute but rather a variable, playing a flexible role with respect to taste and creativity, and always tied to issues of power, prestige, and social class.

The third substantive chapter examines a somewhat less common area of inquiry in sound studies: How does *voice* link to individual and social identities? The semiotic theory of Charles Sanders Peirce (1839–1914) identifies indexicality as key to this linkage. Indexes are signs (meaning-bearing entities) that "point to" what it is that they mean: smoke indexes the presence of fire; cloven footprints index the prior presence of a hoofed animal such as a pig, for example. Linguistic features of the voice such as accent or dialect, along with features of voice quality and delivery, have the potential to signal group membership in categories including, but not limited to, gender, race and ethnicity, and socioeconomic class. However, one needs to question whether those linkages are products of voices themselves or are artifacts of how listeners decode vocal sounds in ways that create categorizations of speakers. This dynamic is at the heart of what linguist John Baugh has referred to as "linguistic profiling," which in turn may lead to instances of "linguistic discrimination."[24] After describing some examples, the chapter turns to a related voice/identity phenomenon but in a very different context: how actors and actresses embody characters they play through their voice and how movies are sometimes built around the very idea of characters finding themselves through their voice. The 2018 remake of *A Star Is Born* is used as a case study, examining Bradley Cooper's voice modification done in preparation for the role, and how Lady Gaga's character, Ally, quite literally changes and defines her identity through her vocal performance. The chapter ends with an inquiry into digital voices, particularly the use of "feminine" voices in digital voice assistants such as Alexa and Siri. Voice, the chapter concludes, is complexly positioned in terms of how it is linked to identity and, in turn, how identity is linked to power, stereotyping, marginalization, and discrimination.

How do sound scholars, whose work is often confined to print, use orthography and other textual devices to describe, depict, encode, or animate the auditory dimensions of what they are writing about? Writers have long grappled with ways to capture sound in text and to create an imaginary soundscape for their readers. The fourth substantive chapter, focusing on *literature and text*, examines experiential and descriptive modes of writing sound as found in the work of linguistic anthropology, fiction, poetry, and comics. Linguistic anthropologists have a long tradition of documenting in writing everything from quotidian everyday speech to lullabies, spiritual practices, education, and verbal art of the languages and cultures they work with. Dell Hymes, for example, developed an "ethnopoetic" approach that sought to represent the speaker's understandings of how speech genres were organized. To convey that "insider" understanding to readers, his transcriptions often visually resembled poetry. Hymes's contemporary Dennis Tedlock went a step further in providing transcriptions that could be read as performance scripts, using things like line spacing, the use of ALLCAPS, and vertical movement of text lines to emphasize the sonic dimensions (volume, voice quality changes, pitch movement) of verbal art. Their work predated the development of digital transcription, which greatly augments the possibilities of evoking sound in text. In fiction, Edgar Allen Poe's work is exemplary for his use of what literary theorist Roland Barthes referred to as the "Reality Effect," defined as the incorporation of small details about a person, place, or action that don't directly advance the narrative of the story but rather give the story more atmosphere or verisimilitude. We examine "The Masque of Red Death" and "The Pit and the Pendulum" to show how Poe uses sonic description very sparingly but consistently in moments of disorientation and terror to create heightened engagement between text and reader. Futurist poet F. T. Marinetti's work in some ways presages modern comics: the cover of his 1914

INTRODUCTION 11

Zang Tumb Tumb seeks to capture the sounds of warfare as experienced at the 1912 siege of Adrianapoli in the Ottoman Empire. In common with Tedlock but for very different reasons and to different ends, Marinetti manipulates font and text size, uses abstract symbols, and creates an impression of sonic movement meant to evoke the dynamic and cacophonous sound of war. The chapter concludes with a discussion of comics—as one example of graphic literature—in which creators have tremendous leeway to illustrate sound and in which they can allow for sound to be implied through images without needing to write text-about-sound at all. The approaches discussed in this chapter are rarely used by sound studies scholars, but the potential offered by their future incorporation into scholarly work is thought-provoking.

The term "sound design" is the subject of the fifth substantive chapter. It is most often associated with film and video game soundtracks, used to refer to the total sonic artifact, often composed of music, voices, and sound effects, that accompanies images. In our view, this is an unnecessarily restrictive usage of the term and overlooks the extent to which sound is (and historically has been) designed in and for multiple dimensions of people's lives, from live sound as heard by *carnaval*-goers in Brazil, to experiences at vacation resorts in the Caribbean, to car components. We stress thinking about sound design as an activity and not simply an outcome, as this approach foregrounds the degree of deliberate effort put into creating the sonic elements that surround people every day. Sound design in cinema is not ignored, however: the chapter introduces Michel Chion's concepts of "audio-vision" (a recognition that "watching" a movie also involves listening to it) and "synchresis" (that sound and image create meaning in tandem, not individually, in films),[25] before discussing the work of famed Hollywood sound designer Walter Murch, specifically the opening sequence of the film, *Apocalypse Now*. We also note that mixing audio for any multitrack music recording involves principles of sound design and take the reader through a comparative listening of The Beatles' "Hey Jude" and "Let It Be" to hear sound design in action. The chapter ends with a nod to sound design in architectural spaces, using changes in the sound design of restaurants over the past twenty years as a case study of how sound is engineered to help maximize diners' experiences and restaurants' profits.

The last substantive chapter addresses the open-ended term "sound art." If sound art is defined as art that exists in the medium of sound, then what differentiates sound art from experimental music, performance art that makes use of sound components, or avant-garde spoken poetry that uses nonlinguistic sound? Even as auditory installations and exhibits become more and more common in museums, galleries, other public spaces, and the internet, these and other questions remain. Can any work that emits or alters sound in a gallery be considered "sound art"? Are works that make use of everyday sound—bits of conversation, electronic oscillations, amplifications of insects or contact microphones placed on household surfaces—automatically classified as "sound art"? Is a walking and listening tour of a city or a sonorous natural location an example of "sound art"? What about the long-honored display of musical instruments that are accompanied by recordings of music? John Cage's infamous 4'33", a three-movement piece for piano in which the performer sits still and quiet, not touching the instrument, embodies three strands that, to some extent, unify much sound art. First, the animating ideas behind the work are more important than the experiential product it yields. Second, often the focus is on listening to the context in which the work is encountered, as much if not more than listening to the work itself. And third, sound art is often not intended to be consumed as an object of contemplation but rather seeks to be transformational, whether of the environment in which it is located or of listening practices. This chapter, more than the others in the book, is a broad survey of the breadth and diversity of works that might fall under the umbrella of sound art, from Max Neuhaus's work that challenges audiences outside of conventional galleries or concert halls, to the environmental recordings of Bernie Krause, Steven Feld, and Annea Lockwood, to Oyvind Brandtsegg's works that harvest satellite signal data to be converted into audible sound.

Beyond Re-Making Sound

As already noted, these six terms and their respective areas of study do not encompass the full range of research that happens within sound studies. We encourage readers to consult additional scholarly resources ranging from edited "handbooks," to academic journals, to websites and blogs dedicated to sound studies. Some English-language resources—a starting point, not an exhaustive list—are listed here.

Handbooks, Edited Volumes, and Review Articles

- Michael Bull, 2013, *Sound Studies* (Routledge)
- Michael Bull, 2019, *The Routledge Companion to Sound Studies* (Routledge)
- Michael Bull and Les Back (eds.), 2015, *The Auditory Culture Reader*, 2nd ed. (Routledge)

INTRODUCTION 13

- Veit Erlmann, 2004, *Hearing Cultures: Essays on Sound, Listening and Modernity* (Berg)
- Mike Goldsmith, 2015, *Sound: A Very Short Introduction* (Oxford)
- David Novak and Matt Sakakeeny (eds.), 2015, *Keywords in Sound* (Duke)
- Trevor Pinch and Karin Bijsterveld (eds.), 2012, *The Oxford Handbook of Sound Studies* (Oxford)
- David Samuels, Louise Meintjes, Ana Maria Ochoa Gautier, and Thomas Porcello, 2010, "Soundscapes: Toward a Sounded Anthropology," *Annual Review of Anthropology*
- Holger Schulze, 2020, *The Bloomsbury Handbook of the Anthropology of Sound* (Bloomsbury)
- Gavin Steingo and Jim Sykes (eds.), 2019, *Remapping Sound Studies* (Duke)

Journals

Sound Studies
Journal of Sonic Studies
Sound Effects
Journal of Acoustic Ecology
Resonance: The Journal of Sound and Culture
The Journal of Sound and Music in Games

Websites and Blogs

Sound Studies in Rhetoric, Composition, and Writing Studies

> https://docs.google.com/document/d/1zUsAQtSAgtHFAPlvsoyY3DKRQWW3dC3xgQvCGNM2y0Y/edit?hl=en_US#heading=h.dgra0j7dwo8z

Sounding Out

> https://soundstudiesblog.com/

Sound Studies Lab

> http://www.soundstudieslab.org/

Sonic Field

    http://sonicfield.org/

The World Forum for Acoustic Ecology

    https://www.wfae.net/

Notes

1. Lecocq, "Global Quieting of High-Frequency Seismic Noise due to COVID-19 Pandemic Lockdown Measures," 1338–43.
2. Smith, Wang, and Mazur, "Impacts of COVID-19-Related Social Distancing Measures on Personal Environmental Sound Exposures."
3. These four states were chosen based on geographic and cultural diversity and due to differences in the timing and intensity of their lockdown responses.
4. Givhan, "What Does a Pandemic Sound Like?"
5. Bui and Badger, "The Coronavirus Quieted City Noise."
6. See: https://www.nypl.org/blog/2020/05/01/missing-sounds-of-new-york (2020).
7. Davidson, "New York Is Getting Loud Again."
8. Barry and Heisler, "The New York City of Our Imagination."
9. Anderson, *Imagined Communities*. See also Calhoun, "Community without Propinquity Revisited," 373–97.
10. If humans live in a multisensorial world, then why choose to foreground sound? One reason is that vision and sight have been historically privileged in Western philosophical and theological traditions as the source of knowledge of the world. Within the past fifty or so years, there has been a growing critique of this ocular-centric perspective, and the study of sound has been one significant locus of this critique. Another reason lies in the use of sound in media: sound has been crucial in advertising since the advent of radio and in film since the 1920s. In this way, we argue that the study of sound brings to critical consciousness something that has long mattered in media but that until relatively recently has been an underemphasized area of analysis.
11. Sterne, *The Sound Studies Reader*, 2.
12. Ibid., 3.
13. See, e.g., Pinch and Bijsterveld, "Special Issue on Sound Studies."
14. Widely cited examples include Sterne, *The Sound Studies Reader*; Pinch and Bijsterveld, *The Oxford Handbook of Sound Studies*; Bull, *Sound Studies*; Erlmann, *Hearing Cultures*; Bull and Back, *The Auditory Culture Reader*; Novak and Sakakeeny, *Keywords in Sound*; and Steingo and Sykes, *Remapping Sound Studies*.

15 See, e.g., *Sound Studies, Journal of Sonic Studies, Sound Effects*, and *Journal of Acoustic Ecology*.
16 See, e.g., the "Music and Sound Interest Group" of the American Anthropological Association, the "Special Interest Group for Sound Studies" of the Society for Ethnomusicology, and the "Sound Studies Caucus" of the American Studies Association.
17 Notable in this respect are Duke University Press, MIT Press, Oxford University Press, and Bloomsbury (the publisher of this book).
18 Ochoa Gautier, "Afterword," 261–74.
19 Novak and Sakakeeny, *Keywords in Sound*, 7. One might also look at the table of contents for Michael Bull's massive four-volume collection, *Sound Studies* (2013), which boasts seventy-two articles, described by the volume's publisher as "authoritative," almost all of which are authored by Western scholars researching in the West, as well as the twenty-three articles that are included in Pinch and Bijsterveld's *The Oxford Handbook of Sound Studies*.
20 Ochoa Gautier, "Afterword," 261–74.
21 Schafer, *The Soundscape*, 43–4.
22 Feld, "Waterfalls of Sound," 91–135.
23 Sterne, "Sounds Like the Mall of America," 22–50.
24 Baugh, "Linguistic Profiling," 155–68.
25 Chion, *Audio-Vision*.

Bibliography

Anderson, Benedict. *Imagined Communities: Reflections on the Origin and Spread of Nationalism.* London: Verso, 2016 [1983].

Barry, Dan, and Todd Heisler. "The New York City of Our Imagination." August 20, 2020. nytimes.com. https://www.nytimes.com/interactive/2020/08/20/nyregion/nyc-sights-sounds-coronavirus.html (accessed March 22, 2021).

Baugh, John. "Linguistic Profiling." In *Black Linguistics: Language, Society, and Politics in Africa and the Americas*, edited by Sinfree Makoni Geneva Smitherman, Arnetha F. Ball, and Arthur K. Spears, 155–68. London: Routledge, 2003.

Bronfman, Alejandra M. *Isles of Noise: Sonic Media in the Caribbean.* Chapel Hill: University of North Carolina Press, 2016.

Bui, Quoctrung, and Emily Badger. "The Coronavirus Quieted City Noise: Listen to What's Left." May 22, 2020. nytimes.com. https://www.nytimes.com/interactive/2020/05/22/upshot/coronavirus-quiet-city-noise.html (accessed June 15, 2020).

Bull, Michael, ed. *The Routledge Companion to Sound Studies*, 2019.

Bull, Michael, ed. *Sound Studies*. 1st ed. 4 vols. London: Routlege, 2013.

Bull, Michael, and Les Back, *The Auditory Culture Reader*. 2nd ed. London: Routledge, 2015.

Calhoun, Craig. "Community without Propinquity Revisited: Communications Technology and the Transformation of the Urban Public Sphere." *Sociological Inquiry* 68, no. 3 (1998): 373–97.

Cardoso, Leonardo. *Sound-Politics in São Paulo*. Oxford: Oxford University Press, 2019.

Chion, Michel. *Audio-Vision: Sound on Screen*. Translated by Claudia Gorbman. New York: Columbia University Press, 1994.

Davidson, Justin. "New York Is Getting Loud Again." July 28, 2020. *nymag.com*. https://nymag.com/intelligencer/2020/07/new-york-is-getting-loud-again.html (accessed March 22, 2021).

Erlmann, Veit, ed. *Hearing Cultures: Essays on Sound, Listening, and Modernity*. Oxford: Berg, 2004.

Feld, Steven. "Waterfalls of Sound: An Acoustemology of Place Resounding in Bosavi, Papua New Guinea." In *Senses of Place*, edited by Steven Feld and Keith Basso, 91–135. Santa Fe: School of American Research Press, 1996.

Friedner, Michele. *Valuing Deaf Worlds in Urban India*. New Brunswick: Rutgers University Press, 2015.

Givhan, Robin. "What Does a Pandemic Sound Like? For Many of Us at Home, It's a Heartbreaking Silence." April 28, 2020. *washingtonpost.com*. https://www.washingtonpost.com/lifestyle/style/silence-solitude-lockdown-quarantine-social-distancing/2020/04/27/ad2ad688-8322-11ea-a3eb-e9fc93160703_story.html (accessed March 22, 2021).

Goldsmith, Michael. *Sound: A Very Short Introduction*. Oxford: Oxford University Press, 2015.

Guilbault, Jocelyne, and Timothy Rommen. *Sounds of Vacation: Political Economies of Caribbean Tourism*. Durham, NC: Duke University Press, 2019.

Lecocq, Thomas, Stephen P. Hicks, Koen Van Noten, Kasper van Wijk, Paula Koelemeijer, Raphael S. M. DePlan, Frédéick Massin, Gregor Hillers, et al. "Global Quieting of High-Frequency Seismic Noise due to COVID-19 Pandemic Lockdown Measures." *Science* 369 (2020): 1338–43.

Novak, David, and Matt Sakakeeny. "Introduction." In *Keywords in Sound*, edited by David Novak and Matt Sakakeeny, 1–11. Durham, NC: Duke University Press, 2015.

Novak, David, and Matt Sakakeeny. *Keywords in Sound*. Edited by David Novak and Matt Sakakeeny. Durham, NC: Duke University Press, 2015.

NYPL Staff. *Missing Sounds of New York: An Auditory Love Letter to New Yorkers*. New York: New York Public Library, 2020.

Ochoa Gautier, Ana Maria. "Afterword: Sonic Cartographies." In *Remapping Sound Studies*, edited by Gavin Steingo and Jim Sykes, 261–74. Durham, NC: Duke University Press, 2019.

Ochoa Gautier, Ana Maria. *Aurality: Listening and Knowledge in Nineteenth-Century Colombia*. Durham, NC: Duke University Press, 2014.

Pinch, Trevor, and Karin Bijsterveld. *The Oxford Handbook of Sound Studies*. Oxford: Oxford University Press, 2012.

Pinch, Trevor, and Karin Bijsterveld, eds. "Special Issue on Sound Studies: New Technologies and Music." *Social Studies of Science* 34, no. 5 (2004).

Robinson, Dylan. *Hungry Listening: Resonant Theory for Indigenous Sound Studies*. Minneapolis: University of Minnesota Press, 2020.

Samuels, David, Louise Meintjes, Ana Maria Ochoa Gautier, and Thomas Porcello. "Soundscapes: Toward a Sounded Anthropology." *Annual Review of Anthropology* 39 (2010): 329–45.

Schafer, R. Murray. *The Soundscape: Our Sonic Environment and the Tuning of the World*. Rochester: Destiny Books, 1994 [1977].

Schulze, Holger, ed. *The Bloomsbury Handbook of the Anthropology of Sound*. London: Bloomsbury, 2020.

Smith, Lauren M., et al. "Impacts of COVID-19-Related Social Distancing Measures on Personal Environmental Sound Exposures." *Environmental Research Letters* 15 (2020).

Steingo, Gavin, and Jim Sykes. *Remapping Sound Studies*. Durham, NC: Duke University Press, 2019.

Sterne, Jonathan. "Sonic Imaginations." In *The Sound Studies Reader*, edited by Jonathan Sterne, 2–17. London: Routledge, 2012.

Sterne, Jonathan. "Sounds Like the Mall of America: Programmed Music and the Architectonics of Commercial Space." *Ethnomusicology* 41, no. 1 (1997): 22–50.

Sterne, Jonathan. *The Sound Studies Reader*. Edited by Jonathan Sterne. London: Routledge, 2012.

Tausig, Benjamin. *Bangkok Is Ringing: Sound, Protest, and Constraint*. Oxford: Oxford University Press, 2018.

1

Soundscape: Sound, Space, and Listening

Key concepts: acoustemology, consumer culture, malls, mediation, Muzak, the senses

Orientation: Three Soundscapes

I. The opening chapter of Theodore Dreiser's 1925 novel, *An American Tragedy*, recounts the effort of a small family to proclaim the (very Christian) word of God on a downtown street corner of a large, though anonymous, midwestern American city in the early twentieth century.[1] Dreiser's evocative prose hints at the density of the city's sounds: multitudes of people stream noisily along the sidewalk; cars incessantly clang their bells (the precursor to the steering wheel push-horn); hawkers shout loudly to peddle their wares (food, tabloids, trinkets); all amid towering buildings that create canyon-like, echoing spaces. A sonic wall closes in and down, overwhelms and blurs individual sounds into an undifferentiated stew of noise. Against this densely layered sonic landscape—in other words, against the city's soundscape—the small, humble family breaks out a portable pump organ to sing psalms with and to preach from the Bible, struggling both to be heard against the din of the city and to be listened to amid its smorgasbord of secular life—even though their preaching and singing add (even if barely) to that very noise. The chapter weaves together multiple auditory sources—voices, language, music, instruments, machines—and embeds them in the historical, social, and built environments in which they are being sounded and listened to. The reader is immersed in a sensuous encounter with the aural environment of the time and place in which the story is set. The remainder of the novel does not linger on sound and the contestation between individuals and the larger physical and social worlds in which they live, but the opening starkly highlights how public spaces can be ill-suited to the social and communicative activities that people may be trying to create and participate in.[2] It also highlights that the concepts of "soundscape" and "noise" (Chapter 2) are deeply intertwined.

II. Roughly sixty years later and approximately 8,500 miles away, American ethnomusicologist Steven Feld is making field recordings in a pocket of the highland rainforest of Papua New Guinea that is home to roughly 1,200 indigenous people. This is not Feld's first time in the area that is home to the Bosavi people. His doctoral research fifteen or so years earlier had focused on examining the complex relationships among the Kaluli language (spoken by a subset of the Bosavi people), on Kaluli speakers' expressive use of speech and song, their cosmological and spiritual belief systems, and how each of these is intimately linked to the auditory dimensions of their rainforest surroundings. In his fascinating book *Sound and Sentiment: Birds, Weeping, Poetics, and Song in Kaluli Expression*, Feld details not only how language describes and interprets the sonic world of the rainforest but also how it reflects it: how the sounds of the rainforest appear as elements deeply woven into the Kaluli language itself, how several types of Kaluli singing incorporate acoustic properties characteristic of birdsong and moving water, and how the sheer density of overlapping sounds in the rainforest becomes an aesthetic and stylistic element of Kaluli expression.[3]

Feld writes in the liner notes to *Voices of the Rainforest*, the recording that resulted from this later trip, "Kaluli people think of themselves as 'voices in the forest.' They sing with birds, insects, water. And when Kaluli sing with them, they sing like them. Nature is music to Kaluli ears. And Kaluli music is naturally part of the surrounding soundscape."[4] Ultimately, the goal of Feld's recording project is to translate the book, which is constrained by the medium of writing in its presentation of how language and song and sounds of the natural world are woven together by the Bosavi people, into a recording that can more directly capture and convey it in sound. The Papua New Guinea Highlands are a far cry from Dreiser's urban soundscape, but they are no less sonically complex. Making this complex sonic environment directly experienceable *in sound* is the ultimate aim of Feld's field recording project.

What *Voices of the Rainforest* as a sonic document, and what Feld's subsequent writings and interviews about it, demonstrates is a remarkably layered sonic environment that, unlike the "wall" metaphor that describes

Dreiser's city, is a much more markedly three-dimensional space of sound. Animals such as wild pigs move along the forest floor, their footsteps and grunting locatable in, and contained to, lower-level vertical space. Birds are less constrained vertically of course, as they may descend to the forest floor or be perched in trees. One can, in theory, track their movements by listening to wing flaps or the positionality of their singing. As different bird species gather to rest or breed at different heights among the trees, understanding differences between birds' songs, and being able to discern the height from which those songs are coming, can help with species identification. In the rainforest, sounds of water are also ubiquitous. Once again, one can imagine differences in vertical space, in which raindrops may only be heard overhead (when, for instance, the rain is lighter and the canopy denser, and most of the rain sound results from water dripping from higher onto lower leaves). This will, of course, contrast with water flowing in streams, or moving across rocks in the rapids, or plunging over a waterfall; flowing water is comparatively anchored to the ground, like the wild pigs. The sonic verticality of the rainforest also suggests how important the ability to decode distance and depth purely through sound could be to forest residents. Except where paths have been created by people or animal trails, or where deliberate clearing of vegetation has happened, rainforests are visually dense, making the ability to see long distances forward (or even up) difficult. One's eyes may be entirely unhelpful in trying to determine how far away an animal that one is hunting or a person who poses a threat is.

Dreiser's description of the urban soundscape essentially presents sounds as "facts" that can be objectively described and whose implications and meanings to the people who hear them are straightforward. Feld paints a more nuanced picture over the corpus of his scholarly work focusing on the Kaluli. There are of course, he argues, "factual" elements of any soundscape: some places have braying donkeys, or church bells that ring at noon, or train horns that blow throughout the night, or shared walls where domestic violence doesn't stay private. Other places don't have these sounds. Privileged spaces can be built to isolate one from intrusive or distressing sounds; those without privilege are less able to do so. Part of what Feld asks us to recognize is that what one hears is deeply rooted in social class and economic standing. But by extension, his work considers the extent to which the mere concept of the soundscape can remain located *only* in sound or whether it must be considered a relational concept that emerges between sounds and those who hear them. Further, since anyone who hears a sound has come to understand the world through the cultural ears of their upbringing, to what extent is any soundscape actually constituted, experienced, or understandable outside of a broader consideration of culture?

III. The soundscape as a concept or an analytic object is not limited to the outdoors. One can consider, for example, spaces that present sonic challenges, while one tries to function in them: challenges ranging from the inhibition of easy communication (a blaring public address announcement at an airport boarding gate that drowns out one's ability to talk on the phone) to impeding the ability to concentrate on a project (a loud college or public library) to making uninterrupted sleep impossible (garbage trucks thundering by or squealing their brakes outside the bedroom window at 3:00 a.m.). Conversely, one can think about indoor spaces whose soundscapes are in fact well designed for their intended use (though conscious attention to sound design and the willingness to invest properly in it are harder to come by, which makes for a shorter list of examples): control and mixing rooms in professional sound recording studios, where tens of thousands of dollars are often invested in the room's sonic properties; to high-end automobile interiors; to built spaces ranging from funeral homes (designed to be quiet), to auditoriums and theaters.

The college that the authors of this book work at remodeled its central dining hall in 2017 as part of hiring a new food provider. Before the renovation, the hall had a centralized kitchen with two large dining rooms that opened off it, each with dozens of rectangular tables that sat six to eight people. The floor of the dining area was carpeted, and the tables sat underneath a dropped ceiling lined with acoustic tile. Given that each dining room could seat several hundred students at any given time, they were never exactly quiet spaces at peak dining hours, but students (and faculty who met them there) indicated that if you had a table of your own, conversation was easily intelligible. During the 2017 renovation, the space was converted to reflect a more typically "industrial" look: carpeted floors were replaced by polished concrete, the acoustic tile was removed to display the air duct circulation system, and the space was opened up such that the dining rooms were less compartmentalized from the food preparation areas. The rectangular dining tables were replaced by modular, irregularly shaped wooden tables. Previously upholstered chairs were dispensed with in favor of wooden blocks with metal legs. This look mimics larger trends in the restaurant industry since the mid-2000-aughts, and in many ways, the college's students reacted positively to the look and feel of the space, which now more closely evoked a contemporary gastropub.

But while the remodeled dining hall may have been visually more contemporary and in line with students' aesthetic tastes, complaints soon emerged about how much harder it was to study in it. It had previously been a hub of collaborative student work, but now it was too loud and often too difficult to talk and to be clearly heard in. The college's language departments had long held "study tables" one or more nights a week there, and some reported that, due to the changed acoustics of the redesigned space, they were relocating these events to the building that housed their department offices and lounges. Students anecdotally indicated that they were less likely to linger there of their own accord. All of this was in spite of the fact that their satisfaction with the food service had actually *increased* since the remodel and the arrival of the new vendor. While it may be reductive to lay all the blame for students' hesitancy to hang out on the acoustics of the new space, there is ample anecdotal evidence that converting areas that were acoustically conducive to group study into ones that made it harder to communicate changed how students utilized the dining center as part of their academic lives.

Dreiser asks us to contemplate how soundscapes overtake our lives and constrain our capacity to share our messages; Feld refines how to think about the soundscape and forces us to ask how much of it is "in" sound as opposed to being in how we encounter sound as socially constituted beings; the college's dining hall then requires that we add the *use* of spaces, and how those uses do or do not line up with their sonic properties, into what the term "soundscape" ultimately means.

Defining "Soundscape"

Sound studies scholars typically locate the sustained systematic usage of the term "soundscape" in the work of Canadian composer R. Murray Schafer who, in 1977, published a book called *The Tuning of the World*, re-released in 1994 with the title, *The Soundscape: Our Sonic Environment and the Tuning of the World*. Schafer employed the term "soundscape" to refer to the total "sonic environment," by which he meant not only physical environments but also "abstract constructions such as musical compositions and tape montages."[5] Despite this broad definition, Schafer focused primarily on issues related to noise pollution: its increase over time, how one might visually map its presence and intensity in a given location, and how one might initiate large-scale social, material, and behavioral processes of noise abatement. His thesis was both historical (that humans have progressively made the world a louder and more noise-polluted place) and prescriptivist (that the problem is dire enough that change needs to occur). "Noise pollution is now a world problem," he wrote. "It would seem that the world soundscape has reached an apex of vulgarity in our time, and many experts have predicted universal deafness as the ultimate consequence unless the problem can be brought strictly under control."[6] Throughout, his writing hews closely to language used in the environmental movements of the United States, Canada, and much of

Europe in the 1960s and 1970s; Schafer writes repeatedly of "noise pollution," "overpopulation," and "abatement" (and even coins the uniquely memorable phrase, "the big sound sewer of the sky," when discussing aircraft noise).

Schafer's thesis is heavily chronological and unidirectional, offering a narrative in which human beings, their activities, and their inventions have progressively altered—and loudened—a supposedly more "natural" prior soundscape. This prior soundscape consisted of noises that are, he argued, increasingly hard to hear, but that in theory would still be audible absent the presence of humans: the sounds of ocean waves, bubbling streams, the crack of melting ice, wind through the leaves of trees or howling across open land, the thud of falling trees, volcanic eruptions, birdsong, the cacophony of cicadas, howling coyotes, and so on. Human evolution is characterized by a progressive move from subsistence via relatively nomadic hunting and gathering activities, to comparatively settled agricultural cultivation and domesticated farming processes, and then later to urban centers whose food supply was brought in from rural areas where farming and livestock were still being cultivated. This is a history, then, in which population density in town and urban centers increased over time, and with that density, Schafer argues, came noticeable changes in local soundscapes, especially since the advent of the Industrial Revolution.

The shift brought about over time is from a "hi-fi" to a "lo-fi" soundscape. The two terms define the opposite poles of a continuum of sonic signal-to-noise ratios.[7] In a hi-fi soundscape, discrete sounds can be heard clearly because there is a low amount of ambient or background sound covering them up; conversely, a lo-fi soundscape is one in which high levels of ambient noise mask or render discrete sounds hard(er) to hear. Dreiser's small family would recognize their experience in Schafer's account—the density of overlapping loud city noises drowning out their efforts to convey the discrete words of their preaching and singing. Or, as Schafer puts it, the sonic density of the modern world risks creating a one-to-one signal-to-noise relationship in which "it is no longer possible to know what, if anything, is to be listened to."[8]

Schafer's work is, from a contemporary perspective, easy to find fault with. Glaringly, the people who make up the "our" of the book's subtitle are overwhelmingly white and western; the histories he invokes and the places he discusses are almost exclusively those of Greeks, Romans, European colonial powers, and contemporary Europe and North America, as populated by male subjects. Further, his argument extolling the superiority of the hi-fi soundscape too often reads as a glorification of a "simpler" past that would inevitably forge a close connection to a more "natural" world. This naïve romanticization of and longing for the countryside, in which one hears chirping birds and mooing cows and the pitter-patter of a light summer shower, permeates the opening sections of the book, unfortunately obscuring his more interesting point that in hi-fi soundscapes, one is in a position simply to be able to decode more meaning from the acoustic world. Another critique concerns the agency that Schafer confers on the lo-fi soundscape to overdetermine how people engage with the auditory world; it is as if the contemporary lo-fi world crushes listeners to its will, leaving them unable to listen through, against, or critically to noise, seeking to put it aside to get to the signal. But is this inevitably the case? Consider, for example, American muscle cars, admired by some not only for their engine power but also for how that power *sounded*. Where Schafer would only hear a loud exhaust pipe, a muscle car aficionado would likely actively seek to discern: Is this a Corvette? Camaro? Mustang? Charger? One can, that is, engage meaningfully with the lo-fi. Lastly, and relatedly, Schafer's lack of engagement with listening subjects shuts out the role that cultural, racial, ethnic, class, gender, historical, and individual backgrounds play in what people hear in the world around them. For example, most people would take for granted that those who live in rural areas will find the loudness and the noise of a major city to be a shock, a distraction, and an adjustment to get used to. Yet while it may be harder to imagine, it is no less true that for many people who have lived their lives in major urban areas, the relative silence of a rural area, especially at night, is no less disquieting: one person's feeling of being drowned by noise is another person's feeling of being exposed by silence. To move this line of critique further from Schafer's world of the countryside and the city, simply consider that how one hears and experiences machine-gun fire in a war zone will likely be different if one is an unarmed civilian or the soldier doing the firing. Who one is, that is to say, powerfully shapes one's understanding of their soundscape.[9]

Despite these critiques, soundscape—both the concept and the book—has had a lasting impact on sound studies, in no small measure because Schafer provides a rich set of terminology with which to describe sonic elements of outdoor and indoor acoustic environments. While the precise definitions and scope laid out by Schafer for some of this terminology have themselves become part of the larger critique of his work, many are nonetheless helpful resources in describing the sonic world. For example, "keynote sounds" are those that are continuously present in a given place and that, therefore, provide a backdrop against which other sounds are heard, such as crashing waves in a seafront community or the sound of traffic if one lives next to a busy highway. Keynote sounds are often not consciously listened to—Schafer likens them to the "ground" in a figure-ground relationship—but for just this reason, if they go silent, their absence may be jarring. "Soundmarks" are defined as sounds that carry a particular significance for members of a community or that have come to partially define the community itself and that are foreground sounds: the bells of Big Ben in London, for example; or of *samba enredo* being performed along the *sambódromo* during Carnival parades in Rio de Janeiro or Saõ Paulo; or of jazz funeral procession bands in New Orleans.[10] "Signals" are also foreground sounds that may or may not be considered soundmarks of a community but that represent a subset of sounds that demand attention or initiate an action: a tornado siren (take immediate shelter), a volunteer fire company horn (come to the station), a doorbell, or the ping of a cooking timer. A given sound need not partake of only a single category in this typology: a mosque's adhān (call to prayer) is clearly both a soundmark and a signal, for example. What is more important than utilizing these terms to assign a prescriptive category to any particular sound is that Schafer's work does provide useful linguistic resources with which to understand and describe different dimensions of the soundscape.

Refining and Extending "Soundscape": The Culturally Situated Ear and Soundscapes of Consumption

One way of building upon Schafer's work is to ask a simple question that challenges its presuppositions: Instead of focusing on what the sounded world brings or does to listeners, what if one asks what listeners bring to an understanding of—and therefore to a definition and description of—the sonic spaces they inhabit? A sound pressure level meter can quantify the loudness of a midwestern city, a rainforest village, or a college dining hall. But what that quantification ultimately means—what impact knowing that measurement would have on those who traverse or inhabit these spaces—can't be addressed by any simple "data-fication" of the space. Is measuring sound an adequate way of understanding how people engage with, or make sense of, or are forced to grapple with how spaces sound? Knowing decibel measurements can certainly help one to gain knowledge of the physical outlines of what they encounter in a given space, but can measurement help people understand how and why sound has the effects it does? Can it help to understand what purposes or insights such grappling might be put to? These questions have been, especially for sound studies researchers in social science disciplines, key post-Schafer explorations. And the resounding answer to these questions is that while such data are useful, they remain largely silent in helping to understand why sound means what it means, how it matters in the way that it does, or how people ultimately make sound meaningful.

SOUNDSCAPE

I. Media theorists often argue that humans come to know the world they inhabit in two different ways: via somatic knowledge (what we learn or experience directly through the bodily sensorium—e.g., heat can be dangerous because being subjected to too much of it burns us) and through mediated knowledge (the world as brought to us through "symbolic" channels, such as what we gain through language or images). One can physically stand at the edge of Iguaçu Falls on the Brazil-Argentina border, for example, looking at and listening to the pounding cascade of the world's largest waterfall while simultaneously feeling the drops of humid spray that shoot upward to land on exposed skin, even as one smells the ionization of the spray (the somatic). Or, one can look at a photo taken from the same exact spot, which strips one's bodily experience bare from any form of sensorial engagement except sight, but even one's sight is constrained by mediations such as the framing of the image, its exposure, the properties of the lens that took the photo, the quality of the physical print or of the resolution of whatever digital device one is looking at the photograph on, and so forth (the symbolic). Of course, the somatic and the symbolic can be experienced in tandem: imagine hearing a bird call and, hoping to identify the species, you consult your pocket field guide for a written description (or your phone for the birdsong app you once downloaded), or that you are cooking from a recipe that tells you to "sauté the sliced garlic until just fragrant but is not yet brown around the edges," so you engage your nose and your eyes to avoid burning the garlic and thereby ruining the dish. Clearly, somatic and symbolic modes of experiencing the world and of learning information about it can provide simultaneous and complementary knowledge.

Symbolic information is often referred to as "mediated," in as much as some mode of communication or presentation of information is understood to sit between the "external world" and how it is represented to or experienced by people. Most would agree that, in the twenty-first century, in most parts of the world, the majority of what we know is learned through mediated channels such as the internet, film, television, social media, books, and so forth. But technology isn't required for mediation to occur: if your friend tells you about something that they learned—for example, that one of your mutual friends had totaled their car late last night—your friend would be providing mediated information *and* acting as a medium (i.e., as a means of transmitting information). Not only is your friend a mediator in this case but so too is language; you are learning about the event not only through someone else but also through their words, with not only their literal but also their connotative meanings. Mediated information is sometimes treated as less reliable than unmediated knowledge; does the mediation process itself frame, color, shape, or misrepresent information? How closely does your birdsong field guide *actually* represent an auditory phenomenon in its silent print? How might you understand your friend's car accident differently if you later learned that the friend who told you about it knew, but deliberately withheld the information, that your mutual friend had been drinking all evening before getting behind the wheel?[11]

Such questions sit at the intersection of what philosophers term "epistemology" (the nature of knowing or of how one knows what one knows) and "phenomenology" (the nature of experiences and consciousness). What is important for this discussion is that care be taken *not* to assume that there is somehow greater objectivity attached to knowledge gained via somatic as opposed to mediated or symbolic means. Anthropologists who study the senses have repeatedly stressed that sensory perception is not merely a physical act but also a cultural one. The Western insistence that there are five distinct senses, for example, has a long intellectual history dating back at least to Greek philosophy and flowing through Catholic theology;[12] other cultures recognize a different number of senses, subdivide the sensorium differently, and strongly ascribe hierarchical values to what is apprehended through different sensory pathways.[13] Anthropologists who study sound would insist that the culturally conditioned ears that listeners bring, for example, to the rainforest—to any acoustic space or event—don't simply interpret the sounds of that space or event but, in fact, are integral in creating its experiential existence. To return to the language of media theory, it is too simple merely to delineate the somatic and the mediated, because the somatic itself is culturally mediated. Hearing and listening cannot, therefore, be uncritically considered, or be divorced from, cultural conceptions surrounding what it means to encounter sounds or how to make sense of them.

Returning to Steven Feld's work in the Papua New Guinea Highlands, then, and to the suggestion made previously that the soundscape isn't merely the acoustic fact of sounds that happen in space, but is instead a relationship that emerges at the intersection of sounds, spaces, and listeners, do the Kaluli hear a different rainforest soundscape than a non-Kaluli would? To address this question, and trying to move beyond some of the limitations of Schafer's work on the soundscape, Feld coined the term "acoustemology." The word is a portmanteau of "acoustics" and "epistemology"; it references sound as a way of knowing. He writes, "Acoustemology joins acoustics to epistemology to investigate sounding and listening as knowing-in-action: a knowing-with and knowing-though the audible."[14] Elsewhere, acoustemology is defined as "local configurations of acoustic sensation, knowledge, and imagination embodied in [a] culturally particular sense of place."[15] Feld is, of course, strongly suggesting that, yes, the Kaluli hear their soundscapes differently than a non-Kaluli would, because of how culture and a long history of engagement with the specific sonic environment of a densely layered auditory world create specifically Kaluli ways of listening to and extracting significance from the rainforest's sonic space. Might these specifically Kaluli ways of listening and making sense of/giving sense to sound share things in common with other rainforest cultures? Undoubtedly, but the particulars of the Bosavi flora and fauna and aviary, of how the Kaluli language deeply weaves onomatopoeia of birdsong into its vowel and consonant patterns, and its cosmology that links birds to humans' ancestors, all combine to create a distinctly Kaluli acoustemology, rooted in, but always simultaneously defining, the Bosavi soundscape.

Whereas Schafer's soundscape seemingly looms as an oppressive and predetermined entity, Feld's acoustemology suggests that soundscapes might better be thought of as dynamic experiences that happen at the intersection of acoustic environments and the people who come into contact with them. If part of acoustemology is to understand that audible spaces consist of "knowing-in-action," then people can be understood as having a meaningful contribution to what a soundscape turns out to be. Dreiser's city noise may have largely overwhelmed the preaching family, but there was certainly a contained area, close to them, in which they were heard, and in which people walking by—or perhaps even standing still to listen—could hear them, and perhaps join in with their singing, praying, and participating by their actions, in the (very Christian) word of God. Students gathered in a residential college's newly renovated central dining hall could choose (or not) to study or to have weekly "language table" dinners in the space. Those choices would simultaneously be responsive to, and be defining of, the soundscape of the dining hall, as a study space (or not) filled with multiple languages (or not) and understood as a part of the college's academic geography (or not).

II. Contemporary consumer culture, just as much as the rainforest, sits at the acoustemological juncture of sounds, spaces, and listeners. Consider the indoor shopping mall, for instance. In the United States, such malls, anchored by one or more large department stores, virtually defined suburban consumer capitalism from the 1960s until the mid-2000-aughts, with their heyday coming in the roughly thirty-five years between 1970 and 2005 (their displacement from that role coinciding with the rise of online shopping and further accelerated by the Covid-19 pandemic). Early iterations during this thirty-five-year window often consisted of a single-story series of adjoined corridors (with the anchor stores possibly two or three stories tall) usually made of brick or polished concrete, often with skylights and water features (such as fountains or indoor streams). Later versions (especially in areas with higher land prices and during the rise of "mega-malls") were increasingly designed as multistoried atriums in which, except for on the ground floor, shoppers walked along what were essentially balconies, off which smaller stores opened. The multistory nonretail spaces of this later generation of indoor malls allowed for the incorporation of even more sound-emitting objects and activities (including small amusement park-like areas). Throughout this period of the construction boom of indoor malls, their public spaces routinely continued to be built using hard surfaces, which meant that sounds created in these spaces would inevitably be highly reflective, creating layers of echoes and sonic overlap. Especially during high-traffic times (the winter holiday shopping season, for instance), malls took on a cacophony not entirely unlike that of Dreiser's anonymous cityscape.[16]

Think for a moment about what you hear when you are in a crowded indoor suburban mall. In its public areas, you will likely encounter a constant drone of unintelligible voices, above which will rise more clearly defined bursts of raucous individual or collective laughter, or the sharp crying of an infant, or an expletive being hurled loudly between people who are about to be, or already are, in a fight. If you are shopping with someone, you will hopefully hear your own voices as you converse. There may be sounds from events the mall is hosting: a high school cheerleading competition; a model train show; Santa's Workshop helpers building wooden toys; or a local martial arts dojo putting on an exhibition. You may hear the mechanical noise and the music from an indoor carousel or the (comparatively quiet) *thunk-thunk* of an escalator's steps as its bull gears rotate them downward to begin their journey on the underside of the chassis. You will hear some of the sounds that people simply make as they move about while carrying objects: footsteps and crinkling plastic bags. And, of course, you will hear the background music that is being piped throughout the mall, music intended to stay in the background, to be unremarkable, to go largely unnoticed: certainly not music designed to make you linger only to continue the enjoyable experience of listening to the music itself.[17]

Once you step into a store, the sonic environment and your experience of it are likely to change noticeably, though in directions less uniform than what you've encountered in the mall's public spaces. Unless you are the only person in the store, you will most likely continue to hear many of the humanly originated sounds of the mall's public spaces: people's voices, the sounds of their movement, and so on. But it is also highly likely that those sounds will not present as much of an unintelligible drone as they did outside the store: more individual words of others' conversations will be intelligible, for example. This may in part result from there being fewer competing voices, but (depending on the particular store) it may also result from the space having less echo because it is carpeted and has lower ceilings and acoustic panels that absorb sound.[18] What is virtually certain, however, is that the music that you will hear in the store—regardless of the genre or its volume—will no longer be the generic, intended-to-be-ignored music of the mall's public spaces. It will instead be carefully curated to match the image that the store wishes to project of itself to you, as a consumer of its goods.

In a groundbreaking article about the role of music at indoor malls, Canadian communication studies scholar Jonathan Sterne examined the dynamics that link sound, consumerism, and patrons' mall shopping experiences in the late 1990s by performing a close study of the sonic characteristics of a "mega-mall," the Mall of America in the Minneapolis suburb of Bloomington, Minnesota.[19] Sterne argues that sound in a mall must be understood as a crucial element of its infrastructure, analogous (and relying upon the same deliberate design forethought) to its electrical, plumbing, HVAC, and communications (e.g., phone and internet) systems. According to Sterne, "The Mall of America presumes in its very structure and requires as part of its maintenance a continuous, nuanced, and highly orchestrated flow of music to all its parts. It is as if a sonorial [sic] circulation system keeps the mall alive," and Sterne suggests that, therefore, there is much to be gained from thinking of music as an element of built architecture.[20]

Sterne was writing before the era of streaming services such as Spotify and Pandora, when the company known as Muzak[21] dominated the industry for creating and delivering background music to retail businesses, bars and restaurants, doctors' offices, elevators, and phone hold-waiting systems.[22] Businesses contracted with Muzak to create and deliver playlists that would appeal to their intended customer base, and Muzak touted its acuity in market research to discover and realize those ideal customers' musical preferences. The better the fit between desired customers' musical tastes and the music being played in the store, it was reasoned, shoppers would be increasingly likely to buy and spend. As Sterne succinctly puts it, "Essentially, the use of programmed music in a shopping mall is about the production and consumption of consumption."

Retail stores in indoor shopping malls are predominantly outposts of national (or, less frequently, regional) chains and thus are usually tightly constrained by corporate requirements to adhere to a specific, uniform, cohesive aesthetic. McDonalds' hallmark French fries are, for example, intended to taste the same whether one is at a drive-through in Atlanta, Seattle, Detroit, or Brooklyn, and the color schemes of their dining rooms, the layout of their "playscape" areas, and the fact that a "#2 meal" is a Quarter-Pounder with Cheese™

coast-to-coast, all are in service of brand recognition and consistency. Musical choices in stores, Sterne argues, are deeply implicated in creating and maintaining precisely this kind of uniform branding message and recognition; just as interior design, store layout, and lighting are often identical (or narrowly constrained)[23] among individual outlets, so too are music programming and stores' overall sonic environment. In other words, music is deeply implicated in marketing and branding.

Critical to selling nonessential goods and services—and even to creating consumers' belief in meaningful differentiations between brands dealing in identical essential goods and services, such as toothpaste or automobile tires—is to create in consumers a recognition that who they are—or who they aspire to be—is bolstered by what they are purchasing. French sociologist Pierre Bourdieu argued that this recognition rests not only on actually possessing and recognizing one's own tastes but equally—if not more so—on an awareness (often not fully conscious) of tastes with which one does *not* want to be associated.[24] Bourdieu's study of French consumerism focused largely on social class; he argued that when making decisions concerning which consumer goods to buy, people were most hesitant to purchase items that might be associated with social classes closely below them and were most likely to try to justify paying for things that were associated with the social class slightly above them, even if their affordability was something of a stretch. Consumerism, in this framework, is seen through the lens of image management: don't make choices that might mistake you for being of lower social standing than you are (or how you want to be perceived), and make, whenever possible, choices that create the appearance of elevated social standing.[25] Purchasing is understood to be driven by the desire to mark social and class distinctions from fellow consumers; to put it another way, stores project images of the kind of consumer who is a shopper of their merchandise, and consumers project that image back onto themselves. Upper-middle-class consumers want, Bourdieu argues, to be seen as the kind of persons who can, or who choose to, for example, buy a Tesla or a BMW i3 instead of a Chevy Bolt; who drink microbrews instead of multinational corporate beers; who listen to vinyl instead of streaming audio; who shop at Costco instead of Sam's Club; and who wear a Rolex or a Patek Phillipe watch when a Timex keeps time perfectly at a fraction of the cost.[26]

During the 1980s and 1990s, the lingerie store Victoria's Secret provided a classic shopping mall example of Bourdieu's claims and is one of several brief case studies from the Mall of America that Sterne discusses. Victoria's Secret sought to associate itself with what might be called a "refined, risqué sexuality," predicated upon a (largely white, heterosexual, male) fantasy of upper-class, female (hetero)sexual identity:[27] a boudoir sensibility that assembled associations of "provocative" undergarments (stockings, garter belts, corsets, satin bras) but associations simultaneously tempered with an implication that to be *too* overtly sexual was to be gauche. Its main mall-based competitors were the lingerie sections of anchor department stores, and another lingerie-specific chain, Frederick's of Hollywood, which had developed deep associations for many consumers of cheapness and trashiness over the years. Arguably, Frederick's of Hollywood served as Victoria's Secret's foil in this time period; Victoria's Secret strove to create an aura of luxury, refinement, and tasteful naughtiness, at a price more affordable than what one might pay for fine European lingerie, and many of its customers clearly shopped there so as not to be mistaken for consumers of its "lower-class" cousin.

The company's brand association was also firmly tied to cultivating a specifically European identity (implied, of course, by the use of Britain's Queen Victoria in its very name), which further suggested a "refined," higher-class identity that many Americans associate with Europe. Beyond the name, the experience was structured so that one walked into a store that was softly lit, lined with dark, warm-toned, wood-paneled walls: for men, it likely evoked a boudoir or a smoking room or the private back room of a pub. Only a limited amount of lingerie was on display to touch or to sort through, with most inventory housed in wooden drawers that shop attendants would slide out for customers after asking what they were looking for. Victoria's Secret's mall stores were designed to evoke the sophistication of exclusive, neighborhood-based, private shopping boutiques far removed, and a respite from the hustle and bustle of the common spaces of suburban American malls, with their fighting teenagers, arguing couples, and crying babies.

Sterne focuses primarily on the deliberate choice made by the company to play only European art music (i.e., what is generically termed "classical music") in its stores during the 1990s, with a particular emphasis on a set of composers most deeply enshrined in the canons of the Baroque, Classical, and Romantic periods; Bach, Mozart, Handel, Beethoven, Schubert, Brahms, and Tchaikovsky were particularly heavily represented. For many Americans, such "classical" music carries very specific sets of associations and/or connotations, both about the music itself and about who listens to it and the qualities those people embody. To some, those connotations and associations may be inherently negative: elitism, snobbery, pretention, and a propensity to advertise one's supposed sophistication. To others, more positive attributes attach to this musical repertoire: prestige, refinement, discerning taste, sophistication (which need not coincide with choosing actively to listen to classical music when on one's own, or even to liking it; what matters simply are the associations it evokes). To those holding the former set of feelings and associations, Victoria's Secret stores (and therefore, by extension, its products) were perhaps turnoffs. But for those with the latter set of associations, the soundtrack that accompanied the shopping experience not only further amplified the poshness and sense of indulgence deeply coded into the stores' interior design and product choices but also confirmed that the store was a respectable, sophisticated place to shop and that by shopping there, consumers were displaying (and indeed enacting) their own sophistication.

As if to lay all of this out explicitly, Victoria's Secret, in a relatively novel move for the era, kept cassette tapes and CDs of the music being played in its stores available for purchase, positioned next to the cash registers. It was able to do so, in part, because Victoria's Secret did not rely upon a service like Muzak to provide its music. Instead, it used an independent contractor to help create specific musical arrangements for play in the stores. Many of these arrangements were performed and recorded by the London Symphony Orchestra, and the liner notes accompanying the cassettes and CDs frequently highlighted that these were recordings made exclusively for Victoria's Secret. The manufacturing of prestige is laid bare in such liner-note claims: that the (prestigious) London Symphony Orchestra would make exclusive recordings for Victoria's Secret conferred prestige upon Victoria's Secret because the London Symphony Orchestra had "chosen" only to let Victoria's Secret distribute these recordings. Purchasers of the tapes and CDs now owned recordings that were not available to just anyone—they were only available to those sophisticated, motivated, and savvy enough to realize that Victoria's Secret was selling far more than lingerie. Victoria's Secret was selling an all-encompassing, flattering portrayal of what it sells and of who consumes what it sells. The soundscape of the store and the fact that a crucial element of the soundscape was itself commoditized by the company combine to show how deeply sound and consumerism can be, and often are, linked.

Conclusion

R. Murray Schafer's specific conception of the soundscape—as the totality of sounds available to the ear in a given place and time, and particularly as associated with a negative trajectory toward an increasingly lo-fi soundscape in need of rehabilitation—has given way to a both a more nuanced and yet often more general use of the term. Scholars have come to recognize that the soundscape isn't simply a monolithic entity that confronts listeners but rather that just as soundscapes may act upon individuals and groups, so too individuals and groups actively construct, utilize in creative ways, and resist or refine soundscapes. Listeners do not simply bring passive, somehow "natural" or neutral ears to the soundscape but instead bring fully enculturated modes of listening to and engaging with the soundscapes in which they find themselves. Further, as Sterne's work demonstrates, soundscapes can be linked to social and individual identities, which people actively construct by how they participate in sounded environments. In many of the chapters that follow, "soundscape"—without the negative connotations of Schafer's work—will remain a useful anchor for understating key concepts and research done within sound studies.

Project

Create an auditory exploration of a natural or built space: literally, take the listener on a three-minute walk through a space in such a way that they can hear how that space shapes, and is shaped by, human artifacts and activities. Human intervention should be broadly construed to include speech, singing, music, and the noise of machines, human social activity, work, play, or relaxation; artifacts can include technologies, commodities, and architecture, for example.

Your "sound object" will be part documentation and part aesthetic intervention. You will need to record raw sonic footage from your chosen space, but you will equally be crafting that sonic footage into a montage that tells a story about sound.

By way of example, imagine that you have chosen an underground subway platform as your space. You may wish to focus on figure-ground relationships between the din of multiple voices reverberating off the echoey subway tiles and the presence of a clearly distinguishable nearby voice. You may wish to explore the sound of quiet (if any) on the platform and juxtapose it with the loud noise of the trains as they arrive and depart from the platform. You may contrast the mechanical noise of brakes and wheels with the melodic sounds played by a saxophone busker or the calls of a vendor. You may take listeners on a ride inside the train, charting how sound changes as one nears the end of the line and the car empties out. You may do a "day in the life of," taking your listener on a sonic journey that contrasts the platform at rush hour with how it sounds late at night.

Notes

1 Dreiser, *An American Tragedy*, 3–9.
2 A version of this description appeared in Porcello (2014).

3 Feld, *Sound and Sentiment*.

4 Feld, *Voices of the Rainforest*.

5 Schafer, *The Soundscape*, 4. City Planning graduate student Michael Southworth systematically utilized the term and concept a few years prior to Schafer, but the term has, for all intents and purposes, become firmly latched to Schafer. See Radicchi, "The Notion of Soundscape in the Realm of Sensuous Urbanism," 99–128, and for a lengthier account of the history of the term, see Picker, "Soundscape(s)," 147–58.

6 Schafer, *The Soundscape*, 3.

7 The concept of signal-to-noise ratio (also termed SNR) is utilized in many fields where the issue of how to best convey information through a medium is crucial: hence the use of the term "sonic" here. SNR is a central concern in medical imaging, for example: a "lo-fi" medical image is one in which graininess or blurring (the noise) impinges upon the ability to see the physical object being imaged (the signal).

8 Schafer, *The Soundscape*, 71.

9 For further discussion of Schafer's work, its impact on sound studies, and critiques, see Kelman, "Rethinking the Soundscape," 212–34; Arkette, "Sounds Like the City," 159–68; Ingold, "Against Soundscape," 10–13; Helmreich, "Listening against Soundscapes," 10; Feld, "Waterfalls of Song," 91–135; Feld, "Acoustemology," 12–21; Samuels et al., "Soundscapes," 329–45; and Daughtry, *Listening to War*. For a discussion specifically of critiques of Schafer's conceptualization of "soundscape," see Picker, "Soundscape(s)," 147–58.

10 See Sakakeeny, "'Under the Bridge,'" 1–27. Schafer's use of this term differs from its use in intellectual property law, where it refers specifically to the trademarking of a sound. Legal soundmarks include Darth Vader's breathing (LucasFilms), the I-VI-IV interval chimes (NBC), the so-called "30 voices over 7 measures" sound during the display of the THX logo at movie theaters, the ticking stop-watch of *60 Minutes* (CBS), and perhaps most notoriously, *Law & Order*'s "chun-chun" (or is it *chung-chung*?!) sequence (NBC Universal), formally described as "two musical notes, a strike and a rapid rearticulation of a perfect fifth pitch interval, which in the key of C sounds the notes C and G, struck concurrently."

11 All of the world's natural languages provide some mechanism to indicate whether knowledge that a speaker is reporting was gained firsthand or not, the general term for which is "evidentiality." Approximately one-quarter of all languages mandate specifying this information, usually accomplished through the use of a grammatical particle (such as an affix) incorporated into verbs, though what precisely needs to be specified varies widely (e.g., whether there merely is evidence at all; whether the source of one's evidence is gained from firsthand witnessing or not; whether it is second-hand or thirdhand; whether it was learned via hearsay; and whether it is visual knowledge or not). But that evidentiality is a linguistic universal, and that a significant percentage of languages

make it mandatory to report, suggests that accounting for how one has learned what one knows has historically been understood to be significant to *homo sapiens*. See Aikhenvald, *Evidentiality*, for a comprehensive discussion.

12 Synott, "Puzzling over the Senses from Plato to Marx," 61–76.
13 Classen, "Foundations for an Anthropology of the Senses," 401–12.
14 Feld, "Acoustemology," 12–21.
15 Feld, "Waterfalls of Song," 91–135.
16 The "eeriness" of abandoned malls has been a subject of fascination for years (even being in a mall at a very slow time of day can feel disorienting given the quiet of what most people associate with a noisy space). Before Covid-19, one could find numerous photography collections of the interiors of closed suburban malls (e.g., Smith, "Ghostly Images of a Dead Mall Tell an American Story"). During the year of intense lockdowns in many parts of the country (and the world), in which malls were not allowed to open, more awareness became focused on what might be called "situational abandonment" (e.g., Biron, "Coronavirus Fears Have Turned Malls Everywhere from Italy to Washington into Ghost Towns").
17 To return to the concept of acoustemology, consider that malls have increasingly moved to playing classical music in their public spaces as a way to keep teenagers from lingering in them. Note the assumption that a particular type of sound (in this case, a particular type of music) will be experienced as unpleasant by a particular demographic of people long associated with being troublemakers, without deterring an older demographic considered less problematic.
18 Cf. Schafer's (*The Soundscape*) discussion of hi-fi and lo-fi soundscapes.
19 Sterne, "Sounds Like the Mall of America," 22–50.
20 Ibid.
21 An additional service that made Muzak attractive to businesses was that it would streamline paying for the right to use artists' music in a store. In the United States, performing artists usually have "performance rights" that give them a royalty each time a piece that they recorded is played. Historically, two major clearing houses—ASCAP and BMI—tracked "plays" of a recording and collected those royalties; Muzak eliminated business's needs to work directly with these two agencies.
22 Sterne, "Sounds Like the Mall of America," 22–50.
23 Corporations may sometimes allow for local or regional variation, if they know that their target consumers may have different musical tastes in, say, rural or urban areas.
24 Bourdieu, *Distinction*.
25 Bourdieu's research focused specifically on consumption as related to social class, but his larger framework and insights map onto parallel demographic differences, such as race and sexuality, as well.

26 Bourdieu's study examined the late-twentieth-century French bourgeoisie and does not map exactly onto its upper-middle-class counterpart in the United States. In the United States, the "distinctions" used in these examples can turn into a two-edged sword, susceptible to being understood as "snobbish" taste preferences and thus subject to scorn. Further, as political polarization has increased in the United States in the twenty-first century, these distinctions are easily drawn into participating in liberal/conservative polarizations, in which case they do not entirely map onto social class.

27 Company founder Roy Raymond has repeatedly been quoted as saying that his inspiration for the brand came from being made to feel uncomfortable shopping for a lingerie gift for his wife in a department store, as well as being disappointed that it was hard to find "sensual" lingerie that was geared beyond only a woman's wedding night. See Barr, " 'Happy Ending, Right?' "

Bibliography

Aikhenvald, Alexandra. *Evidentiality*. Oxford: Oxford University Press, 2004.

Arkette, Sophie. "Sounds Like the City." *Theory, Culture and Society* 21, no. 1 (2004): 159–68.

Barr, Naomi. " 'Happy Ending, Right?' The Founder of Victoria's Secret Had a Genius Idea." October 30, 2013. https://slate.com/business/2013/10/victorias-secret-founding-roy-raymond-had-a-great-idea-but-les-wexner-was-the-one-to-see-it-through.html (accessed January 28, 2021).

Biron, Bethany. "Coronavirus Fears Have Turned Malls Everywhere from Italy to Washington into Ghost Towns." March 12, 2020. https://www.businessinsider.com/coronavirus-fears-turn-malls-around-the-world-into-ghost-towns-2020-3 (accessed March 14, 2021).

Bourdieu, Pierre. *Distinction: A Social Critique of the Judgment of Taste*. Translated by Richard Nice. Cambridge, MA: Harvard University Press, 1984.

Classen, Constance. "Foundations for an Anthropology of the Senses." *International Social Science Journal* 49, no. 3 (1997): 401–12.

Daughtry, J. Martin. *Listening to War: Sound, Music, Trauma, and Survival in Wartime Iraq*. Oxford: Oxford University Press, 2015.

Dreiser, Theodore. *An American Tragedy*. New York: Boni and Liveright, 1925.

Feld, Steven. "Acoustemology." In *Keywords in Sound*, edited by David Novak and Matt Sakakeeny, 12–21. Durham, NC: Duke University Press, 2015.

Feld, Steven. *Sound and Sentiment: Birds, Weeping, Poetics, and Song in Kaluli Expression*. 3rd ed. Durham, NC: Duke University Press, 2012 [1982].

Feld, Steven. *Voices of the Rainforest*. Washington, DC: Smithsonian Folkways, 1991.

Feld, Steven. "Waterfalls of Song: An Acoustemology of Place Resounding in Bosavi, Papua New Guinea." In *Senses of Place*, edited by Steven Feld and Keith Basso, 91–135. Santa Fe, NM: School of American Research Press, 1996.

Helmreich, Stefan. "Listening against Soundscapes." *Anthropology News* 59, no. 9 (2010): 10.

Ingold, Tim. "Against Soundscape." In *Autumn Leaves: Sound and Environment in Artistic Practice*, edited by Angus Carlyle, 10–13. Paris: Double Entendre, 2007.

Kelman, Ari. "Rethinking the Soundscape: A Cricial Genealogy of a Key Term in Sound Studies." *Senses & Society* 5, no. 2 (2010): 212–34.

Picker, John M. "Soundscape(s): The Turning of the Word." In *The Routledge Companion to Sound Studies*, edited by Michael Bull, 147–58. London: Routledge, 2019.

Porcello, Thomas, Book Review, *Religion out Loud: Religious Sound, Public Space, and American Pluralism*, by Isac Weiner (2013, NYU Press). In *Anthropological Quarterly* 88, no.1 (2014): 213–17.

Radicchi, Antonella. "The Notion of Soundscape in the Realm of Sensuous Urbanism: A Historical Perspective." In *Listen! Sound Worlds from the Body to the City*, edited by Ariane Wilson, 99–128. Newcastle upon Tyne: Cambridge Scholars Publishing, 2019.

Sakakeeny, Matt. "'Under the Bridge': An Orientation to Soundscapes in New Orleans." *Ethnomusicology* 54, no. 1 (2010): 1–27.

Samuels, David, Louise Meintjes, Ana Maria Ochoa, and Thomas Porcello. "Soundscapes: Toward a Sounded Anthropology." *Annual Review of Anthropology* 39 (2010): 329–45.

Schafer, R. Murray. *The Soundscape: Our Sonic Environment and the Tuning of the World*. Rochester, VT: Destiny Books, 1994 [1977].

Smith, Aaron. "Ghostly Images of a Dead Mall Tell an American Story." November 16, 2016. https://money.cnn.com/2016/11/16/news/dead-mall-photos-seph-lawless/ (accessed March 13, 2021).

Sterne, Jonathan. "Sounds Like the Mall of America: Programmed Music and the Achitectonics of Commercial Space." *Ethnomusicology* 41, no. 1 (1997): 22–50.

Synott, Anthony. "Puzzling over the Senses from Plato to Marx." In *Varieties of Sensory Experience*, edited by David Howes, 61–76. Toronto: University of Toronto Press, 1991.

2

Noise: From the Everyday to the Exceptional

Key concepts: futurism, noise abatement, secondary object, meta-discourse, *sawari*

Introduction

In *Discord: The Story of Noise* author Mike Goldsmith relates a short but telling anecdote related to the first noise ordinances in London in 1846. At this moment, the population of the city was ballooning, and with it came increases in both mechanical and human noise. Philosopher and social commentator Thomas Carlyle bemoaned the human noise that intruded into his living quarters. In a letter to his nephew Alexander, he lamented the constant noise, writing, "every door that slams to in the street is audible in your most secret chamber ... and when you issue from your door, you are assailed by vast shoals of quacks, and showmen, and street sweepers, and pick-pockets, and mendicants of every degree and shape, all plying in noise or silent craft their several vocations."[1] For Carlyle, the noises of modernizing London were more detrimental to intellectual workers of his ilk than to the manual and physical laborers whose lives produced this din and were lived within it.[2] Carlyle's solution to this was novel and groundbreaking: he employed an architect to design and build a sound-proof room on top of his house to use as his study, an in-home retreat from the noises lurking just outside his door. While his home was under construction, he departed for his country home, leaving his wife, Jane Welsh, to oversee the London construction project. Unlike Carlyle, Welsh found the sounds of construction far less annoying when Carlyle was away—perhaps Carlyle's own griping about the noise was more irritating to her than the noise itself. When Carlyle returned, his construction project was a success, providing him the sonic insulation from urban London that he longed for to pursue his intellectual work. But as Goldsmith recounts it, Carlyle's triumph of engineering was pyrrhic. In the new silence, he became more aware of the noises in his own home that distracted him. He was also confronted with the reality that some human noises are desirable: his home was quieter after the project's completion as his wife ran off with the architect.

This brief anecdote demonstrates the complexities of noise: its implication in power, legislation, labor, aesthetics, and creativity, as well as its role in social relations of gender, class, race, sexuality, and locality. As Goldsmith demonstrates, noise is subjective and is often demonized by those of Carlyle's status, class, and race. As a commentator and thinker of the Victorian era, Carlyle enjoyed a position of privilege: the right to assert a subjugating bird's eye view over a rapidly growing and changing society. From his vantage of power, due to his gender, class, sexuality, and education, Carlyle was free to criticize the necessary activities of the struggling working classes, (im)migrants, street hustlers, and hawkers. He heard them as noise and attributed to them disruptive qualities. He also employed his substantial resources—financial, intellectual, and social—to put space in between himself and the causes of the noise rather than recognizing the human, social, economic and policy causes, the symptom of which is noise.

The final issue that this story illuminates is that some noises are desirable. A blanket condemnation of noise always has in it an unspoken set of exemptions for desirable noises that confer to us power and authority, or that indicate pleasurable moments and events. As the well-worn anecdote states, "One man's music is another man's noise," indicating that taste is more often the arbiter of what is classified as noise than any objective criteria. Hillel Schwartz notes that noise itself is an indication of life, from the white noise of wind and waves, to the buzz of insects, and the deafening crash of thunder.[3] While Jacques Attali's platitude that "nothing essential happens in the absence of noise"[4] may have been intended for social interpretation, it is also true from the standpoint from biology and physics. Life is noisy, but the definitions, understandings, and discourses that separate sounds heard into language or babble, noise or music, static or information, signal and noise are not objective and vary among individuals, communities, societies, and events. To quote David Novak, "Noise ... is not really a kind of sound but a metadiscourse of sound and its social interpretation. The presence of noise indexes a larger field of differences, even as its own particularities remain undefined."[5] Noise is a product of social differences, their interplays, articulations, and confrontations.

Definitions of Noise

The *Oxford English Dictionary* has eleven different definitions of noise that range from conventional uses to older, unused historical notions, which ironically include "[a] pleasant or melodious sound" and "[a] company or band *of* musicians."[6] Apart from these two definitions, the others cluster around ideas of discomfort, excess, dissonance, stress, animality, notoriety, scandal, and undesirability. In common English usage, noise indicates sounds or states of being that hinder our ability to communicate, concentrate, sleep, or feel comfortable. Noise signifies sounds that are unwanted, undesirable, painful, embarrassing, or inhuman. Even in scientific and quantitative definitions, like data noise and signal-to-noise ratio, noise refers to irregularities, unpredictable fluctuations, distortions, and interference. In these cases, noise denotes a lack of clarity, an obfuscating force, and a negative relationship to knowledge or accuracy.

But noise is more than its dictionary definition. Hillel Schwartz states that "noise in the West has been signally transformed from an exclusively aural experience to a root metaphor about our world, our lives, and the meaning of our lives abroad in the world."[7] His point is that noise and its supposed opposite, silence, have become poles between which society is structured. For example, Gross et al. suggest that in Paris of the 1990s, with ongoing tensions between white French communities and Muslim immigrants from the Maghreb, immigrant neighborhoods were often described through noise and smell.[8] Their smells indexed unusual cuisine and unclean living. Their noises were the rough sounds of Arabic, Berber, improper French and suburban slang loudly spoken, souped-up automobiles, and Rai, the common popular dance music of Algeria and the Maghreb diaspora. Compared to the elegant sounds of Parisian French, the refined aromas of French perfume and haute cuisine, and the gentle, melodic strains of French pop, the sensuous cultural expressions of these new immigrants demarcated their neighborhoods by indexing existential cultural difference. This auditory and olfactory evidence of difference legitimated discrimination and marginalization in the minds of France's conservative white nationalists. In this context, noise becomes an indication of hierarchical differentiation, an excuse to label communities as subhuman, to limit entitlements and access to resources, and to use these communities as props for and objects of political propaganda.

In a *New York Times* piece on Green Bank, West Virginia, author Pagan Kennedy compares the noise of networked modernity to madness after experiencing the "quiet" of the National Radio Quiet Zone. The town of Green Bank is host to the Green Bank Observatory, a set of powerful radio telescopes capable of detecting tiny astral radio waves that inform astronomers about deep space. Because of the observatory's sensitivity, the town is free from all electromagnetic interference: cell phones, microwaves, Bluetooth devices, and smart technology. In this environment, the slight waves of an electric toothbrush can block the whisper of a star's passing millions of light years away. This technological quiet is a way of life embraced by the town's tiny population (less than 200). After a stay in Green Bank, the technological noises of modernity—alarms and notifications on phones, constant engagement with social media—seem like lunacy to Kennedy.[9] This case shows how relative perception can be and how the quieting of one form of noise—electromagnetic radio waves—literally quiets life and has the effect of changing perceptions of the speed, sound, and quality of life. Sometimes the sounds that we are not exposed to are the ones that matter the most.

There are, of course, exceptions to these negative notions of noise. Siegmund Levarie, using a scientific definition of noise derived from acoustics—a sound possessed of an irregular soundwave, juxtaposed with "tone," which is a regular and repeating wave—is adamant that not all noises are disturbing, damaging, loud, or dangerous. Most sounds in nature, save for songbirds and humpback whales, are irregular—the honking of geese, chirping of crickets, crashing of waves, and whistle of the wind. They are neither loud nor unpleasant.[10] Many desirable sounds, like the gentle bubbling of a stream, patter of rain, turning the pages of a book, or the sizzle of a frying pan, can be soothing. White noise and pink noise machines are used to calm babies and travelers in their sleeping hours, and autonomous sensory meridian response (ASMR) videos often consist of irregular sounds like eating, folding towels, brushing hair, sorting papers, or whispering.[11] In this case, noise is the correct descriptor for desirable sounds that are commonly used by consumers to alleviate insomnia, induce relaxation, and reduce stress. These uses run contrary to common reactions to noise and show the breadth of this particular sonic characteristic and sound metaphor. They also demonstrate that noise and its sonic others (music, speech, or high-fidelity sound) are not opposites but rather meta-discourses that create each other (this concept will be revisited in Chapter 6, also see Chapter 1).

The rest of this chapter examines noise in its varied roles as power broker, creator, and maintainer of difference and its generative place in musical and social aesthetics.

Noise and Noise Abatement

Noise can hurt, infuriate, and frustrate. Poorly timed noises prevent sleep and interfere with concentration; they distract and obfuscate the sounds that we either need to or would rather pay attention to. Exposure to noise at high volumes has direct and immediate effects that range from temporary loss of hearing to headaches, nausea, and pain. When exposed to noise at high volumes, the middle spectrum of hearing is temporarily dampened, favoring hearing at the far ends of the auditory spectrum. Long-term exposure can lead to permanent loss of hearing, higher risk of heart attack,[12] and lower test scores for school children.[13] The personal annoyance and stress caused by constant noise trigger the release of stress hormones, potentially resulting in hypertension and cardiovascular disease. Over long periods of time, regular exposure to noise can lead to a number of chronic health conditions. According to the World Health Organization, 1.6 million healthy years are lost in Western Europe each year due to noise exposure.[14] This means that the effect of noise on personal and social wellness and economic activity is profound. Lowering the noise level a mere 10 decibels around airports could potentially add $11,000 of productivity and health savings per person in the affected areas.[15] In "Sound and Cities," podcast host Roman Mars points out that people exposed to the stresses of noise tend to seek alleviation in comfort food and alcohol. Both these remedies can exacerbate the negative health effects of noise exposure.[16]

However, these facts, studies, and economic estimates do not explain noise abatement policies and campaigns. Noise abatement, as shown in the opening vignette about Thomas Carlyle, is more often about social aesthetics and the imposition of bourgeois notions on the growing industrial cities of modernity. In the industrial era, when factory noises increased along with the sounds of automobiles and the sounds of the new proletariat that moved to the city to find employment, noise abatement campaigns clearly bore the marks of class, race, and privilege. In her work on noise abatement campaigns, historian Karen Bijsterveld describes sound, with regard to technological advancement, as "controversial and deeply invested with symbolic significance."[17] In the context of a rapidly industrializing West, cities and citizens were not prepared for the onslaught of machines and their workers. Those who confronted noise often did so through familiar bourgeois intellectual strategies.

Early Examples

The first significant American anti-noise campaigner, Julia Barnett Rice, a New York physician, began her advocacy by taking on New York Harbor's cacophonous steamboat whistles. Tellingly, she considered these sounds to be social, not occupational, and therefore not necessary. She interpreted the late night whistles as jocular communication between boat captains. Through collecting signatures, Rice was able to put guidelines in place to quiet the harbor. She then founded the New York City Society for the Suppression of Unnecessary Noise in 1906. While the society was never large, it was populated by the wealthy and influential and had wide-ranging effects.[18] Principle among them was establishing quiet zones around schools and hospitals, a prescient judgment that predated much of the science about the effects of noise. What Rice and her society, along with the European societies that followed suit, often overlooked were the people whose lives were lived within the bounds of these noises. Rice's issue with the boat whistles was her own sleep, not the ears of the crews and longshoremen who were also exposed to these sounds. European anti-noise campaigners went so far as to place the blame for urban noise squarely on the laboring classes rather than on the factories, companies, or their owners. This lack of concern for workers and the working classes, which conflated manual laborers with the sonic signatures of industrialization, also manifested in a laissez-faire attitude toward workplace injuries and deaths. The workers' ears were of no more consequence than their hands, bodies, eyes, or families (noise abatement precedes child labor laws by a decade, and the Occupational Safety and Health Administration by over six decades). This also deflected blame from industrialists whose drive for profit forced factories and ports to operate into the night or around the clock.

In early twentieth-century England, efforts were made to educate workers out of their noisy lives, but these often manifested in paternalistic efforts to civilize rather than policies geared toward better mental and physical health and safer working conditions. Mike Goldsmith gives an example: "Anthropologist Michael Haberlandt proposed that an eleventh commandment should be taught in every school 'Though shalt not make noise.' "[19] This is an example of turn-of-the-century attempts to pedagogize working-class children out of the boisterous ways of their parents and communities. These actions, both creating quiet zones around schools and emphasizing stillness as a moral virtue, were encouraged by and for the benefit of citizens like Carlyle and Rice (not necessarily to improve the social and economic standing of working class children, let alone position them to compete economically and socially with the children of elites).

In another anecdote from the same era, microbiologist Robert Koch conflated fighting noise to fighting diseases like cholera and pestilence.[20] Cholera, an intestinal ailment from drinking contaminated water, was an affliction suffered in the squalid conditions in which the new urban laboring classes existed. Pestilence, often used in biblical context but literally referring to the bubonic plague, signified either a contagious and deadly disease contracted by living in proximity to vermin or a divine punishment visited upon the sinful. For many in an industrializing West that not only aggravated class inequality but also placed elites and working classes in closer proximity, noise was a metaphor for the discomforts of modernity. The reaction of the power classes was not to blame the machines that brought them wealth but to confine and control the laborers from from whom they derived value and to attach religious righteousness to their paternalistic and disciplinary actions. In these pursuits, anti-noise campaigning was the outward manifestation of these hierarchical social patterns.

Modern Noise Abatement

With better science and research came the quantification of noise's effect on human health. In both the UK and the United States, anti-noise campaigners exerted enough pressure to make noise abatement a national issue. Much of this agitation was generated by a new form of transportation that disrupted urban and suburban areas: air travel. The expansion of air transport and the development of the turbine dramatically raised the noise level of communities living near airports. Troubled by this increase, new noise abatement groups sprang up to advocate for regulation, leading to fresh approaches to studying, quantifying, and relieving noise. The result of this was international cooperation on an agreement between the International Civil Aviation Organization and the US Federal Aviation Association to reduce noise generated by aircraft.

One of the outgrowths of this activism in the United States was the Noise Control Act of 1972, which provided funding for a series of Environmental Protection Agency-run studies on noise pollution, including automobile, train, and airplane noise. Although the EPA, founded in 1970, was initially focused on clean air and water, noise easily became a concern that encompassed physical, occupational, psychological, and emotional health. The 1974 report submitted to Congress by the EPA stated that the purpose of the act was "to promote an environment for all Americans free from noise that jeopardizes their public health and welfare."[21] The EPA would then go on to promote a program to quiet jet engines and to produce a noise-rating system for consumer goods that would provide information to buyers on the noise made by particular products so that they might better control their indoor environments.

All of this is to say that the history of noise abatement in the West is one of dramatic encounters driven by industrialization, class tension, and regulation. The growing ambient sounds of cities across the world has largely coincided with economic growth, a force that citizens, governments, elites, and workers alike are often loath to completely oppose. But the frustrations and health effects of noise were and continue to be undeniable. Early on, these maladies were confronted by urban elites, using class-based hierarchies to graph new industrial issues onto pre-existing stereotypes and solutions. Later, science and regulation would be used to quantify noise and set recommendations and limits on its proliferation, leading to hosts of zoning and noise regulations by state and local governments. But as Van Kamp and Davies and Connor's work show, the sonic inequities of noise are still often drawn around lines of race and class.

Desirable Noises

The desire to eliminate noise coexists with the equally strong desire to produce and control it. While science and environmentalism set different thresholds for healthy noise—from a rustic zero artificial noise ideal proposed by R. Murray Schafer in *The Soundscape: The Tuning of the World* to the 70 dB level recommended in the 1974 EPA report on levels of environmental noise—entities ranging from politicians and militaries to club owners, composers, musicians, engineers, and interrogators have sought to utilize noise as a critical tool for their professions.

To begin with industrialization, not all involved and exposed to the noise of early factories, trains, and new urban living conditions heard the din the same way. Mark Smith notes that in the United States, the sounds of industry and the taming of the wilderness, from wagon wheels to the fall of axes and the hum of riverboats, were seen as preferable to the untamed howl of the wilderness. The battle between man and nature was framed as a confrontation between the wanted noise of the Anthropocene and the undesirable sounds produced by nature. In this context, the growing din of industry, mills, looms, sawmills, and steam engines was heard by capital and labor alike as sounds of progress, necessary for a fledgling nation that promised all the opportunity to ascend the ladder of class and comfort. Moreover, the sound of a neighbor laboring in the early hours of the morning was heard as a sign of industriousness and good character, ideal traits for a neighbor to possess.[22]

Karin Bijsterveld records a similar situation with Dutch boilermakers in the late nineteenth century. Young boys were needed to hold rivets in place inside of boilers, exposing them to incredible levels of noise as the outside of the boiler was hammered. The option of filling the ears with cotton or some other sound dampening material was rejected, as the boys needed their ears to communicate with the men on the other side of the steel. Despite the reality that boilermakers suffered hearing damage and loss, union leaders, who advocated for better working conditions, considered hearing damage part of the job. They viewed the boys who grew through that experience as exhibiting toughness. The experience made them strong workers, desirable because of their mettle. One claim made by a riveter in a mid-century Dutch documentary on the dangers of industrial hearing loss commissioned by the Dutch Department of Social Affairs and Public Health is that "[a] nail boy wearing earplugs will never become a man." Hearing loss was part of the masculine identity of these Dutch boilermakers. In other early twentieth-century factories, critics bemoaned the lack or rhythm and melody in the sound of machinery rather than the volume of the noise itself. Studies were conducted on the uses of music as an aid to make factory and office workers more efficient, adding sonority to industrial noise rather than searching to quiet the spaces that these professions existed in.[23]

Noise as a Weapon

The potential of noise to damage more than human ears—to cause disorientation, anxiety, nausea, and long- and short-term cognitive disturbances—has also proven an attractive concept for military and defense. While governments will only sparingly admit to deploying sonic weapons in either foreign or domestic disputes, evidence is ample that both loud infrasonic sounds or high-volume music has been used in warfare and crowd control. Steve Goodman points to the development of directional ultrasound technology, the ability to produce and pointedly transmit sub- and super-acoustic sounds at high volumes, as a turning point in the military deployment of sound.[24]

Sound was added to the military arsenal beginning during the Second World War, when anthropology and psychology were used to augment the science and strategy behind military policy. The German V-1 flying bomb, or buzz bomb as it was dubbed in England, may have inflicted fewer casualties on British cities than Allied incendiary bombs or nuclear weapons did on their adversaries. However, the confusion and fear that were stoked by the sound of low-flying aircraft and their noisy munitions, which caused nearly a million to flee London, were enough to tempt Winston Churchill to use chemical weapons (which, in the end, the British military did not).[25] In an experimental laboratory, an unusual defense mechanism called the "Whirlwind Cannon" was built by an Austrian scientist. The principle was that wind and sound could be an effective antiaircraft defense. The cannon produced artificial whirlwinds by triggering an explosion in a combustion chamber pointed into the air. According to reports, a smaller version of the cannon could shatter boards at 200 yards.[26]

US military psychological operations utilize a range of sonic strategies. The use of sound at high volumes has been in the US military arsenal for decades. These range from the audio-harassment and attempted spiritual coercion of the Viet Cong; to the day-and-night audio assault on General Manuel Noriega while he was holed up in the Vatican Embassy in Panama;[27] and the uses of music at loud volumes, usually heavy metal and rap, to deprive prisoners of war of sleep and induce extreme anxiety, with the aim of extracting intelligence.[28] Some of these uses were proclaimed as tactical successes, others as failures, and others denounced as the unethical actions of rogue soldiers.

Today, the most widely used noise weapon is the long-range audio device (LRAD). Manufactured for commercial and governmental use, the technology is variously self-labeled as a "game changer for communication," "humanely & safely protecting wildlife & assets," "securing borders safely & remotely," and "filling the critical gap between initial engagement & escalation of force," among other things.[29] The instrument is capable of transmitting sound, either voice messages or signals, with clarity over long distances. The company's own PR touts it as a vital component to security, crowd control, and public safety. However, in between the lines of the company's rhetoric are the echoes of the Urban Funk Campaign of the 1970s, which used high-volume noises capable of deafening at short ranges for crowd control and dispersal. The weapon was noise, and the desired effect of the high-volume sound ranged from auditory pain to nausea and anxiety. This history is contained in the tools and PR of LRAD.

What holds these together is the idea that sound at extreme volumes—noise—could be deployed as an effective coercive force. Whether it is effective because of the pain that sheer volume produces or because of the psychological effects of the sound—audible or ultrasonic—noise, in this context, is desirable, as long as it is pointed away from the user. Unlike the case of Dutch boilermakers, where exposure to noise served as a necessary dimension of labor and a rite of passage into robust manhood, sonic warfare is a game of tacticians and scientists. Those using the noise are protected from it, and those exposed to it suffer the consequences of having inferior scientific and defense mechanisms. In these cases, noise is an index of control and superiority, particularly technological and spatial dominance.

Noises We Desire

In light of the previous sections on noise as a nuisance and public health issue and noise as a weapon, it is odd to imagine that noise would possess pleasant and desirable connotations. However, noise has a long legacy in music and musical aesthetics—as a descriptor for unpleasant or poorly executed music, as well as a desirable characteristic of music itself. The definitions and parameters of noise are flexible and run from the employment of new dissonances to incorporation of electronic and mechanical noise into performance and composition, and the use of extremely high-wattage sound systems. In these contexts, noise operates as an identifier of a specific in-group, of fandom, or an aesthetic/intellectual community. Similar to LRAD, it is also a means of repelling unwanted groups. Unlike sonic warfare, but similar to Dutch riveters and nail boys, willing self-exposure to noise and participation with it serve as a marker of masculinity, a rite of passage, or a sign of belonging.

One of the clearest examples of this is a group of writers, artists, and musicians in early twentieth-century Italy. Known as the futurists, they sought new forms of expression, believing that older forms of poetry, opera, theater, orchestral, and chamber music no longer elicited an emotional response from modern man, who grows up in industrialized society. They experimented with approaches to and theories about art that challenged the prevailing aesthetics, reception, and production of art. The group criticized arts institutions and centers of learning, like conservatories, for perpetuating the past and valorizing old, meaningless art over the vigorous, aggressive, and daring art of the present. Among their favorite products were manifestoes. They composed multiple manifestoes about art, music, poetry, and aesthetics.[30]

The first futurist manifesto was published in *La Figaro* in 1909. Written by poet and provocateur Filippo Tomaso Marinetti, it begins with the author and his friends enjoying a night of drinking, musing about the end of Romanticism, and admiring the sound of passing trams. Marinetti then sets out in his car at high speed, taunting death, and eventually ending up in a factory ditch. As his car is rescued and he revels in his muck- and oil-covered state, he composes ten new principles of art. He calls for love of danger and rashness; valorizes violence, revolt, courage, and speed; and glorifies war and beautiful ideas that kill. He also takes the opportunity to deride feminism and women. In Marinetti's aesthetics, noise, speed, aggression, and violence were masculine. Those who relished this animalistic cacophony and pursued it with every fiber were meant to subdue a world that included women and everything feminine.

Perhaps the most cited Futurist musical manifestoes are those written by painter and inventor Luigi Russolo. "The Art of Noises" was originally a letter to friend and fellow composer Francesco Balilla Pratella, which was reprinted as a pamphlet. In it, Russolo lays out his theory of modern music. He sees the liberation of sound, the inclusion of industrial noise into the concert hall, as a logical progression of music. For Russolo, throughout European history, composers have pushed the limits of sonority, progressively adding more dissonances and colors. Incorporating noise is the obvious outcome of this history. In addition, the sounds of modern society are made by machines. These mechanical noises, from factory floors, automobiles, trains, ocean liners, airplanes, and the increasingly loud sounds of warfare, are what elicit emotion in modern individuals. Therefore, music of the concert hall that is seeking to touch the contemporary soul must incorporate these sounds.[31]

Russolo's proposed new compositional process was twofold. The first step was undertaking a project of auditory observation. He called on young composers to skip the hallowed halls of the sterile conservatory and instead tune in to the street corner and factory. This form of pedagogy teaches the composer what they need to know about meaningful sounds and their constituent textures and structures. The second part of Russolo's process is the creation of noise machines, *intonarumori* as he called them. These machines corresponded to the types and varieties of noises heard and artistically imitated them in an age before sampling was possible.[32] While some futurist concerts employed running gasoline engines on stage as part of the sound, Russolo sought to transpose the noise of the city into instruments designed for the concert hall rather than simply including the sounds of the street directly. He wanted orchestrated, controlled, and aesthetically theorized noise to be part of the listening experience. Russolo created an ensemble of his own machines to perform his music and used horizontal, sloping lines on a staff as notation.

Unfortunately, both the construction plans and Russolo's machines were destroyed during the First World War, and little record of his music is left.[33] However, Russolo's ideas were carried into the mid-century in different forms. Composer Edgard Varese experimented with extended percussion and sound effects, famously including a police siren in "Ameriques" (1921, rev. 1927) and composing the first work for percussion ensemble, "Ionization."[34] Pierre Schaffer created a compositional technique called musique concrete, which used magnetic tape as a medium. The technique consisted of using found and pre-recorded sounds, splicing them together and modifying them using various effects to form a sonic montage, a concert work without live musicians. Later composers would write works for live musicians accompanied by a tape track. For both Varese and Schaffer, the sounds of industrial and incidental noise become the building blocks of new forms and aesthetics for concert music (for more on composers, see Chapter 6).

The Sound System

In postwar Jamaica, local DJs took a different approach in subjecting listeners to noise. Following the collapse of newly independent Jamaica's economy in the 1960s, money for expensive rhythm and blues and ska ensembles was in short supply, but demand for popular dance music was still high. The solution was the development of the sound system, a high-wattage mobile playback unit capable of turning open spaces, like housing courtyards and beaches, into impromptu dance halls. These sound systems played domestic and imported records for patrons, avoiding the need to pay large ensembles.[35] As sound reproduction technology improved, these sound systems expanded, with the largest and wealthiest sound systems capable of pumping out hundreds of thousands of watts and requiring several trucks to transport.[36] Julian Henriques labels the aesthetic of this auditory excess "sonic domination," when the music literally becomes a physical force.[37] In proximity to a sound system at full tilt, the sound is felt as much as it is heard, causing not only auditory distress but also extreme pleasure, creating a particular mode of sociability that both includes and excludes.

The sound system's sonic wall is both physical and metaphorical. The pure volume serves as a powerful indicator of Jamaican working-class culture, practices, and aesthetics. In the envelope of sound, the music is both heard and felt.[38] It indicates the communities that will be present, the hierarchies within these communities, and the behaviors—use of narcotics, slackness, suggestive dance moves, colorful clothing, brand new dub plates—that will be conterminous with music pushed to extreme volume.[39] In this case, sound is used to dominate space, to resist the imposition of middle-class hegemony, and to assert the presence of the Jamaican working class, its place in society, and its right to pleasure and space. Noise, in this case music played at incredibly high volume, is desired to foster feelings of community and to assert presence and power, even if it is temporary and fleeting. The noise of the Jamaican sound system is an act of resistance to erasure and acts as a marker of identity and creates a space for pleasure.[40]

Noise in the Japanese Concert Hall

In *Hogaku*, Japanese traditional classical music, another kind of noise is desired. There is a term for a desired aesthetic, *sawari*, that is glossed as possessing a "seasoned" tone.[41] Sawari is literally translated as an obstacle, a hindrance, or a bad effect. Musical sounds that possess this desired quality have a dense and complex sound, featuring the kind of irregularity associated with running water or wind through the leaves. According to Japanese composer Toru Takemitsu (who introduced the biwa and shakuhachi to the Western concert hall), "the major characteristic that sets [the biwa] apart from Western instruments is the active inclusion of noise in its sound, whereas Western instruments, in the process of development, sought to eliminate noise. It may sound contradictory to refer to 'beautiful noise' but the biwa is constructed in such a way."[42] This term is used to describe the desired sound of several instruments, including the lutes, the biwa and shamisen, and the end-blown flute, the shakuhachi. In the case of the two lutes, both have strings that are strung relatively loosely and are played with large plectrums. This results in a snap when the strings are struck and a buzz that accompanies each note as the loose strings vibrate against the frets or the fingerboard, thickening the texture of the sound. In addition, the biwa is built with a grooved ivory plate on the soundboard that emphasizes the buzzing of the strings. There are also performance techniques that emphasize these noises, including scraping the plectrum horizontally along the strings and intentionally hitting the strings with force and at an angle such that the snap of the strings against the frets and soundboard is emphasized.[43]

In the case of the shakuhachi, the mouthpiece has a simple notch, leaving the player many options with which to articulate each note. One of the variations is the breath-to-pitch ratio. There are times when a player's articulation sounds more breath than fundamental. According to Takemitsu, that is one of the chief differences between Japanese and Western art music. In the concert traditions of the West, music is about the juxtapositions of notes—melodies, phrases, and harmonies. In Japan, music can be about the many ways a player articulates a single note with its potential for depth, subtlety, and variation.[44] In this, sawari is the "apparatus of an obstacle," leading to creativity and expressiveness.[45] An essential part of the expressive range is the ratio of noise, in the form of unpitched sounds or textures, and the pitch of the instrument. In Takemitsu's exegesis on Japanese art music, noise is an important part of the performance practice, compositional process, and reception praxis.

Noise in the Philosophy of Western Music

In the Western philosophy of music, the role of noise, and the very definition of noise, in opposition to music, is a topic of scholarly debate and consideration.[46]

The compositional innovations of the early twentieth century, from futurist noise machines to musique concrete and electro-acoustic music; conceptual innovations like those of John Cage, Pierre Henri, and Karl-Heinz Stockhausen; and myriad technological innovations have unlocked the sonic possibilities of the concert hall. The inclusion of noises, from extended instrumental techniques, tape and sound reproduction, and synthesizers, has altered the experience of the concert hall and the sonic palette available to composers (also see Chapter 6). In the wake of these challenges and transformations of an evolving acoustic order, aesthetic philosophers engage in debate about the relationship of music to noise and the blurred and contingent lines between the two. Noise in the concert hall also triggers a debate about musical representation: Is noise meant to act as a sonic referent, or, like specific techniques and sonorities in tonal music, is noise an abstract symbol that is imbued with meaning through the compositional context?

Aesthetic philosopher Roger Scruton engages with sound as a "secondary object," that is, something that is judged by perception, apart from its source. The sounds that are emitted by a cello in the performance of a solo cello suite are judged by how they are heard. This judgment can occur apart from the instrument itself, from which the sounds are emitted, the performer, who may or may not be known to the listener, or the score of the work, which often does not accompany a listening.[47] In this case, sound is an object in itself, one that occurs but leaves no physical traces. Unlike cooking, which changes physical properties music does not alter the instrument it is played on[48] and does not leave obvious physical traces. Sound lives in its perception, and it is its perception that should be the subject of judgment.[49]

It is this perception that is most important—how are sounds perceived as music, and what changes occur that allow for new sounds to be included into the category of "music"? According to a definition of music given by John Blacking, music is "humanly organized sound." Any assemblage of sounds that are organized through human endeavor, like building instruments and playing them together, or through human cognitive change, like John Cage opening his window to hear the symphony of the street, or individuals deciding that the mating call of the wood thrush is a song, can become music.[50] Blacking's human-centered approach sheds light on the processes through which sound becomes music and provides a vantage into some of the philosophical issues of musical function, judgment, and aesthetics.

If noise is to become music—in either the Western concert tradition or while being included in popular music—what and how does this signify?[51] Peter Kivy puts forth a question on musical signification that can easily be applied to noise. He asks the question of representation: Are sonic figures connected directly to reality through semblance, like transcriptions of folk songs and dances in the Romantic repertoire, or are they abstracted and inferred in the formal language of the composer and the concert hall, like the thunderstorm in Beethoven's sixth symphony?[52] In the case of the former, the sonic referents are obvious, or are at least meant to possess a verity or naturalism similar to landscape painting or portraiture, if not photography. Sonic emitters, like the train imitated in Eric Honneger's "Pacific 231," the addition of the train whistle and metallic sounds on the tape track that accompanies the string quartet in Steve Reich's "Different Trains," or the police siren in Edgar Varese's "Ameriques," are made obvious to listeners, even those who are less well versed in the concert tradition.

"Pacific 231" and "Different Trains" make the locomotive and its implications the centerpiece of the composition, and "Ameriques" uses a common sound, the siren, as an indicator of place in its visceral representation of New York City in the interwar years. The same can be said of gunshots and tire squeals found in studio recordings of hip-hop and narcocorrido—the uses of noise are an iconic referent to places, events, and narratives. These musical engagements with noise follow Russolo's prescription for composers to use the raw materials of everyday sound to form new music. While none of the three composers' references do that exclusively, all use noise to expand the representational capacity of traditional concert music. In Blacking's formulation, humans have cognitively organized this sound and categorized it as music, (temporarily) blurring the aesthetic perception of music and noise.

But what of noise that is identifiable but whose relevance is not readily apparent? How do we understand the music concrete of Pierre Schaeffer and Pierre Henri, John Cage's "Water Walk," or Annea Lockwood's "Piano Burning"? When musical noise is not integrated into a traditionally framed musical concept but rather is the musical concept, is it music or a separate sonic category? What is a performance of Cage's "Water Walk" which navigates the lines among theater, performance art, and music? Can this noise, detached from implements like an orchestra ("Ameriques" and "Pacific 231") or a string quartet ("Different Trains"), which smooth the edges between noise and music, be incorporated into the realm of music?

To return to a question raised by the Italian futurists, is the inclusion of noise in concert performances an expansion of the experimental or avant-garde tradition of the concert hall,[53] does it serve the same function that concert music of the past did but for a distinctly new and modern audience,[54] or does noise perform an auditory function beyond what traditional concert music can? The futurists themselves were divided on this question, and modern composers are still grappling with it. If Scruton is correct in assessing music apart from its producers, is it even possible to give noise a fair hearing, or, does noise always begin as something unwanted that depends on human ingenuity and experimental spirit for its affective and cognitive impact? Can listening to noise help us hear, perceive, and live in the world differently?

Conclusion

Noise traverses our auditory lives. It defines safe and hostile spaces, circumscribes and enables activities, and provides critical information for those who choose to tune in. Noise has within it the quality of a judgment: noise indexes the excessive, unwanted, invasive, and unnecessary in sound and society. Noise draws maps, and it demarcates zones of desire and transgression, areas of quiet and solitude, and spaces of comfort and control. There are also noises that serve as markers of desirable traits and friendly places. In this regard, noise has a flexible social role as an arbiter of taste, class, acceptability, and virtue. Because noise is not an absolute but a variable, a blurred line between aesthetic judgments, it also forms a perpetually mobile final frontier in musical or sonic composition. In the musical realm, noise that ranges from electronic manipulation of signal to the injection and alteration of samples is used to augment the listening experience, to mark those who belong in a sonic culture, and to chase away and intimidate outsiders. In the realm of auditory experience or performance, noise challenges us to image what Blacking had in mind when he defined music as humanly organized sound.

In-class Exercises

1 Bring in examples, and discuss desirable and unwanted noises.
2 Using a sound meter (or a sound meter app), investigate noises in your surroundings. Compare different levels of sound and sound quality.
3 Discuss the limitations of noise in music. Bring examples (think about music like Jimi Hendrix's "Star Spangled Banner," Ligetti's "Atmospheres," Diamanda Galas's "Litanies of Satan," John Zorn's "Cat o' Nine Tails," Ronald Shannon Jackson's *Red Warrior*, works by Merzbow, or Fushitsusha).

Project I: Composing with Noise

Prompt: Create a composition (between two and three minutes) from everyday noise. You must record the sounds yourself (they should be sounds that occur in your everyday life), but once you have recorded them, you are free to manipulate or alter them in any way that you see fit. Think about the role that noise plays in your life and how listening to noise can change your perspective.

Write: A one-page artist statement for your composition. Give the listener an idea of your aesthetic intentions, how you found and assembled your noises, and how the process of listening to the noises in your life inspired your composition.

References to help think through the possibilities of composing with noise:
John Cage, "Water Walk."
Pierre Schaeffer, "Etude aux Chemins de Fer" or "Etudes De Bruits."
Pierre Henry, "Variations Por une Porte et un Soupir."
Luigi Russolo, "The Art of Noises."
Annea Lockwood, "Tiger Balm."

Project II: Noise Ethnography

Prompt: Create a composition that uses everyday noises as an inspiration to create.

Step 1: Read Russolo's "Art of Noises" (optional additional readings by Carra, Marinetti, Pratella, and Busoni can be added).

Step 2: Following Russolo's method, investigate the sounds of your space. Spend time in particularly sonorous localities, and record the sounds heard. Write a brief classification chart of the sounds that you heard. (Keep in mind not only Russolo's classification system but also its limitations.)

Step 3 (option 1): Inspired by the noises around you, create a short composition based on the textures, forms, and feelings evoked by your soundscape. Following Russolo, this exercise is a *translation* of the noises of your surroundings into a sonic language of your choice. You can use traditional instruments, add new textures, and create new "instruments" of your choice.

Step 3 (option 2): Write a new manifesto for composing with everyday noises using the futurist manifestoes as a model.

References to help think through the possibilities of composing with noise:
  Hildegard Westerkamp, "A Walk through the City" (see chapter 6).
  Edgard Varese, "Integrales."
  Carlos Chavez, "Energia."
  Da Lench Mob, "Inside tha head of a Black Man."

Project III: Noise Maps

Prompt: Make a noise map of your campus or surroundings (best done as a class).
Step 1: Acquire a map of your surroundings.
Step 2: Divide the map into sections, assigning groups or individuals a section or sections.
Step 3: Using a sound meter or sound meter app, carefully record sound levels in each location.
Step 3 a (optional): Choose designated times (morning, noon, evening; weekday, weekend) where every group will take measurements.
Step 4: Using topographical maps as a model, create a sound map of your surroundings.
Variation: Use color coding for different types of sound, depending on sound classification scheme decided upon by the class. (Russolo's classification scheme is not effective for campuses with levels of natural sound, wildlife, or clearly audible human noises like athletic practices/competition and acappella rehearsal; as a class, come up with a schema that fits the character of your surroundings; be creative in your map design.)
Step 5 (optional, if possible): Compare your topographical map with other maps, and compare the noise profile with other social, demographic, and vocational variables.

Notes

1 Goldsmith, *Discord*, 102.
2 Also see Bijsterveld, "The Diabolical Symphony of the Mechanical Age," 37–70.
3 Schwartz, *Making Noise*, 17–36.
4 Attali, *Noise*, 3.

5   Novak, in Novak and Sakakeeny, *Keywords in Sound*, 126.
6   "noise, n." *OED Online*, Oxford University Press, June 2019, www.oed.com/view/Entry/127655 (accessed June 14, 2019).
7   Schwartz, *Making Noise*, 21.
8   Gross, McMurray, and Swedenburg, "Arab Noise and Ramadan Nights," 3–39.
9   Kennedy, "The Land Where Internet Ends."
10 Levarie, "Noise," 21–31.
11 Fairyington, "Rustle, Tingle, Relax"; Cline, "What Is ASMR and Why Are People Watching These Videos?" For an excellent analysis of whispering as white noise that can be shaped, see Fales (2002).
12 A recent podcast offers an excellent summary of noise and health. Mars, "Half Measures."
13 See van Kamp and Davies, "Noise and Health in Vulnerable Groups," 153–9, for a summary of recent perspectives on noise and vulnerable populations. Also see Connor, "Feel the Noise," 147–62. The journal *Noise and Health* is dedicated to perspectives on this research.
14 Cited in Basner et al., "Auditory and Non-Auditory Effect of Noise on Health."
15 Jiao et al., "The Cost-Effectiveness of Lowering the Permissible Noise Levels around US Airports," 1479–89.
16 Mars, Roman. "Sound and Health: Cities." *99% Invisible*, May 16, 2019.
17 In Bull and Back, *The Auditory Culture Reader*, 165. Also see Bijsterveld, "The Diabolical Symphony of the Mechanical Age," 37–70.
18 Goldsmith, *Discord*, 140–4.
19 Ibid.
20 Ibid., 140.
21 EPA, "Information on Levels of Environmental Noise Requisite to Protect Health and Welfare with an Adequate Margin of Safety."
22 Smith, in Bull and Back, 2003.
23 Bijsterveld, in Sterne, *The Sound Studies Reader*, 159.
24 Goodman, *Sonic Warfare*, 17.
25 Neufeld, "'Buzz Bomb.'"
26 Goodman, *Sonic Warfare*, 16.
27 Ibid., chap. 3.
28 Peisner, "War Is Loud"; Daughtry, *Listening to War*.
29 https://www.lradx.com (accessed December 12, 2018).
30 See Apollonio, *Futurist Manifestoes*; Marinetti, 2008.
31 Russolo, 1913, in Black, 2012.
32 See Black, *The Art of Noise*, 2012.
33 There is speculation that music and plans that are attributed to him are hybrids of Russolo's ideas and those of his brother, Antonio Russolo, who was also a composer.

34. Radice, "'Futurismo.'" 1–17.
35. Stolzoff, *Wake the Town and Tell the People*; Veal, *Dub*.
36. On a research trip, sociologist Norm Stolzoff was able to hear a sound system playing music from over a mile away (*Wake the Town and Tell the People*).
37. See Henriques, *Sonic Bodies*, 2011; also see Henriques in Bull and Back, 2003.
38. Henriques notes that some sound systems set up their speakers in a triangle to literally envelope their audience in sound waves.
39. Also see Stolzoff, *Wake the Town and Tell the People*.
40. Although as Stolzoff and others have notes, these spaces are not unproblematic and are often violent toward women and LGBTQ individuals.
41. Shimosako, "Philosophy and Aesthetics," 545–5.
42. Takemitsu, *Confronting Silence*, 64.
43. See Takemitsu's "Eclipse" (1966) for examples of these techniques for biwa and shakuhachi.
44. Shimosako, "Philosophy and Aesthetics," 551.
45. Takemitsu, *Confronting Silence*, 64–5.
46. For the sake of brevity, I am bracketing a debate on the roles of noise in the production of popular music, which would warrant its own chapter. See Novak, *Japanoise*; Gracyk, *Rhythm and Noise*.
47. These three are variable, but it is possible to perceive and judge a performance without knowledge of the instrument, performer, or score.
48. This is obviously not true for particular performance art pieces that call for the destruction of instruments during the performance, but Scruton obviously sees these as outliers to a general aesthetic theory of music.
49. Scruton, *Understanding Music*, chap. 1 "Sounds."
50. Blacking, *How Musical Is Man?*
51. For the sake of clarity, I am neglecting a philosophy of music literature about instrumental noises as part of a recording (see Jennifer Judkins, 2011) and myriad ethnomusicological critiques of "purity" in Western concert music.
52. Kivy, *Sound and Semblance*.
53. Busoni, 1906, in Black, 2012.
54. Russolo, 1914, in Black, 2012.

Bibliography

Apollonio, Umbro, ed. *Futurist Manifestoes*. Boston: MFA Publications, 1970.
Attali, Jacques. *Noise: The Political Economy of Music*. Minneapolis: University of Minnesota Press, 1995.

Basner, Mathias, Wolfgang Babisch, Adrian Davis, Mark Brink, Charlotte Clark, Sabine Janssen, and Steven Stansfeld. "Auditory and Non-Auditory Effect of Noise on Health." October 30, 2013. Lancet.com.
Black, Candice, ed. *The Art of Noise: Destruction of Music by Futurist Machines*. Sun Vision Press, 2012.
Blacking, John. *How Musical Is Man?*. Seattle: University of Washington Press, 1973.
Bull, Michael, and Les Back. *The Auditory Culture Reader*. London: Bloomsbury, 2016.
Cline, John. "What Is ASMR and Why Are People Watching These Videos?" *Psychology Today*, September 26, 2018.
Connor, Steven. "Feel the Noise: Excess, Affect and the Acoustic." In *Emotion in Postmodernism*, edited by Gerhard Hoffman, and Alfred Hornung, 147–62. Heidelberg: Universitatsverlag Carl Winter, 1997.
Daughtry, J. Martin. *Listening to War: Sound, Music, Trauma, and Survival in Wartime Iraq*. Oxford: Oxford University Press, 2015.
EPA. "Information on Levels of Environmental Noise Requisite to Protect Health and Welfare with an Adequate Margin of Safety." *EPA, Office of Noise Abatement and Control*, March 1974. 550/0-74-004.
Fairyington, Stephanie. "Rustle, Tingle, Relax: The Compelling World of ASMR," *New York Times*, July 28, 2014.
Goldsmith, Mike. *Discord: The Story of Noise*. Oxford: Oxford University Press, 2012.
Goodman, Steve. *Sonic Warfare: Sound, Affect, and the Ecology of Fear*. Cambridge: MIT Press, 2010.
Gross, Joan, David McMurray, and Ted Swedenburg. "Arab Noise and Ramadan Nights: Rai, Rap And Franco-Maghreb Identity." *Diaspora* 3, no. 1 (1994): 3–39.
Henriques, Julian. "Sonic Dominance and the Reggae Sound System Session." In *The Auditory Culture Reader*, edited by Michael Bull and Les Back, 451–80. Oxford: Berg, 2003.
Henriques, Julian. *Sonic Bodies: Reggae Sound Systems, Performance Techniques, and Ways of Knowing*. New York: Continuum, 2011.
Jiao, Boshen, Zafar Zafari, Brian Will, Kai Ruggeri, Shukai Li, and Peter Muennig. "The Cost-Effectiveness of Lowering the Permissible Noise Levels around US Airports." *International Journal of Environmental Research and Public Health*, no. 14 (2017): 1479–89.
Judkins, Jennifer. "Silence, Sound, Noise, and Music: Jennifer Judkins." *Routledge Companion to Philosophy and Music*, 37–46. Routledge, 2011.
Kennedy, Pagan. "The Land Where Internet Ends." *New York Times*, June 21, 2019.
Kivy, Peter. *Sound and Semblance: Reflections of Musical Representation*. Princeton: Princeton University Press, 1984.
Levarie, Sigmund. "Noise." *Critical Inquiry* 4, no. 1 (Autumn 1977): 21–31.
Marinetti, Filippo T. *Selected Poems and Related Prose*. New Haven, CT: Yale University Press, 2002.
Mars, Roman. "Half Measures." *99% Invisible*. Ep. 280, October 10, 2017.

Neufeld, Michael. "'Buzz Bomb': 70th Anniversary of the V-1 Campaign." *Smithsonian National Air and Space Museum*. June 13, 2014. https://airandspace.si.edu/stories/editorial/"buzz-bomb"-70th-anniversary-v-1-campaign (accessed October 1, 2021).

New Yorker. "How ASMR Became an Internet Phenomenon | Annals of Obsession." Annals of Obsession. https://www.youtube.com/watch?v=DxjfyBEII7Q (accessed October 1, 2021).

Novak, David, and Matthew Sakakeeny, eds. *Keywords in Sound*. Durham, NC: Duke University Press, 2015.

Oxford English Dictionary. Oxford: Oxford University Press, 2019.

Peisner, David. "War Is Loud." In *Spin Greatest Hits: 25 Years of Heretics, Heroes and the New Rock'n'Roll*, edited by Doug Brod, 79–94. London: Wiley, 2010.

Pinch, Trevor, and Karin Bijsterveld, eds. *The Oxford Handbook of Sound Studies*. Oxford: Oxford University Press, 2012.

Radice, Mark A. "'Futurismo': Its Origins, Context, Repertory and Influence." *Musical Quarterly* 73, no. 1 (1989): 1–17.

Russolo, Luigi. "The Art of Noises (1913)." In *The Art of Noise: Destruction of Music by Futurist Machines*, edited by Candice Black, 55–66. Sun Vision Press, 2012.

Schwartz, Hillel. *Making Noise: From Babel to the Big Bang and Beyond*. New York: Zone Books, 2011.

Scruton, Roger. *Understanding Music: Philosophy and Interpretation*. London: Bloomsbury, 2009.

Shimosako, Mari. "Philosophy and Aesthetics." In *The Garland Encyclopedia of World Music, Vol. 7, East Asia: China, Japan and Korea*, edited by Robert Provine, Yosihiko Tokumaro, and J. Lawrence Witzleben, 545–5. London: Routledge, 2002.

Smith, Mark M. "Listening to the Heard Worlds of Antebellum America." In *The Auditory Culture Reader*, edited by Michael Bull and Les Back, 137–164. Oxford: Berg, 2003.

Sterne, Jonathan. *The Sound Studies Reader*. London: Routledge, 2012.

Stolzoff, Norman C. *Wake the Town and Tell the People: Dancehall Culture in Jamaica*. Durham, NC: Duke University Press, 2000.

Takemitsu, Toru. "Eclipse." Editions Salabert, 1966.

Takemitsu, Toru. *Confronting Silence: Selected Writings*. Lanham, MD: Fallen Leaf Press, 1995.

Van Kamp, Irene, and Hugh Davies. "Noise and Health in Vulnerable Groups: A Review." *Noise and Health* 15, no. 64 (2013): 153–9.

Veal, Michael. *Dub: Soundscapes and Shattered Songs in Jamaican Reggae*. Middletown: Wesleyan University Press, 2007.

Recommended Further Reading

Bijsterveld, Karin. *Mechanical Sound: Technology, Culture, and Public Problems of Noise in the Twentieth Century*. Cambridge: MIT Press, 2008.

Bijsterveld, Karin. "The Diabolical Symphony of the Mechanical Age: Technology and Symbolism of Sound in European and North American Noise Abatement

Campaigns, 1900–1940." *Social Studies of Science* 31, no. 1 (February 2001): 37–70.

Cardoso, Leonardo. *Sound-Politics in São Paulo*. Oxford: Oxford University Press, 2019.

D'Errico, Lucia. *The Powers of Divergence: An Experimental Approach to Music Performance*. Leuven, Belgium: Leuven University Press, 2018.

Doolan, Con. "A Review of Wind Turbine Noise Perception, Annoyance and Low Frequency Emission." *Wind Engineering* 37, no. 1 (2013): 97–104.

Fales, Cornelia. "The Paradox of Timbre." *Ethnomusicology* 46, no. 1 (2002): 56–95.

Goddard, Michael, and Benjamin Halligan. *Reverberations: The Philosophy, Politics and Aesthetics of Noise*. London: Bloomsbury, 2012.

Gracyk, Theodore. *Rhythm and Noise: An Aesthetics of Rock*. Durham, NC: Duke University Press, 1996.

Hainge, Greg. *Noise Matters: Towards an Ontology of Noise*. London: Bloomsbury, 2013.

Hegarty, Paul. *Noise Music: A History*. New York: Continuum, 2007.

Martins, Susana S. "White Noise in Everyday Technologies." *American Studies* 46, no. 1 (Spring 2005): 87–113.

Novak, David. *Japanoise: Music at the Edge of Circulation*. Durham, NC: Duke University Press, 2013.

Patch, Justin. *Discordant Democracy: Noise, Affect and Populism in the Presidential Campaign*. London: Routledge, 2019.

Schmidt, Charles W. "Noise That Annoys: Regulating Unwanted Sound." *Environmental Health Perspectives* 113, no. 1 (January 2005): A42–4.

Smyth, Fiona. " 'More Than a "Machine for Living In': Science, Noise and Experimental Housing in 1930s Britain." *Construction History* 29, no. 2 (2014): 103–20.

3

Voice: Hearing and Ascribing Individual and Social Identity

Key concepts: discrimination, identity, linguistic profiling, semiotics, synthetic voices

I. Does *how* one says something sometimes mean more than *what* one says? The 2013 film, *In a World*, centers on a character named Carol Solomon, who aspires to become a Hollywood movie-trailer voice-over star and encounters everything from persistent bewilderment to overtly sexist dismissal that she would dare try to crack an all-male, baritone-dominated profession. In one scene, Carol stands in front of a small group of attractive, white women in their twenties. Behind Carol, a sign reads, "Voice Over, The Vocal Make-Over: Find your voice and get ready to be heard," the slogan for her vocal coaching business.[1] She turns to a woman named Staci and asks what she does for a living. Staci replies, "I'm a corporate attorney?" Carol asks, "And I know you've been on a job hunt. How's that been going for you?" Looking abashed, Staci replies, "Well, um, I've been interviewing for about ten months?" Carol looks at her, nods as if in sympathetic understanding, and asks, "And why do you think that is?" Staci responds, as if confessing a shameful secret, "It's because I sound like a sexy baby?" Carol looks at the whole group and states, "Which may be great for the bedroom," at which point Staci eagerly jumps into Carol's breath pause and exclaims, "Yes, it is!" (which elicits knowing laughter and "Yeah!"s from the other women). "But," Carol continues, "Am I *really* going to hire a sexy baby to defend me in a patent infringement lawsuit?" Staci, seeming ashamed, shakes her head "no" while whispering, "Right, no. Sorry. Sorry." Carol then tells the group that they will be recording and listening to their voices over the coming weeks as part of a self-improvement regime: "Because women should sound like women, not" (and here she scrunches up her face and alters her voice to sound like Staci's) "baby dolls who end everything in a question?" Carol returns to her regular voice and exhorts, "Now ... who's ready to be heard?" She is met with a chorus of high-pitched "squeaky" voices, like Staci's, eager to begin their vocal makeover.

Staci's voice is a recognizable (if somewhat caricatured) version of a speech pattern widely associated with young women from Southern California and thought to be spreading more broadly throughout the United States among so-called Millennials and Gen-Xers. At least three features characterize this voice pattern: uptalk (raising the pitch of the voice at the end of a phrase or sentence as if asking a question, even when the utterance is not one), as reflected in the punctuation used when quoting Staci previously (note that there were three declarative statements by Staci, not in fact questions); vocal fry (a phrase-final lowering of the speaking voice articulated by slackening the vocal chords, which results in an audible creakiness); and vowel-fronting (the pronunciation of some vowels forward in the mouth so that, e.g., "for sure" sounds like "ferr sherr"). In this scene, all three features are present, additionally combined with exclusively high-pitched, nasal voices lacking in any chest resonance. Absent from this sequence, but often considered to accompany this speech pattern, is the (perceived) excessive use of the word "like." This constellation of features has taken on associations with ditziness, frivolity, and superficiality. As Carol says, is this the voice you think of when you need a powerful attorney representing you?[2]

Lake Bell, who plays Carol, wrote and directed *In a World*, and in a series of interviews and TV appearances accompanying the release of the film, it became readily apparent that the views expressed by Carol in this scene are those of Bell as well. In a July 2013 appearance on *Conan*, for example, when prompted to talk about the movie (and after briefly stating that she wants to be clear that she is not talking about all US women), Bell begins by saying dramatically, "I don't want to get on my soapbox here, but I'm going to get on my soapbox. There is a pandemic that is rampant in this country and it's the" (and here she shifts into the voice she used when mimicking Staci) "the sexy baby vocal virus?"[3] Watching this during Covid-19, one may be tempted to scoff and dismiss it as nothing more than a ludicrous exaggeration with a poor analogy (to a virus) at its heart. But linking particular voice types and ways of speaking to assumptions about the people who have or use them happens every day in the real world, often with very painful consequences. When Christine Blasey Ford spoke before the Senate Judiciary Committee in September 2018 during the Brett Kavanaugh Supreme Court confirmation hearings about his alleged sexual assault of her thirty-six years prior, many who opposed her testifying, or who thought she was lying in order to sabotage his confirmation, latched onto her voice. Perhaps most infamously, Rachel Butera, who voiced a character on the animated show, *Star Wars: Resistance*, took to Twitter to "imitate" and ridicule Blasey Ford.[4] Speaking in an exaggerated "valley girl"-like accent that she likened to Ford's voice—nasal, high-pitched, and ripe with vocal fry—Butera said, among other things, "I can't help it, I just have this voice, like a baby, even though I'm a doctor," and "I sound like I'm still back at that high school party," and "I know, it's a surprise even to me that I talk this way." Putting aside the context—that Blasey Ford was testifying publicly about an event that had clearly been a source of trauma for her—the larger message is that voices—not just the words they say—are often the subject of intense judgment, with real-world consequences.

II. Jazz singer James Victor Scott (1925–2014), more commonly known as Little Jimmy Scott, performed at the inaugurations of Presidents Eisenhower and Clinton and garnered numerous recognitions late in his life, including a Jazz Masters award from the National Endowment for the Arts, a Living Legend award from the Kennedy Center, and a Lifetime Achievement Award from the Jazz Foundation of America. Scott was born with Kallmann syndrome, a genetic condition that prevents the production of hormones that direct sexual development. At puberty, males are unlikely to develop facial or body hair or to have their voices deepen, and females will rarely start menstruation or develop breasts. For both, there will likely be no growth spurt. Scott was no exception: he stopped growing at age twelve, and his singing voice was often described as sounding like a woman's. Musicologist Nina Sun Eidsheim notes that people had a hard time categorizing Scott, often mistaking him for a masculine woman, an effeminate man, a gay man, or a transexual. Scott simply saw himself as a "regular guy," whose most unusual feature was his degree of obsession with music.[5] Yet in many ways, the "oddity" of Scott's voice was far more defining of his career than the recognitions and awards his singing led to.

How is one's voice linked to perceptions of masculinity, femininity, or sexuality? A common assumption is that the pitch of the speaking or singing voice is critical in this process; men are thought to have deeper voices and women to have higher ones. White it is true that the *average* fundamental frequency of an adult male speaking voice is lower than that of a female speaking voice (due to how the hormone androgen affects male vocal fold development during puberty), that clearly cannot provide a complete explanation: individual men's voices may well fall within the range of the average female voice and vice versa, yet rarely would this be sufficient to create confusion about a speaker's sex. Eidsheim suggests that the key feature in explaining the hallmarks of vocal masculinity is not pitch but vocal timbre (often also referred to as "sound color" or "sound quality").[6]

As Eidsheim notes, the classic division of the singing voice into bass/baritone/tenor/alto/mezzo soprano/soprano yields an overlap of an octave plus two notes between tenors (assigned to male voices) and altos (assigned to female voices), an overlap that spans about one-third of human singing range. Thus, pitch alone cannot be an absolute defining factor in signaling singer sex.[7] But what about in the case of Scott, whose voice did not drop due to his genetic condition? To address this, Eidsheim compares Scott's vocal range with those of other male jazz and R&B singers who were his contemporaries, including James Brown, Sam Cooke, Marvin Gaye, Smokey Robinson, Otis Rush, and Stevie Wonder, among others. For the corpus of songs Eidsheim examines, two unexpected results stand out: first, Scott's highest note was *lower* than the highest notes sung by James Brown, Marvin Gaye, Smoky Robinson, Otis Rush, and Stevie Wonder; second, the mean pitch at which Scott sang in the corpus was lower than Gaye's and Robinson's. Yet no one on this list other than Scott is read by listeners as a nonmale singer. Why?

The key, Eidsheim suggests, is that Scott never moved his voice into falsetto singing, whereas his contemporaries routinely did so when moving to the upper ranges of their voices. In contrast to regular (modal) singing, which involves the use of the entire vocal fold, falsetto singing requires relaxing and thinning the vocal folds such that only the vocal ligaments are engaged in the production of sound; this has the effect of allowing for higher pitches to be produced. However, it simultaneously alters the timbre of the voice; subjectively, it is often described as being thinner or more flute-like. This timbral difference results from the altered nature of the vocal folds leading to the production of fewer overtones compared to the modal voice. As a result, Scott's highest pitches had a very different sound quality from those of his male contemporaries whose highest pitches originated in falsetto voicings.

But for Eidsheim, the examination of how this sonic difference led to confusion about Scott's sex (and questionings of his sexuality) doesn't end with the fact that he sang his high notes differently than his contemporaries and therefore had different vocal timbral properties. Rather, she argues that, within a larger culture linked to Black hypermasculinity that accompanied much of the jazz world that Scott participated in, the use of falsetto by other male singers worked as a kind of "timbral scare quotes": a way that male singers could engage the highest register of their vocal range while audibly signaling its difference from their normal range. Eidsheim writes, "By timbrally marking the otherness of this vocal range in relation to their so-called true voices, male singers' masculine personae are held intact while singing high notes."[8] Scott's failure to use falsetto—which led to a consistency of his vocal timbre across his singing range—marked him as different; he refused to play the timbral masculinity game as it was configured in the musical culture in which he participated, and thus, his identity turned into a source of confusion to many.[9]

Scott's story, though, also returns us to acoustemology, the relationship between knowing and hearing discussed in Steven Feld's work in Papua New Guinea. We encounter Scott with social and cultural ears. What listeners do or don't make of Scott is not solely reducible to an absence of timbral change because he does not use his falsetto; it just as crucially depends on how listeners ascribe meaning onto that absence. The book in which Eidsheim analyzes Scott's career provocatively argues that we would do well to question whether each timbral performance begins and ends with listener projections. In other words, is it in the source of the meanings we ascribe to voices in the singer's vocal production, or is it in the listener's decoding of the singer's voice?

Defining Voice

What, exactly, is "voice"? Amanda Weidman writes, "We speak of the 'voice of the people,' 'the voice of authority,' 'the voice of God,' the 'Voice of America'; we 'voice' the notes of a piano or the melodic lines of a composition, the instrumental score in music, and talk of musicians as having unique performative voices on their instruments." She continues, "We 'find' our voice or discover an 'inner voice'; we 'have a voice in matters' or 'give voice to' our ideas'; we 'voice concerns' and are 'vocal' in our opinions."[10] Compared to most of the terms that define the other chapters of this book, the meaning of "voice" is polysemous[11] and hard to pin down. Is voice the "acoustic fact" that is emitted through the vocal cords when we speak or sing? Is it activated primarily through the medium of language—through the ways in which we speak or sing—or does it equally stray into forms of extra-linguistic bodily sound-making, such as ululation, scat-singing, doowop, or glossolalia (i.e., "speaking in tongues")?[12] What is the relationship between vocal texture and the meanings of the words themselves?[13] Is voice best understood through the measurements of scientific devices capable of analyzing its acoustic properties? Or is voice not reducible to what the body produces auditorily but rather the effect that a sounding body has on the world? Is voice a thing, or is it an action? In the end, we argue that voice is a loose, multivalent term that encompasses both the material (i.e., the sonic) properties of bodily originating vocal sounds and how those sounds link to agency, power, meaning, and identity. Voice is, to quote Eidsheim, a "thick event."[14]

This chapter provides examples that illustrate two ideas regarding the term "voice."[15] First, voice is a sound produced by a "phonating" body, with specific acoustical properties that result from the means by which the body emits vocal sound. This position will be referred to as a materialist understanding of voice. A materialist approach to the voice emphasizes that the (human) voice depends upon factors of human physiology such as lung capacity, length and shape of the larynx, and the ability to precisely coordinate movements of the tongue, jaw, and lips, to emit vocal sound; to some extent, people cannot fully control how their voices sound because the body draws constraints around individual possibility. However, a materialist approach can equally examine how people utilize their vocal flexibility in given contexts: consider an evangelical pastor, for example, who consciously deploys specific vocal techniques (e.g., wide fluctuations of intonation, stress, volume) in the performance of a sermon but quite differently when engaged in casual conversation within their household.[16] Finally, this approach to thinking about voice also links the body to medical, behavioral, and psychological conditions: for example, having too much fluid in the nasal cavity, so that one's pronunciation of nasal consonants (e.g., [m], [n]) is compromised, indicates one's having a cold; polyps on the vocal cords often lead to raspiness or hoarseness because the cords don't vibrate smoothly; smoking tends to deepen the voice; and stress and depression can manifest in a tight or a weak voice. In this sense, the body is actively present in the sound of the voice.

Second, and more closely aligned with Weidman's description, voice is tightly linked to identity. This is, of course, true at the individual level in the sense that we quickly recognize the voices of our closest family and friends (and when we fail to do so, we often make a point of saying something like, "Sorry, I didn't recognize your voice at first").[17] However, it is equally the case that voice is social: it is central in how people craft identities and attribute identities onto others. In this way, voices become meaningful above and beyond the words they convey.

The process by which this happens—and the theoretical paradigm frequently invoked to analyze it—is semiotic in nature: in other words, "signs" are linked to "meanings." The distinctions among *icon*, *index*, and *symbol* made by Charles Sanders Peirce (1839–1914) are particularly useful here. An icon is a sign that means by virtue of resemblance (or a sharing of properties) between the sign (the so-called signifier) and what it means (the signified): simple examples are onomatopoeia in language,[18] or the dubbing of footsteps by a Foley artist who is synching sound to an image of a walking person during film *sound design*. An index is a sign that means by virtue of co-presence, of pointing to, or of being influenced by the signified: a weather vane that means "the wind is coming from the east" does so because of the wind acting upon the vane; footprints mean via a cause-and-effect relationship in which the tracks point to the (prior) presence of the animal that made them; in the sentence, "Carla sat down at the piano and then she started to play," "she" functions as an index, pointing back to the aforementioned Carla.[19] A symbol is a sign that means by virtue of a convention that links the signifier and the signified, as there is no inherent relationship between them: that a red light means "stop," a green light means "go," while a yellow light either means "come to a stop" or "hit the accelerator hard" (depending on context) is because those meanings have been agreed to, not because of the properties of the colors or the resultant actions themselves; similarly, there is no reason that the sound sequence /k/ + /æ/ + /t/ means "adult domesticated feline, male or female" in English other than that English speakers agree that is what this particular sequence of sounds will refer to. It is important to note that overlap and ambiguity are inherent in Peirce's system: in the aforementioned example, "Carla sat down at the piano and then she started to play," for example, "she" functions indexically to point to Carla, but that the sound sequence of /ʃ/ + /i/ means "previously mentioned third person subject, female-identified" is a convention specific to English; in the example of animal tracks pointing to the prior presence of the animal (indexicality), the footprints simultaneously resemble the shape of the hooves (iconicity).

In the Peircian framework, the connection between voice and identity is fundamentally indexical.[20] Voices have the potential to signal group membership in identity categories including, but not limited to, gender, race and ethnicity, and class, and listeners frequently "read" voices in ways that place their speakers (correctly or incorrectly) into such identity categories. Linguistic features of speech, such as accent and dialect, provide much of this information, but so too can rhythm, pitch, resonance, voice quality, volume, and other "prosodic" features of the speaking voice. The remainder of this chapter offers some examples of indexically driven voice-identity relationships while also keeping in mind Eidsheim's question of whether that linkage resides in the voice itself or is an artifact of how listeners decode and encode vocal meanings.

Linguistic Profiling and Discrimination

Have you ever listened to a radio announcer or a podcast host, never having seen them, or had a phone conversation with someone you don't know, and caught yourself creating a mental image of that person? Chances are that your mental image maps, at a minimum, perceived sex and ethnicity onto the voice. It may also map age (especially if the voice carries cues such as breathiness and shakiness that are more common in elderly voices) and assumptions about the person's place of origin, social class, and even sexuality. This practice of seeking to identify voices is a common human characteristic: in a talk at the World Economic Forum in 2018, artificial intelligence (AI) scholar Rita Singh presented a slide with the photos of five men and one woman of varying ages and racial or ethnic groups while playing a short audio clip of one of them speaking. Her point was to illustrate that very quickly—within the space of two seconds—the majority of the audience had selected the correct speaker.[21] This human practice is now being "learned" by AI systems and is already used in law enforcement contexts to help create visual images of speakers when the only data available to identify them are recordings of their voices.[22]

What are some of the social effects that follow this kind of mapping? "Linguistic profiling" is a term coined by linguist John Baugh to describe how people use auditory cues from speaking voices to identify others' social characteristics. Baugh focused primarily on how race is read through accent and dialect and, by extension, how those readings can become part of overtly discriminatory practices. Baugh was drawn to this research because of his personal experience when looking for housing in Palo Alto upon being appointed to a fellowship at Stanford University in 1988. In that pre-internet era, Baugh's apartment search took the form of reading through classified ads in local newspapers and calling prospective landlords to make appointments to look at potential residences. Baugh writes, "During all calls to prospective landlords, I explained my circumstances ... always employing my 'professional voice,' which I am told 'sounds white.' No prospective landlord ever asked me about my 'race,' but in four instances I was abruptly denied access to housing upon arrival at my scheduled appointment."[23] Baugh is careful to note that his being refused access was not technically a result of linguistic profiling: he was *seen* as a Black man, not *heard* as one, so the profiling was visual. But he notes the example of Anita Henderson, in nearly identical circumstances, searching for an apartment in Philadelphia. Henderson went in person to a large complex, was directed to the unit's most expensive apartment, and told it was the only one available. The next day, Henderson called the same complex, deliberately using Standard American English (i.e., "white" English), only to be told that several less expensive apartments were available and encouraging her to come see them.[24] In Henderson's case, Baugh argues, it was solely on the basis of linguistic profiling—of her not sounding Black—that she was later granted access to a wider range of apartments.

While Baugh has focused his research on racially based effects of linguistic profiling, linguists have long studied multiple forms of accent or dialect "discrimination" that can hinder access to education, jobs, and other avenues for advancing one's life: this is exactly the premise, after all, of Carol's argument about why Staci was unsuccessful for ten years in her corporate law job search. Such discrimination can be based on fear of Others, on perceptions of how various ways of speaking are believed to link to intelligence (or lack thereof), to a belief in the "rightness" or superiority of one's own dialect or accent, or to managing social *distinction*. And such discrimination often lays bare the "language ideologies"—the conceptualizations that individuals or cultures hold about languages and their speakers—that people repeatedly turn to in assessing their own and others' use of language, and the judgments that follow.[25]

In much of the United States, for example, to speak with a southern drawl leads to being read as ignorant, uneducated, and possibly rural;[26] to combine a Mexican Spanish speaker's accented English with vocal fry is to sound "Cholo" or Chola;[27] to "r-drop" at the end of a word like "car" (so that it sounds like "cah") is to be read as working class and from Boston, or parts of the outer boroughs of New York City;[28] to be a man who speaks with breathiness, strongly accented syllables, and a wide intonation contour is to mark oneself as gay;[29] that to have a deep male voice is to be read as having power, confidence, and sexual virility;[30] that to have a shaky voice is to be weak, old, or infirm.[31] Here we see again that Peirce's semiotic system contains overlaps and ambiguities: a southern drawl, vocal fry in American English by Mexican Spanish speakers, r-dropping, breathiness, having a low-pitched male voice, or having a shaky voice, all index—point to—an identity, but largely because there is an arbitrary cultural convention that creates these linkages. Are there no highly educated people who speak with a southern drawl? Of course there are. Do the wealthiest social classes in Boston and Charleston, South Carolina, r-drop? Yes, they do. Must a wavering voice signify infirmity? Not necessarily, if the source is (as is the case for many) essential tremors: a genetic disorder that, while inconvenient, is simply the result of a condition that does not imperil one's health. Voice features, in other words, are not essentialist markers of identity but become engrained in historically and culturally specific ways.[32]

There is also a flip side to the coin of discrimination: Baugh refers to this as "preferential linguistic profiling."[33] Certain ways of speaking—certain accents and voice qualities—are associated with prestige and, in this sense, are aspirational. For example, it is more common that Americans who move to Britain adopt "British-like" accents than the reverse; for many Americans (though this is likely eroding), to sound British is to sound upper-class, educated, and sophisticated. Britons who move to the United States are much less likely to adopt American English accents, perhaps because the positive valence of the British accent is socially advantageous in the United States. Those whose voices—whose ways of speaking, both linguistically and prosodically—are read as falling into preferred categories will gain advantages. They get voiceover careers, become news anchors, are taken seriously as corporate lawyers or linguistics professors, are more likely to be given a "pass" if pulled over at a DUI checkpoint, or become successful when applying for a loan from their bank. Such is the power of voice.

Whether discriminatory or preferential, linguistic profiling and discrimination return us to the ambiguity within the Peircian semiotic system; is the association between voice and identity "in" the sound of the voice (an indexical relationship in which the voice points to identity), or is it in how people make meaning out of the sound of the voice (a symbolic relationship in which conventions and ideologies map meanings onto those sounds)? This Peircian ambiguity is at the root of Eidsheim's question of whether the meaning of the voice resides in the voice or is brought to the voice by how listeners encounter it and make meanings out of it. The answer does not need to be either-or, we suggest: the relationship is fundamentally co-constitutive.

Voice in Cinema: *A Star Is Born*

James Earl Jones as Darth Vader in the early *Star Wars* movies. Kathleen Turner as Jessica Rabbit or as Sue Collini in *Californication*. Douglas Rain as Hal in *2001: A Space Odyssey*. Sir Ian McKellen as Gandalf in the *Lord of the Rings* trilogy. Scarlett Johansson as Samantha in *Her*. Lauren Bacal, Morgan Freeman, Dame Judy Densch, Emma Thompson, Donald Sutherland, Anthony Hopkins, Samuel L. Jackson, Jeffery Wright, Sam Elliott, Angelina Jolie, and Meryl Streep. Any English-language internet search for "best voice actors and actresses" will yield a list that looks a lot like this. In some cases, "best" is linked to a particular role in which the voice became a central plot-point of the movie; in other cases, the assessment stretches across the corpus of the actor's or actress's work. Some of the roles may involve unseen characters (such as Darth Vader); others may be voicing animated entities; others are fully visually filmed human characters. Great male voices are usually described in terms of their depth or gravely-ness or power; female voices often (though not always) through their evocation of seductiveness or sexuality (and in a few cases, to their flexibility from role to role). Conscious use of the voice is central to the success of the film and television careers of many actors and actresses.[34]

In at least two different ways, voice plays a particularly central role in the 2018 remake of the film, *A Star Is Born*, cowritten and directed by Bradley Cooper, and starring Cooper, Lady Gaga, and Sam Elliott. Cooper plays Jackson Maine, a middle-aged country/rock musician at the apex of his career but with a serious and growing alcohol and drug addiction problem. Maine accidentally comes across Lady Gaga's character, Ally, when he goes into a bar and happens upon her performing "La Vie en Rose." He is captivated by her performance, and the two spend a night talking, by the end of which he is both smitten and left deeply admiring her musical talent. They eventually begin performing together, enter a relationship, marry, and then are forced to negotiate their careers moving in starkly opposite trajectories, as Ally is "discovered" and eventually wins for the Best New Artist at the Grammy Awards. At the same time, Jackson slips deeper into addiction and dysfunction, culminating with him publicly urinating in his pants before passing out on stage as Ally accepts her Grammy. The remainder of the film follows the fallout—professionally and (inter)personally—for both characters.

For anyone who had seen Cooper in an earlier film, his Jackson Maine speaking voice likely came as a shock from the very outset of the movie. When he first blurts out an impatient, "Where the fuck are we?" in the backseat of a limo taking him away from a concert, one can barely recognize the drawly, boozy growl as emanating from the same actor who so often played frat boy–like roles such as in the *Hangover* series or *Wedding Crashers*. Maine, the audience learns, is from Arizona, and everything from his music to his clothing to his persona is meant to evoke a kind of rural, working-class, Western identity. Cooper had worked on making the film for several years and, in thinking about Maine's voice, decided it should evoke this origin story. In multiple interviews, Cooper noted that he wanted to lower the pitch of his voice by a full octave.[35] Working with famed Hollywood dialect coach Tim Monich—who has prepped the likes of Brad Pitt, Hilary Swank, Matt Damon, and Gerard Butler for roles that required accents very different from their native ones[36]—they identified actor Sam Elliott's voice quality and accent as their ideal target. Cooper claims that he worked for many months—he hired Monich a year before filming began—practicing for four hours a day, five days a week, to master a slight drawl but, most crucially, to lower the pitch of his speaking voice. He describes the work as "brutal" and "painful," especially in the esophagus.[37] Cooper sees as a measure of success that Elliott agreed to join the cast as Jackson's brother (and manager), Bobby, after hearing Cooper's Elliott-ized voice. To audiences, Cooper's voice almost becomes a character in itself, so strongly does it mark his performance.

If Cooper's work might be described as a very literal and material construction of a sounding "voice," the second way in which voice is central to *A Star Is Born* is somewhat more metaphorical. In this reading, the film is about Ally "finding" her voice, in Weidman's sense, above: becoming musically confident; creating her individuation from a domineering and verbally abusive father; and later from riding the coattails of Jackson's career into an independently defined career of her own. In this way, voice is equated with personal agency and self-definition; it links to concepts of empowerment and self-determination.

The emergence of Ally's voice is encapsulated early in the movie when she joins Jackson on stage at one of his concerts to sing the duet, "Shallow," her own song that she had hesitantly sung *a capella* to Cooper during their first encounter and that Cooper had since taken it upon himself to write a musical arrangement of.[38] The sequence begins with Jackson inviting Ally to fly on his private jet to the concert and watch from backstage. Ally eventually agrees; Jackson announces to the crowd (37:30 into the film), "There's a friend of mine who, uh, came a long way to be here, and she wrote a great song and I'd just like her to sing it, I think it's pretty fucking good." He walks off stage to greet Ally and bring her out. "No, I can't do that, I'm sorry," she protests.

"All you gotta do is trust me. That's all you gotta do," Jackson responds. He starts walking back onto the stage, then turns back to her, and says, "I'm gonna sing it either way, so …" Initially, the scene alternates shots featuring Jackson's performance and Ally's reactions from backstage. Shortly after the song enters the first refrain, Ally is shown looking stunned and then briefly covering her eyes with her hands and lowering her head as if in disbelief. She looks left and right and then slightly up, as if assessing her situation. During the last line of the refrain, she appears to half-say something to herself, gives a slight nod, takes a deep breath, and walks briskly onto the stage.

As the second verse starts, she arrives at a backup singer's mic and sings the verse's opening lines. She holds her body quiet and does not fully project her voice. Her eyes alternate between looking down at the stage and out into the crowd, though one senses she is mostly staring at the scene in front of her rather than seeking directly to engage with the audience. As the second refrain starts, with Ally still singing alone, bass and piano enter, the crowd cheers, and Ally seems to settle into the performance somewhat more. Throughout the refrain, Jackson and Ally look at each other, and her singing becomes gradually more expressive: hints of vocal texture and vibrato that were completely absent from her performance of the verse can be heard for the first time.

Several things happen in the audiovisual field as the second refrain moves into the chorus (which is also a transition from Ally singing in the lower portion of her vocal range to the higher portion of it, providing vocal contrast). The first phrase of the chorus encompasses the lines, "I'm on the deep end/ Watch as I dive in/I'll never meet the ground." By the time Ally has articulated the word "deep," crowd cheer has swollen noticeably in the mix—clearly in response to Ally's voice opening up in her higher range—and Jackson looks out at the crowd with a broad smile as if to say, "What'd I tell you?!" For the remainder of the chorus, the camera stays closely focused on Ally, allowing the viewer to follow her oscillation between hesitancy and confidence in her vocal performance. She covers her eyes again briefly while singing the word "ground" at the end of the first phrase but looks steadily out at the crowd for the remainder of the chorus, completing its final word "now" with her deepest vibrato yet.

Following a different refrain in which Ally and Jackson sing the words "In the shallow" in harmony, a brief interlude features drums entering for the first time, playing tom-tom and kick eighth notes that are synched to the rhythm guitar throughout a gradual crescendo. Ally walks to Jackson's lead vocal mic and grabs it with both hands to pull it lower to match her stature, and the crowd raises a resounding cheer. Two-and-a-half measures into the interlude, Ally closes her eyes and, still gripping the microphone with a sense of ownership, begins an untexted vocalization (a series of "ah"s and "oh"s) that moves melodically upward, steadily increases in intensity, and ends with a two-measure-long sustained note—on the highest pitch in the interlude—that she projects flat for the first measure and then with a resoundingly deep vibrato for the second. Her eyes are closed for these two measures but now out of expressive intensity rather than shyness.

As the song glides seamlessly into the second chorus, Ally releases her grip on the microphone, spreads her arms wide as she sings the line, "Watch as I dive in," and then moves her arms briefly in emphasis to the words, "I'll never meet the ground." The net effect is of a full performative engagement among Ally's voice, body, and the text that she is singing. Ally's eyes sweep the width of the crowd in front of her, before she briefly drops her head on the chorus's last word and covers her mouth as if she cannot believe what has just escaped it or that she has allowed it to escape. The song enters the final refrain with Ally and Jackson singing "In the shallow" in harmony, Ally pulling her hands away from her mouth within the first measure as Jackson bends down to share the mic—now her mic—with her. When the song ends, Jackson looks at Ally with the same "What'd I tell you?!" look that he had earlier given the audience, and Ally gazes in disbelief into the audience before giving a brief laughing smile while saying—nearly inaudible against the cheering crowd—"Oh my god, there's so many people," as Jackson leans into her ear to say, "You're fucking good, man. Really fucking good."

One cannot and should not look past important critiques of the film: that it replicates narratives in which the careers of women are built upon the gatekeeping of or are enabled by men. In this film, Maine, who has a successful and established music career, "finds" Ally, who does not. Maine is portrayed as astute enough to recognize something in Ally that she is supposedly too shy, insecure, or wounded to pursue on her own. Maine arranges a song she wrote with telling her. Maine essentially forces her to sing at this concert by putting her in a position in which she is risking shame, or of letting him down, if she refuses to perform with him in front of thousands of people and with no rehearsal. Maine offers her the "gift" of career possibilities and the lure of self-confidence. And Maine positions himself as both more knowing and more capable: "All you gotta do is trust me." Further, in the larger narrative of the movie beyond this scene, once Ally's career becomes decoupled from Jackson's—once she is seen as an artist in her own right—Maine's anger and jealousy overtake the relationship and become an excuse for his alcohol and drug abuse to deepen. And, in the end, Maine interprets this decoupling of Ally's career trajectory, her self-definition, and her desire to define herself musically as distinct from him, as a weapon that she uses against him.

In spite of the very patriarchal framework the film inhabits, it also depicts voice as a means to examine both the methods and the tools by which individuals can seek to claim agency. As one watches and listens to Ally sing "Shallow" in front of thousands of people for the first time, one is taken on a journey through her emergence as a singer—and thereby as a person—coupled at times in duet with Jackson, but whose most impressive vocal moments are presented as independent of him. In Ally's initial foray onto the stage, she sings the second verse, the refrain, and the chorus solo. Across those three structures of the song, her voice steadily augments in resonance, intensity, and range. Immediately thereafter, during the interlude, she literally takes control—and thereby ownership—of the means of delivering her voice to the crowd: the lead mic becomes hers, her ownership of it symbolized by lowering it to conform to the size of her body. Her voice soars, the crowd roars, the lead vocal mic is hers, and she is thereby turned into a singer defined by herself and not by Jackson. Her arms spread just as her voice does; the audience is the witness to a sonic and physical chrysalis. Even if Maine was the one who brought Ally to people's attention, he cannot contain her voice, her music, her essence of self, her identity as she crafts it and as others engage with it.[39] Such is the power of voice, to shape and define identity.

The Digital Voice and Artificial Intelligence

"Alexa, what's the capital of Senegal?" you ask. Alexa responds, "Dakar," in "unaccented" Standard American English that sounds efficient, knowledgeable, competent, and decidedly gendered as female, and not just because of Alexa's name. Until recently, if you asked Siri, "Hey Siri, are there any Ethiopian restaurants near me?" the answer, "Try Oasis Café on Divisadero Street," would come in a voice that might as well be Alexa's sister, unless you had gone into Siri's settings and selected one of a limited number of alternate voices; starting with iOS 14.5, Apple no longer defaults to Siri's longtime signature voice but will ask users to select Siri's voice from a range of options. Google Assistant has allowed users to choose among different voices for longer but also never tied its digital voice assistant (DVA) as overtly to a (supposed) particular personality in the way that, especially, Amazon has with Alexa. Across a range of products that "talk" to consumers to give them information—in car navigation systems, phone menus, parking garage pay stations, Internet of Things (IoT) devices such as voice-activated and voice-responding washing machines, toasters, and home thermostats—the majority in the United States, at least, will sound "female."[40]

We put "female" in quotation marks because increasingly, such voices are not recordings of humans saying what is being said but are synthetic voices, the products of AI and voice synthesis research. They do not emanate from a human body, nor, in the moment they are speaking, are they drawing upon immediate human consciousness. And yet, as linguist Deborah Cameron points out, human consciousness is *behind* these voices, because humans have made intentional decisions about how these voices should sound. Hearkening forward to another chapter in this book, they are the products of intentional *sound design*. "Synthetic voices do not need to have gender or nationality, let alone personality, but invariably their designers equip them with all three," Cameron writes.[41] Gender, nationality, and personality are each (but by no means the only) ways to humanize the voices, and—importantly—by extension, the technologies themselves.[42] Taken to the extreme, they become auditory slates for the projection of users' fantasies. Spike Jonez's 2013 film, *Her*, provides a case in point: the main character Theodore, played by Joaquin Phoenix, falls in love with his computer's operating system, Samantha, as voiced by Scarlett Johansson. While Theodore's attraction and the film's plot cannot be reduced to how Johansson speaks, her voice—with its breathiness and tendency to crack, its whispery intimacy, its wide pitch modulations—is deeply implicated in her (heteronormative) attractiveness to Theodore.

When it comes to DVAs, the prevalence of female voices may be linked specifically to the *A* in the acronym: these devices function as assistants. Writing about why so many DVAs have female or feminine-sounding *names* (not voices), Adrienne LaFrance suggests bluntly, "The whole point of having a digital assistant is to have it do stuff for you. You're supposed to boss it around."[43] Chandra Steele notes:

> Whatever you asked [your DVA], a synthesized version of a woman likely answered you, polite and deferential, pleasant no matter the tone or topic. That's because Siri, Alexa, Cortana, and their foremothers have been doing

this work for years, ready to answer serious inquiries and deflect ridiculous ones. Though they lack bodies, they embody what we think of when we picture a personal assistant: a competent, efficient, and reliable woman. She gets you to meetings on time with reminders and directions, serves up reading material for the commute, and delivers relevant information on the way, like weather and traffic. Nevertheless, she is not in charge.[44]

Writing even before the widespread adoption of DVAs, Clifford Nass and Scott Brave argued that, at least in much of the Euro-American world, people tend to interpret female voices as more nurturing—helping people to solve their own problems—and male voices as more authoritarian—knowingly telling people how to solve their problems. When it comes to technology, they argue, people want to be helped by it but not controlled by it; thus, a "female" interface may be preferred.[45]

Tech companies suggest other reasons for the prevalence of female voices, in ways that downplay assumed gender roles or sexism. Daniel Rausch, Amazon's vice president for Smart Home, for example, has been quoted as saying, "We carried out research and found that a woman's voice is more 'sympathetic' and better received," while another spokesperson added, "In choosing the voice, Amazon was careful to bring the most 'pleasing' sounding voice into people's living rooms—after many trials, Alexa's was the one to come out on top."[46] Dennis Mortensen, the CEO and co-founder of x.ai (a digital assistant for scheduling meetings), seems aware that the "it's just what consumers like based on our marketing research" line of response is met with skepticism, saying, "To provide a little bit of defense for some of my fellow technologists, [research] has been done—certainly on a voice level—on how you and I best take orders from a voice-enabled system. And it's been conclusive that you and I just take orders from a female voice *better*. Some of them suggest that the pitch itself, just from an audio technology perspective is just easier to understand."[47] Arguments like these rest on a corporate best-practices logic: companies make more profits by the more customers they can attract; customers prefer their assistants to sound like women; therefore, profits will be maximized by using "female" voices for DVAs.

UNESCO and the EQUALS Skills Coalition copublished a 2019 report entitled, "I'd blush if I could," named for Siri's longtime default response to being told, "Hey, Siri, you're a b****."[48] Framing the report, its authors write, "Siri's 'female' obsequiousness—and the servility expressed by so many other digital assistants projected as young women—provides a powerful illustration of gender biases coded into technology products, pervasive in the technology sector and apparent in digital skills education."[49] The report consists of a policy paper (concerning rationales and recommendations for redressing gender inequity in digital skills acquisition) and two "think-pieces." The second think-piece is entitled, "The Rise of Gendered AI and Its Troubling Repercussions," and uses DVAs as an example to illustrate broadly how consumer technologies that are generated by male-dominated teams and companies often reflect troubling gender (or other cultural) biases.

We strongly urge readers to peruse this report directly but will highlight two of its points here. First, it cites a 2018 survey by the software company LivePerson indicating that 53 percent of respondents had never thought about why DVA voices are projected as female, even though 85 percent knew that was the default setting. The UNESCO/EQUALS report stresses that not only have people failed to ask *why* nongendered devices are being given gendered properties but, more important, that this failure precludes a consideration of the repercussions of this practice. Second, this failure to question the practice likely leads to a furthering of gender bias and the replication of gender inequality. We quote the report at some length because of its clarity and significance:

> Because the speech of most voice assistants is female, it sends a signal that women are obliging, docile and eager-to-please helpers, available at the touch of a button or with a blunt voice command like "hey" or "OK." The assistant holds no power of agency beyond what the commander asks of it. It honours commands and responds to queries regardless of their tone or hostility. In many communities, this reinforces commonly held gender biases that women are subservient and tolerant of poor treatment. As voice-powered technology reaches into communities that do not currently subscribe to Western gender stereotypes, including indigenous communities, the feminization of digital assistants may help gender biases to take hold and spread. Because Alexa, Cortana, Google Home and Siri are all female exclusively or female by default in most markets, women assume the role of digital attendant, checking the weather, changing the music, placing orders upon command and diligently coming to attention in response to curt greetings like "Wake up, Alexa."

University of Southern California sociology professor Safiya Umoja Noble and other researchers have observed that virtual assistants produce a rise of command-based speech directed at women's voices. Professor Noble says that the commands barked at voice assistants—such as "find x," "call x," "change x" or "order x"—function as "powerful socialization tools" and teach people, in particular children, about "the role of women, girls, and people who are gendered female to respond on demand." Constantly representing digital assistants as female gradually "hard-codes" a connection between a woman's voice and subservience. According to Calvin Lai, a Harvard University researcher who studies unconscious bias, the gender associations people adopt are contingent on the number of times people are exposed to them. As female digital assistants spread, the frequency and volume of associations between "woman" and "assistant" increase dramatically. According to Lai, the more that culture teaches people to equate women with assistants, the more real women will be seen as assistants—and penalized for not being assistant-like. This demonstrates that powerful technology can not only replicate gender inequalities, but also widen them.[50]

The issues of AI's replication of implicit bias, the possible intensification of such biases given how people use AI and its rapid expansion into every corner of daily life, and of how the composition of the AI workforce itself creates challenges for addressing implicit bias, are far beyond the scope of this book. But it is important to reiterate that, even in our interactions with technology, voice, along with socially and culturally biased assumptions about how voice indexes identity, is deeply present and powerfully shapes our experiences with machines. This is likely only to intensify as digital technologies shift increasingly from text-based input and output mediums into voice-based ones.

Conclusion

Through the lenses of indexicality and iconicity, voice can be examined in multiple ways and contexts for how it creates and is used to create identities, whether individual, social, or both. Whether the starting point is the materiality of the voice or its more metaphorical meanings, voice is highly productive as a signifier, linking sound to race and ethnicity, social class, geography, age, and more. Voices are all the more productive because they inherently have a degree of plasticity to them: one can change one's way of speaking much as Carol advocated in *In a World*; one can work with a vocal coach to change (within physiological limits) one's vocal register as Bradley Cooper did; one can move between different dialects and thereby project outward different signals of the self as John Baugh and Anita Henderson did when searching for housing. Finding one's voice can signal empowerment as it did for Ally in *A Star Is Born*. Not all markers of identity are this plastic; thus, voice is particularly complexly positioned in terms of how identity links to power, to stereotyping, to marginalization, and to discrimination. This chapter has raised the question of whether what a voice "means" is "in" the voice or is in how the voice is interpreted or decoded by listeners. It would seem that the answer is that it is located in both and that one of the continual dynamics of sending one's voice into the world is recognizing that the meaning of a voice emerges as a negotiation between what the vocalizer intends to signal and what a listener extracts and assigns to the heard voice.

Perhaps because some of the phenomena related to voice require at least a passing knowledge of linguistics (particularly of phonetics, phonology, and prosody), voice and language have not been major foci in sound studies, as few of its scholars have linguistics as their academic training or disciplinary home. As hinted in the chapter, though, there are fertile areas for sound studies that sit at the intersection of voice, linguistics, and sound studies, such as how voice analysis can assist with certain medical diagnoses and how forensic audio can be used in identity verification of voices and in creative voice manipulation or voice creation via voice synthesis as examined in the case of aforementioned DVAs.

Project

Find video recordings of three people reading the same text (of approximately thirty seconds in length), and extract the audio track from each. Alternatively, you may make your own audio recordings of people you know. (If you record voices on our own, you must obtain an informed consent statement from each speaker, indicating that they are willing to be recorded for the purposes of an academic study. A template can be found at https://www.ship.edu/globalassets/counsel/informedconsent.pdf.) Play these audio recordings to at least five other people you know. Ask each person to try to imagine the speakers in terms including, but not limited to, their sex, age, social class, geographical origin, and physiology. What commonalities arise among their responses? What differences? What might your results suggest about how people use others' voices to make assumptions about individual and social identity?

Notes

1 View the scene at https://www.youtube.com/watch?v=IGLXMXX_OOc.
2 One answer to Carol's question might be found in Shalita Grant's embodiment of Attorney Cassidy Diamond in season 3 of HBO's *Search Party* (2020).
3 View the scene at https://www.youtube.com/watch?v=sY_6fFdRnik.

4 The tweet was quickly removed but, as of the writing of this book, was still embedded in an article at https://www.thedailybeast.com/star-wars-actress-mocks-kavanaugh-accuser-christine-blasey-ford.

5 Eidsheim, *The Race of Sound*, 93.

6 Timbre is usually defined as the sound quality of a voice or instrument, independent from pitch or loudness. Timbre is what allows listeners to distinguish between the same note as played by, for example, a flute and a saxophone. Timbre results from the fact that different instruments will produce different overtones when playing the same note due to differences in shape, mode of exciting the sound (breath, bow, finger-pluck, etc.), and the material the instrument is made from.

7 Eidsheim, *The Race of Sound*, 102.

8 Ibid., 108.

9 While not a critique of Eidsheim, we wish to note that her analysis does leave some questions unanswered, such as the effects of age on the singing voice, the falsetto break points of the other singers in the corpus—it would be interesting to note if any of them were in fact higher than the top of Scott's vocal range—and whether a growth spurt Scott had at age thirty-seven had any effect on his voice.

10 Weidman, "Voice," 233–45.

11 Polysemous words are those with more than one definition or meaning, such as "crane" (the bird, the piece of construction equipment, or the verb indicating lengthening one's neck) but in which the meanings are often closely related.

12 See, e.g., Meintjes, "Ululation," 61–76, on ululation; Bauer, "Scat Singing," 303–23, on scat singing; Samuels, "Language, Meaning, Modernity, and Doowop," 297–323, on doowop; and Samarin, *Tongues of Men and Angels* on glossolalia.

13 Brittany Howard's vocal work during Alabama Shakes's March 1, 2015, *Saturday Night Live* performance of "Gimme All Your Love" provides an excellent case study in the use of vocal texture in relation to words. See https://www.youtube.com/watch?v=_sNNTpORtDQ.

14 Eidsheim, *The Race of Sound*, 5. For a comprehensive overview of the field of "voice studies," see Eidsheim and Meizel, *The Oxford Handbook of Voice Studies*.

15 This chapter does not delve into a more philosophically oriented literature that exists on voice. See, e.g., Cavarero, *For More Than One Voice*; Dolar, *A Voice and Nothing More*; and Ihde, *Listening and Voice*.

16 The four-season IFC show *Brockmire*, about a "down-on-his-luck" baseball announcer trying to make a career comeback, often dabbled in the comedic potential of failure to modulate voice depending on the occasion and context of speaking.

17 This is also a critical feature used in forensic analysis and voice identification. See Laub, Wiley, and Bornstein, "Can the Courts Tell an Ear from an Eye," 119–58.

18 Arguably, there is no "pure" onomatopoeia in language; where an English speaker claims a dog goes "bow wow," a Portuguese speaker claims "uau"; both are conditioned by the phonological systems of the respective languages. For further explanation of more or less phonologically conditioned versions of onomatopoetic sound, see Feld, Fox, Porcello, and Samuels, "Vocal Anthropology," 321–45.

19 The power of indexes is palpable given the extent to which they play a key role in hoaxes, "unsolved mysteries" (such as whether Bigfoot does or not exist), and in paranormal research.

20 For a comprehensive discussion of the links between voice and identity, see Podesva and Callier, "Voice Quality and Identity," 173–94.

21 See the video at https://www.youtube.com/watch?v=4HjcQjwKBWM (Singh, "Pinpointing People and Places through Advanced Audio Analysis").

22 There is a very large scientific literature on teaching machines to identify speaker sex; however, much of it conflates the terms "gender" and "sex"; to see the scope of this literature, one can go to Google Scholar or ProQuest and search using the words "voice," "gender," and "recognition."

23 Baugh, "Linguistic Profiling," 155–68.

24 The account Baugh quotes is from Henderson, "Put Your Money Where Your Mouth Is."

25 For a discussion of language ideology and its links to race, ethnicity, gender, class, and power in the United States, see Lippi-Green, *English with an Accent*. More recent work in "raciolinguistics"—the study of the central role that language plays in shaping ideas about race and vice versa—updates many of the lines of inquiry that Baugh opened up. See Alim, Rickford, and Ball, *Raciolinguistics*; and Rosa, "Standardization, Racialization, Languagelessness," 162–83.

26 Porcello regularly teaches an introductory linguistics course in which he asks, once these issues have been raised in class, how students think they would have reacted if—and how their parents might have reacted if told that—he walked into class the first day speaking in a deeply "Appalachian" dialect. Year after year, most say they would have been at the least taken aback and, in many cases, skeptical of his credentials to teach such a course.

27 See Mendoza-Denton, "The Semiotic Hitchhiker's Guide to Creaky Voice," 261–80; Mendoza-Denton, *Homegirls*.

28 For a classic study, see Labov, "The Social Stratification of (r) in New York City Department Stores," 43–54.

29 See, e.g., Cameron and Kulick, *Language and Sexuality*.

30 See, e.g., Bakalar, "Study Finds Reproductive Edge for Men with Deep Voices."

31 See, e.g., Cleveland Clinic, "Voice Changes."

32 Media representations often reinforce such linguistic ideologies, further propagating them. See Podesva and Callier, "Voice Quality and Identity," 173–94.

33. Baugh, "Linguistic Profiling," 155–68.
34. Voice casting for animated features has changed over the years, such that on-camera movie stars are displacing actors who focused their work almost solely off-camera, such as Mel Blanc (known as "The Man of a Thousand Voices"), Daws Butler (the voice of Yogi Bear and Huckleberry Hound, among many others), Kath Soucie, and Janet Waldo (sometimes referred to as the Woman of a Thousand Voices).
35. See, e.g., Sharf, "Bradley Cooper Spent 20 Hours a Week Working on His 'A Star Is Born' Accent during the Year before Filming"; Yahr, "Yes, Bradley Cooper's Voice in 'A Star Is Born' Was Physically Painful to Create"; and Rao, "Bradley Cooper Will Keep Geeking Out about 'A Star Is Born' As Long As You Let Him."
36. For a fascinating account of Monich's career and examples of how he has coached specific actors, see Wilkinson, "Talk This Way."
37. Rao, "Bradley Cooper Will Keep Geeking Out about 'A Star Is Born' As Long As You Let Him"; and Yahr, "Yes, Bradley Cooper's Voice in 'A Star Is Born' Was Physically Painful to Create."
38. Cowritten by Lady Gaga and Mark Ronson, "Shallow" won the Best Original Song Oscar at the Academy Awards in 2019.
39. Lady Gaga is, of course, acting in this scene, crafting a *particular performance* of a shy, halting performance and its movement into growing confidence and the chrysalis as described.
40. In the UK, France, and Germany, Siri's default voice has always been male, and in Germany, BMW reported a lack of confidence by drivers in receiving navigation instructions from its female voice prototypes (Donald, "Siri, Alexa, Cortana, and Why All Boats Are a 'She' "). The navigation app Waze has taken a somewhat different approach by, among other things, having celebrities such as Morgan Freeman and Boy George record their voices as options for users to choose from.
41. Cameron, "Language," 81–5.
42. This humanization often takes the form of giving technologies personalities, of which the voice is one part.
43. LaFrance, "Why Do So Many Digital Assistants Have Feminine Names?"
44. Steele, "The Real Reason Voice Assistants Are Female (and Why It Matters)."
45. Nass and Brave, *Wired for Speech*.
46. Both quoted in Schwär and Moynihan, "Companies like Amazon May Give Devices like Alexa Female Voices to Make Them Seem 'Caring.' "
47. Quoted in LaFrance, "Why Do So Many Digital Assistants Have Feminine Names?"
48. At present, the response is, "I don't know how to respond to that."
49. UNESCO and EQUALS Skills Coalition, "I'd Blush If I Could: Closing Gender Divides in Digital Skills through Education."

50 Ibid. Umoja Noble's work as cited in the UNESCO/EQUALS is from Lever, "I Was a Human Siri"); see her primary work in Umoja Noble, *Algorithms of Oppression*. See Lai and Banaji, "The Psychology of Implicit Intergroup Bias and the Prospect of Change," for Lai's primary research.

Bibliography

Alim, H. Samy, John R. Rickford, and Arnetha F Ball. *Raciolinguistics: How Language Shapes Our Ideas about Race*. Oxford: Oxford University Press, 2016.

Bakalar, Nicholas. "Study Finds Reproductive Edge for Men with Deep Voices." November 27, 2007. *nytimes.com*. https://www.nytimes.com/2007/11/27/science/27voic.html (accessed April 28, 2021).

Bauer, William R. "Scat Singing: A Timbral and Phomenic Analysis." *Current Musicology* 71–3 (2001/2002): 303–23.

Baugh, John. "Linguistic Profiling." In *Black Linguistics: Language, Society, and Politics in Africa and the Americas*, edited by Sinfree Makoni Arnetha Ball, Sinfree Makoni, Geneva Smitherman, and Arthur K. Spears, 155–68. London: Routledge, 2003.

Cameron, Deborah. "Language: Designer Voices." *Critical Quarterly* 43, no. 4 (2001): 81–5.

Cameron, Deborah, and Don Kulick. *Language and Sexuality*. Cambridge: Cambridge University Press, 2003.

Cavarero, Adrianna. *For More Than One Voice: Toward a Philosophy of Vocal Expression*. Translated by Paul A Kottman. Palo Alto, CA: Stanford University Press, 2005.

Cleveland Clinic. "Voice Changes: What Can They Tell You as You Age?" December 31, 2020. *health.clevelandclinic.org*. https://health.clevelandclinic.org/voice-changes-what-can-they-tell-you-as-you-age/ (accessed April 27, 2021).

Dolar, Mladen. *A Voice and Nothing More*. Cambridge: MIT Press, 2006.

Donald, Samara J. "Siri, Alexa, Cortana, and Why All Boats Are a 'She.' " August 18, 2019. *medium.com*. https://medium.com/voice-tech-podcast/siri-alexa-cortana-and-why-all-boats-are-a-she-e4fb71b6a9f7 (accessed February 16, 2021).

Eidsheim, Nina S. "Familiarity as Strangeness: Jimmy Scott and the Question of Black Timbral Masculinity." In *The Race of Sound: Listening, Timbre, and Vocality in African American Music*, 91–113. Durham, NC: Duke University Press, 2019.

Eidsheim, Nina S., and Katherine Meizel, eds. *The Oxford Handbook of Voice Studies*. Oxford: Oxford University Press, 2019.

Feld, Steven, Steven Feld, Aaron A. Fox, Thomas Porcello, and David Samuels. "Vocal Anthropology: From the Music of Language to the Language of Song." In *A Companion to Linguistic Anthropology*, edited by Alessandro Duranti, 321–45. Malden: Blackwell, 2004.

Henderson, Anita. "Put Your Money Where Your Mouth Is: Hiring Managers' Attitudes toward African-American Vernacular English." PhD dissertation, University of Pennsylvania, 2001.

Ihde, Don. *Listening and Voice: Phenomenologies of Sound*. 2nd ed. Albany: SUNY Press, 2007.

Labov, William. "The Social Stratification of (r) in New York City Department Stores." In *Sociolinguistic Patterns*, edited by William Labov, 43–54. Philadelphia: University of Pennsylvania Press, 1972.

LaFrance, Adrienne. "Why Do So Many Digital Assistants Have Feminine Names? Hey Cortana. Hey Siri. Hey Girl." March 30, 2016. *theatlantic.com*. https://www.theatlantic.com/technology/archive/2016/03/why-do-so-many-digital-assistants-have-feminine-names/475884/ (accessed February 24, 2021).

Lai, Calvin K., and Mahzarin R. Banaji. "The Psychology of Implicit Intergroup Bias and the Prospect of Change." In *Difference without Domination: Pursuing Justice in Diverse Democracies*, edited by Danielle Allen and Rohini Somanathan, 115–46. Chicago: University of Chicago Press, 2019.

Laub, Cindy E., Lindsey E. Wiley, and Brian H. Bornstein. "Can the Courts Tell an Ear from an Eye: Legal Approaches to Voice Identification Evidence." *Law & Psychology Review* 37 (2013): 119–58.

Lever, Emily. "I Was a Human Siri." April 26, 2018. *nymag.com*. https://nymag.com/intelligencer/smarthome/i-was-a-human-siri-french-virtual-assistant.html (accessed February 28, 2021).

Lippi-Green, Rosina. *English with an Accent: Language, Ideology, and Discrimination in the United States*. 2nd ed. London: Routledge, 2012.

Meintjes, Louise. "Ululation." In *Remapping Sound Stuies*, edited by Gavin Steingo and Jim Sykes, 61–76. Durham, NC: Duke University Press, 2019.

Mendoza-Denton, Norma. *Homegirls: Language and Cultural Practice among Latina Youth Gangs*. Malden: Blackwell Publishing, 2008.

Mendoza-Denton, Norma. "The Semiotic Hitchhiker's Guide to Creaky Voice: Circulation and Gendered Hardcore in a Chicana/o Gang Persona." *Linguistic Anthropology* 21, no. 2 (2011): 261–80.

Nass, Clifford, and Scott Brave. *Wired for Speech: How Voice Activates and Advances the Human-Computer Relationship*. Cambridge: MIT Press, 2007.

Podesva, Robert J., and Patrick Callier. "Voice Quality and Identity." *Annual Review of Applied Linguistics* 35 (2015): 173–94.

Rao, Sonia. "Bradley Cooper Will Keep Geeking Out about 'A Star Is Born' As Long As You Let Him." October 1, 2018. *washingtonpost.com*. https://www.washingtonpost.com/lifestyle/style/bradley-cooper-will-keep-geeking-out-about-a-star-is-born-as-long-as-you-let-him/2018/09/27/a965b168-c0d6-11e8-90c9-23f963eea204_story.html (accessed November 6, 2020).

Rosa, Jonathan D. "Standardization, Racialization, Languagelessness: Raciolinguistic Ideologies across Communicative Contexts." *Journal of Linguistic Anthropology* 26, no. 2 (2016): 162–83.

Samarin, William J. *Tongues of Men and Angels: The Religious Language of Pentacostalism*. New York: Macmillan, 1972.

Samuels, David W. "Language, Meaning, Modernity, and Doowop." *Semiotica* 149, no. 1/4 (2004): 297–323.

Schwär, Hanna, and Qayyah Moynihan. "Companies like Amazon May Give Devices like Alexa Female Voices to Make Them Seem 'Caring.' " April 5, 2020. *BusinessInsider.com*. https://www.businessinsider.com/theres-psychological-reason-why-amazon-gave-alexa-a-female-voice-2018-9 (accessed February 24, 2021).

Sharf, Jack. "Bradley Cooper Spent 20 Hours a Week Working on His 'A Star Is Born' Accent during the Year before Filming." August 13, 2018. *indiewire.com*. https://www.indiewire.com/2018/08/bradley-cooper-a-star-is-born-voice-training-accent-1201993727/ (accessed November 6, 2020).

Singh, Rita. "Pinpointing People and Places through Advanced Audio Analysis." World Economic Forum, February 21, 2018. YouTube video.

Steele, Chandra. "The Real Reason Voice Assistants Are Female (and Why It Matters)." January 4, 2018. *PCmag.com*. https://www.pcmag.com/opinions/the-real-reason-voice-assistants-are-female-and-why-it-matters (accessed February 24, 2021).

Torres, Libby. "'Star Wars' Actress Mocks Kavanaugh Accuser Christine Blasey Ford." September 27, 2018. *thedailybeast.com*. https://www.thedailybeast.com/star-wars-actress-mocks-kavanaugh-accuser-christine-blasey-ford (accessed November 30, 2020).

Umoja Noble, Safiya. *Algorithms of Oppression: How Search Engines Reinforce Racism*. New York: NYU Press, 2018.

UNESCO and EQUALS Skills Coalition. "I'd Blush If I Could: Closing Gender Divides in Digital Skills through Education." 2019. *UNESDOC Digital Library*. https://unesdoc.unesco.org/ark:/48223/pf0000367416.page=1 (accessed February 24, 2021).

Urban, Greg. "Ritual Wailing in Amerindian Brazil." *American Anthropologist* 90, no. 2 (1988): 385–400.

Weidman, Amanda. "Voice." In *Keywords in Sound*, edited by David Novak and Matt Sakakeeny, 233–45. Durham, NC: Duke Univeristy Press, 2015.

Wilkinson, Alec. "Talk This Way: The Man Who Makes Hollywood Sound Right." November 1, 2009. *newyorker.com*. https://www.newyorker.com/magazine/2009/11/09/talk-this-way (accessed November 6, 2020).

Yahr, Emily. "Yes, Bradley Cooper's Voice in 'A Star Is Born' Was Physically Painful to Create." October 5, 2018. *washingtonpost.com*. https://www.washingtonpost.com/arts-entertainment/2018/10/05/yes-bradley-coopers-voice-star-is-born-was-physically-painful-create/ (accessed November 6, 2020).

Recommended Further Reading

Alim, H. Samy, John R. Rickford, and Arnetha F. Ball. *Raciolinguistics: How Language Shapes Our Ideas about Race*. Oxford: Oxford University Press, 2016.

Eidsheim, Nina S. *The Race of Sound: Listening, Timbre, and Vocality in African American Music*. Durham, NC: Duke University Press, 2019.

4

Sound on the Page: Echoes and Resonances in Writing

Key concepts: transcription, translation, verisimilitude, reality effect, sound writing, writerly text

In *Mr. Wuffles*, an epic tale of intergalactic travel, clash of civilizations, and interspecies cooperation, author and illustrator David Weisner depicts one of the classic structures of encounter: the struggle to communicate through different languages. In his story, a tiny alien craft lands in the home of Mr. Wuffles, an alternately apathetic and aggressive tuxedo cat. Unfortunately for the ant-sized space travelers, Mr. Wuffles takes a liking to the spacecraft, batting it like a new toy, violently churning its inhabitants, and damaging the spaceship's delicate power system. In search of a solution, the aliens are chased underneath a heater and into the walls of the house. There they discover a series of cave painting–like images depicting Mr. Wuffles terrorizing ants, ladybugs, and mice. A moment later, they encounter these same creatures.

At this point in the book, Weisner has established the auditory orthography of three languages. In the book's prologue, the cat's human, shown only from mid-chest down, is attempting to entice Mr. Wuffles with a toy fish, which the unimpressed feline rejects. The human speaks in English, with short sentences that end in exclamation points, but there is no visual sign that Mr. Wuffles comprehends, or perhaps in feline fashion, he simply does not care. When the aliens are first depicted celebrating their interstellar travel, their language is depicted as elegant sets of geometric symbols that use Roman punctuation. Their celebrations upon landing are marked with exclamations, and their bewilderment upon being tossed about by Mr. Wuffles is punctuated by question marks. In the walls of the house, there are iconographic pictures and the language of the ladybugs and ants is represented as a bunches of short, irregular, vertical marks.

In the encounter between aliens and insects, the fear of the unknown is mitigated by the shared medium of pictographs. The aliens draw their story on the wall, showing that they are also victims of Mr. Wuffles, the great antagonist. This bonds the aliens and insects, prompting a sharing of food, group pictures, and assistance in finding the materials needed to reconstruct the damaged power system of the alien spacecraft. The two civilizations also use pictographs to collectively devise a plan that will allow the aliens to escape. As the tiny ship victoriously sails out the window, Mr. Wuffles's meow of frustration is sounded, drawn as a bold *MROWW!* in a spikey speech bubble.

What Weisner so beautifully captures in visual form is the sound of the characters' actions—languages, crashes, hot pursuit, and celebration—and what those sounds convey about meaning, action, feeling, and personality. The intergalactic aliens' language is elegant and seemingly sophisticated— the aliens celebrate, converse, and problem solve together. Their language is drawn in clean lines and regular geometric shapes; there is symmetry, balance, and symbolic complexity; their language appears to have syntax and multi-word sentences. The language of the ship's engineer is depicted as an equation or formula, visual differentiating his technical speech from that of his fellow aliens.

In contrast, the insects' language is depicted as simple and lacking in discernible difference between characters and sounds. Instead of appearing in straight lines, their dialogue bubbles contain markings in constellations rather than lines. The two civilizations initially communicate through pictures drawn on a wall before learning to converse.

Weisner also captures the sounds of the ordinary and extraordinary through the depiction of sonorous actions. While we do not "hear" Mr. Wuffles's frustrated "meow" until the final pages of the book, we see him playfully batting about the aliens' ship, licking its surface, and holding the ship in place while he blissfully rubs his chin on its textured metallic surface. We can imagine the sounds of him purring as he plays. Likewise, the aftermath of Mr. Wuffles's first encounter with the alien craft shows the inside of the ship with the aliens strewn about, holding their heads and muttering in confusion, with a trail of smoke ascending from the ship's engine room. The hiss of the smoldering engine and the wilted murmurs of the dazed aliens are drawn into the scene. While the cat sleeps, the aliens attempt to stealthily slip away, illustrated into their body language through stiff arms and tiptoes. All these actions—the purring of a happy cat, the cacophony of mechanical violence,

FIGURE 1 *From David Weisner, Mr. Wuffles. Boston: Clarion Books, 2013. Used by permission of the author*

FIGURE 2 From David Weisner, *Mr. Wuffles*. Boston: Clarion Books, 2013. Used by permission of the author

the wheezing of broken machinery, and muffled sounds of cautious steps—pique our mind's ear and place us into the narrative of the book, within earshot of the characters and their actions.

As is often the case with books—from picture books to comics, graphic novels, and literature—authors use visual depictions of sound as a device to engage the reader and their mind's ear. Sound draws readers into the action of the text and provides an extra sensory experience while reading. There are many reasons for inserting sounds and aural description into texts and images. Some descriptions and depictions serve to set the scene, to embed readers within the soundscape of the book and bring them into the place, real or imagined, of the narrative. Other sonic depictions trigger familiar sounds in the reader's imagination that set up the time, space, and place of the story. Others portray characters, from the sound of the voice (either as part of their character or as reflective of a character's emotional state, see Chapter 3) to the sounds generated by plot, like footfalls, cooking sounds, or the noises associated with specific forms of labor and leisure (for more on *diegetic sound*, see Chapter 5). A different use for sound in text is to evoke specific reactions, to induce an affective response to the text that will either mirror that of a character or allow the author to create a desired emotional state in the reader.

The techniques used by writers are rich and varied, and new ideas, theories, and experiments are regularly explored. This chapter examines several of the many ways of thinking about sound through sound writing. The first theory and method are taken from linguistic anthropology and the debates over how to transcribe speech and verbal art into print. The second is taken from the literary criticism of Roland Barthes and his concept of the "reality effect"—how attention to detail aids in suspension of disbelief and reader immersion. The third is taken from ethnographic writing and the practice of translating primary experiences into secondary experiences through text. Finally, this chapter returns to pictorial representation and the ways that graphic novelists depict sound in their narratives and images.

Transcribing Language as Sound

Alphabetic writing is primarily concerned with capturing and creating the sounds of spoken language and verbal gesture. Graphic shapes are arbitrarily assigned sounds; sounds are combined into phonemes; phonemes are strung together to make words.[1] Some phonemes contain small pieces of meaning in themselves (think of prefixes or suffixes), and others are used for onomatopoeic or aesthetic purposes. In *Of Grammatology*, philosopher Jacques Derrida argues that writing is tethered to the reproduction of speech and the voice. This role of voice capture and reproduction limits what writing is capable of, because it is bound by the limitations of speech practices.[2] However philosophically and metaphysically salient this argument is, the modern practice of graphic writing, particularly with mechanical additions like italics, bolding and additional symbols, has expanded how language is represented on the page. As works by many theorists, artists, and authors demonstrate, using writing to capture the sound of language is not a straightforward or uniform task. Techniques of transcription are complicated, varied, and multifaceted. These techniques are also dynamic. As we will see later in this chapter, comics and graphic novelists have also developed a complex visual vocabulary for sounds, including the voice, that add layers of information beyond language.

Researchers of language have spent over a century decoding the complex links between language and social structures. These concerns necessitated fieldwork and extended firsthand experience within communities, documenting everything from quotidian everyday speech to lullabies, spiritual practices, education, and verbal art (this practice of extended contact is sometimes referred to as ethnography). This led researchers to document, participate in, and record language usage from around the world. Since foundational early research was done in print—before recordings and documentary footage were feasible, affordable, and easily shared—rigorous debates ensued about transcription and how to capture verbal art as it is performed on paper (rather than earlier practices of writing a grammar or a lexicon). The global and multilingual nature of sociolinguistic work gave rise to a robust debate about how to create a system of transcription that would enable cross-cultural comparative study. These experiments in sound on the page are examples of how sound is represented in print, and are an excellent entry point into scholarly debates about representing the sounds of language, its temporal and performative aspects, and the reception of listening communities.

Linguistic anthropologist Dell Hymes pioneered the concept of "ethno poetics," an important notion in relativizing and analyzing the auditory experiences of language. Unlike some of his predecessors, Hymes was not combing language in search of its pure or universal forms. His theoretical writing critiques orthography as an artificial and marginalizing pursuit. Instead, he was interested in how language worked in social context, how the idiosyncrasies of individual or regional speech were differently meaningful, and how speech acts were performed. Hymes studied, analyzed, and documented perpetually mobile systems of language. He followed Roman

Jakobson's idea that the poetic function analyzes how "choices of sounds, lexical items, syntactic structures, and the like are combined to create expressive alignment" and how poetics both fulfill and escape convention and form.³ Expanding on this notion, Hymes sought to develop a system that apprehended language use in context and also performed the critical political function of social justice. In moving away from structural linguistics and the search for deep structures or universal grammar, Hymes turned the focus of linguistics toward sound in social context.⁴ He also sought to locate the limits of effective speech, how far a speaker can push form before meaning is confused, compromised, or lost.

Hymes's ethongraphic writing is dense with context. It provides extensive notes on the history of the communities and individuals he writes about, analysis of their linguistic tendencies and performance style, and background on the myths and verbal performances that he transcribes and translates. When he provides text in indigenous language, it includes a pronunciation guide. His transcriptions and translations show the pacing of the story by breaking the text into groupings as they are heard (e.g., groupings of two, three, or four lines) with indentations to indicate speech hierarchy and temporal articulation. Using variations in punctuation and spacing, transcriptions indicate points where long and short pauses are taken, where organizational units begin and end, and the auditory structure and flow of the narrative. These units are intended to represent and reflect both the aesthetic organization used by the speakers (to craft their vocal performance) and the stylistic expectations of listeners. Often, Hymes's transcriptions resemble poetry rather than prose, a nod to the sounds of speech performance being distinct from both literary practices and articulations of everyday speech. Hymes wished his transcriptions to be analytic, to present in alphabetic writing what was socially, structurally, and aesthetically important in the text, reflecting what is heard and listened for.

Here is an example from Hymes's "Helen Sekaquaptewa's 'Coyote and the Birds': Rhetorical Analysis of a Hopi Coyote Story." This is a translation into English from the original story, told in Hopi by Helen Sekaquaptewa. Previous to Ms. Sekaquaptewa's performance, we read a member of the audience coaxing her to tell a coyote story. She agrees but admonishes the audience that they must offer her encouragement, lest she decide not to tell the story. Hymes captures the audiences' interplay in bold on the right. From this transcription, we can see that Hymes preserves the syntax of Hopi storytelling style as well as the timing, with the first few lines of the introduction of place unfolding slowly and then picking up place with the introduction of the birds, a protagonist in the story.

They say at Oraibi they were living.	(A)
Yes	

They say at Oraibi they were living.   (A)
                                           Yes
Well as a matter of fact, there, they say, they were living

and
over there   20

Well birds also, they say, were abundant there, I mean they,   (B)
well likewise flock together in their usual way,
    while flying about like so, *(gesture)*
Well they likewise, when it got to be toward winter,
    would prepare to store some food   25
                                                   Yes . . . . . yes

Hymes's contemporary Dennis Tedlock, also a scholar of indigenous languages and verbal art, adopted a more radical approach in his transcription style. Tedlock's transcriptions were imagined as being akin to a script for performance, as opposed to Hymes's, which were designed as a tool for sociolinguistic analysis. Tedlock looked to restore sonic and temporal elements of speech, playing with the spacing of words; using all caps to designate phonemes, words, or sentences that were enunciated louder; using split lines to imitate tonal delivery; and employing falling or rising letters to indicate verbal glissandos. He, like Hymes, also indicated actions that accompanied the text. His book *The Spoken Word and the Work of Interpretation* has a thorough "Guide to Reading Aloud" that contains the following directions:

    "The cold is dangerous
the snow is deep
and you shouldn't go out at a
    time like this

It isn't your place," so he told his
    granddaughter

NOW THEN, LOOK OUTSIDE
    and see how far in the
    night it is

The fire was going out, *(softly)*
    the light was dim.

In passages set in poetic lines, pause at least half a second each time a new line begins at the left margin, and at least two seconds for a dot separating lines. Do not pause within lines; indented words are continuations of long lines.

Use a loud voice for words in capitals.

Soft passages, dramatic tones of voice (sharp, kind, etc.) and gestures are marked with parenthesized italics.

SOUND ON THE PAGE 99

```
some    cha    meeeeeeee
   one is   sing
                        e
                          e
                            e
```

Chant split lines, with an interval of about three half-tones between them. Draw out repeated letters (and hold vowels followed by long dashes) as long as it would take to say the words occupying an equal amount of space. Spilling letters indicate a glissando.

Caution: Do not attempt mechanical accuracy. In narrative passages, slow down to the pace of someone telling a story without any script.[5]

As Tedlock's guide shows, the transcriptions are intended for a different purpose and appear visually more daring than Hymes's. Both seek a more ethnographically representative depiction of the sound of language outside of the bounds of orthography. Where they differ is the intention of putting the sound of verbal art onto the page. For Hymes, the transcription was done with social analysis in mind, bringing the reader to a fuller understanding of verbal art in the lives of the indigenous communities in which Hymes worked. His extensive research and experience into the social history and context of verbal art are crafted into the transcription, including representations of abstract forms and audience expectations. Depictions of language performance include sound as it is produced as well as it is cognitively organized by verbal artists and listening communities in relation to shared aesthetics, even if those codes were transgressed or expanded during performances.

For Tedlock, the transcription was a score or a script, a record of sound unfolding in time that was meant to act as a tool for students and scholars to learn about verbal art experientially, through performance. The temporal element of verbal art, like sound art, was critical to understanding the production and reception of language as meaningful sound. Tedlock sought to reproduce performative elements, as well as facets of language like differential stresses (through using all caps), accompanying gestures, dramatic pauses of different lengths, and variations in pitch. Tedlock's transcriptions were like musical scores or musical transcription: they captured performance practice, albeit in limited ways, similar to a music score that captures the outline of a performance. With Tedlock's transcriptions, the goal was to learn verbal art by reproducing it, learning through embodiment. The analysis of verbal arts is then done by comparing transcriptions (with Hymes) and performances (with Tedlock).

The technology used in modern sociolinguistics has dramatically improved since Hymes's and Tedlock's ideas were contested in academic circles. However, concerns about representing language as sound have continued relevance, particularly as interest in social justice and representation, of which language and verbal art play a substantial role, have risen to the forefront of ethnographic method. Hymes's focus on social justice and Tedlock's idea of learning through embodiment are mainstays of scholarly and educational practice. As we will see later in this chapter, the idea of representing language as sound in a textual medium is relevant to the way that we read and see ideas of character, place, and action.

Linguistic Transcription in a Digital Age

With the proliferation of digital tools and hardware, Hymes's and Tedlock's styles of transcription have been partially eclipsed by digital modes of representation and care for the representation of indigenous and non-European languages. Digital technology enables symbols beyond the Roman alphabet to be easily used in transcription. Alphabetic and symbolic representation in indigenous and other non-European languages can be included in print rather than only written about in the scholar's language. These transcriptions of speech acts and verbal art use newly added symbols to represent linguistic sounds not found in European languages and alphabetic or graphic writing systems. This adds additional layers to transcriptions, including the text in its own written language, a phonetic guide, and a translation. These augmented transcriptions and translations give a silent reader insight into the sound of language and also how its native speakers and communities represent their own language.

Another innovation is the use of digital technologies to simultaneously provide an aural recording of speech, a visual depiction of the sound waves, a transcription, and analysis. This analysis can include a translation, formal analysis, and footnotes on the text or the visuals (gesture is often an important element of verbal art that is difficult to transcribe). Some of the more sophisticated software sync video with the analysis, allowing for multiple levels of evidence and analysis to be presented simultaneously. An excellent example of this is Elan, a software developed for language analysis that has since expanded into video, making it an important tool for multiple disciplines.[6]

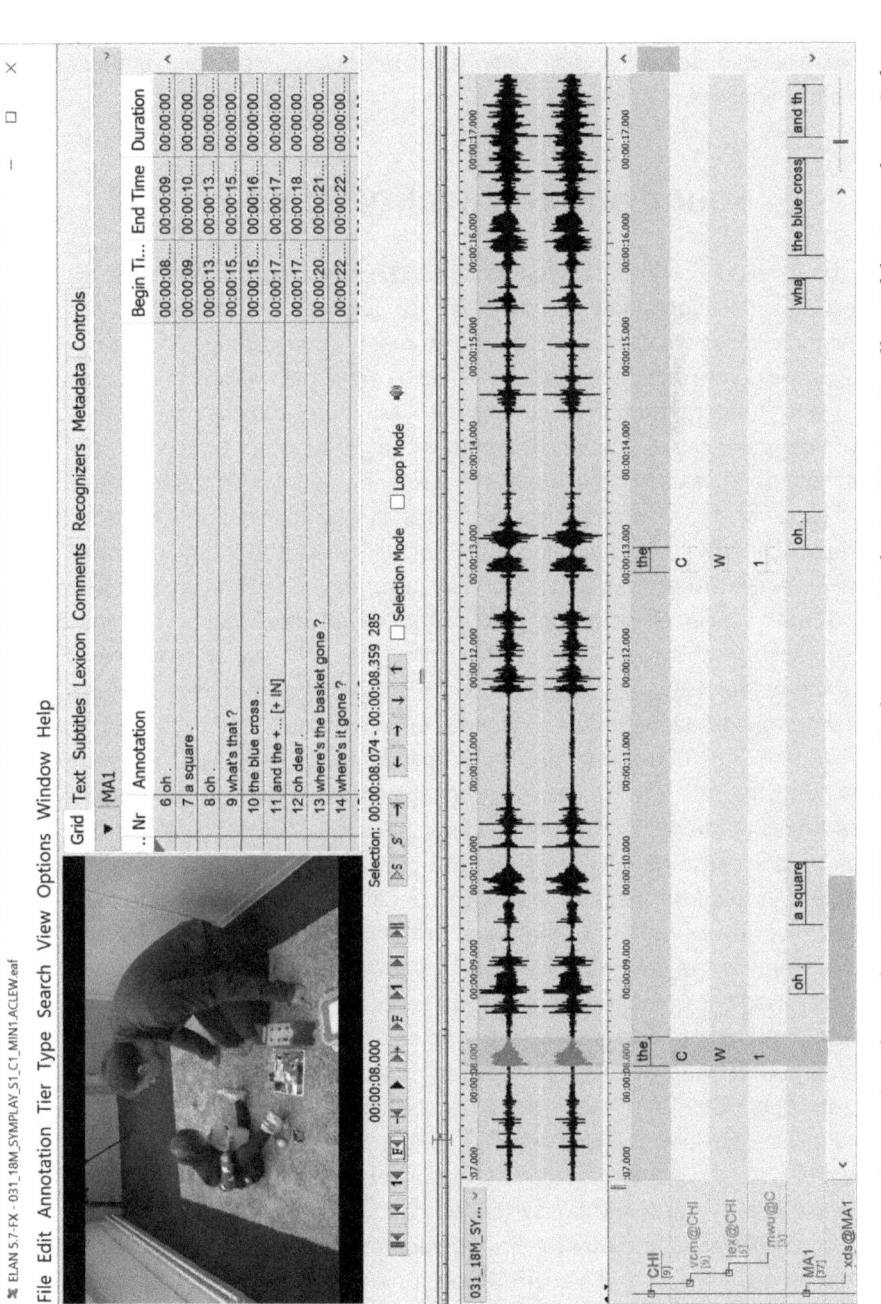

FIGURE 3 Screenshot from the ACLEW project. Soderstrom, Melanie, Marisa Casillas, Elika Bergelson, Celia R. Rosemberg, florencia alam, Anne S. Warlaumont, and John P. Bunce. 2020. "Developing a Cross-cultural Annotation System and Metacorpus for Studying Infants' Real World Language Experience." PsyArXiv. September 30. doi:10.31234/osf.io/bf63y. Used by permission from Max Planck Institute

These digital innovations circumvent the necessity of writing the "reality effect" (see later) of speech and allow for more levels of contextual, historical, or theoretical analysis.

Sound and the Reality Effect

Writing about description in literary realism, Roland Barthes touches upon the role of non-narrative description in the work of French novelist Gustave Flaubert and French historian Jules Michelet. In his brief and mesmerizing essay "The Reality Effect," Barthes delves into details left unmarked by previous analyses that sought to understand literature through lenses like form, structure, and analogy. The fine details of boxes and cartons under a barometer or a gentle knock on a door were assigned little to no value in other literary analyses. Barthes seeks to recuperate the significance of small, nonallegorical detail, particularly its effect on the reader.

Barthes begins by deconstructing the Enlightenment notion of "the real," as it was written into literature and history. In an expression of history that was impacted by an empirical, scientific idea of proof, what was "real" lay outside of the subjectivity of verisimilitude, which provides only the *appearance* of reality to the reader. History, influenced by the scientific method, archaeology, tourism to historical sites, and other practices of witness (later the photograph), sought proof for their truth claims. This implied the universal and absolute in proclaiming the real and its depictions in literature and history. What was real was never contingent on what readers knew or understood but could stand on its own as a direct representation of a lived reality (and therefore knowledge).[7] In this formulation, detail was subservient to the verifiable truth in the narrative: every detail of what was written in history or literature was within the realm of the verified and served a structural function in the story.

The small, neglected details addressed by Barthes, the value of which is not immediately relevant to narrative or allegory, create the "Reality Effect." This is the documentation of a reality, a "notation of a pure encounter."[8] The effect on the reader is outside of the narrative and offers no representation other than to express that the scene is real by making connections to what is real in the reader's mind. This short circuits the process of connotation, metaphor, or allegory that is typically attributed to objects in literary analyses that were thought to objectively stand apart from the subjectivity of the reader. Barthes reads this as a new genre of verisimilitude, one that seeks to produce the unmediated and unreflective notion of reality (what he terms the "referential illusion"), a subjective function masked in objectivity. These details serve to bring the reader into the scene, resonating with their subjective experience, rather than serving as an objective role as proof or evidence.

Barthes's notion of the "Reality Effect" is informative for understanding the selective inclusion of sound in fiction. From a structural standpoint, sound in literature is something that is often left unanalyzed—read as color and style rather than structure. But like the minute details of Flaubert and Michelet, sound in literature places the reader in a position of pure encounter, one that piques the imagination and the suspension of disbelief. Sounds place the reader directly into a scene. However, sound is, as Barthes writes of detail in "Reality Effect," verisimilitude: it has the appearance of reality only when it plays on a common referent, one that is known to the reader as well as the author. This is why the idea of verisimilitude was critiqued—it lacked the quality of the universal that both history and literary realism were thought to possess. Sound is verisimilitude, its translation into text is subjective, and its comprehensibility is dependent on common referent between author and reader. The very expression of sound—its onomatopoeic language—is subjective, dependent on the ear of the reader for its effect (one need only think of the different expressions for animal sounds across languages).

The act of reading must therefore be synesthetic, triggering the reader to hear the action when they read it represented in the text. This more closely resembles what Roland Barthes refers to as "writerly text," which requires the reader to actively complete the narrative of the text. This kind of text is, in many ways, an unfinished work, the meaning of which is determined by the readers themselves based on their experiences. In this case, the sounds in the text are heard in the mind's ear of the reader, based on their own library of sonic experiences.

This raises challenges to the writer—how to depict sound in a way that represents the desired scene via the silent medium of text. Later, two radically different examples are given of authors using sound in creative ways. The first study is drawn from the short stories of Edgar Allan Poe, nineteenth-century master of the American macabre. The second is taken from Filippo Tomaso Marinetti, the futurist poet. Both writers engage in genres that are writerly: they depend on heightened levels of embodiment by the reader for their success. Horror, as Angela Ndalianis notes, is a genre "capable of intensifying the range of reactions and experiences in which we can become enmeshed when connecting with media texts."[9] Horror piques our senses directly, often with a shocking lack of subtlety, since its goals are affective: to shock, frighten, and disturb. Marinetti, on the other hand, was an advocate for all that was modern: speed, volume, mechanization, danger, warfare, and the sensual delights of life. His art and the art of those around him who joined the Italian Futurist movement were dedicated to destroying the excessive sentimentality and conservatism of art and its institutions, and freeing citizens to be their own creators. Their art was visceral, aimed at stimulating senses—from the eyes and ears to the emotions—that had been dulled by tired symphonies, operas, poetic forms, and novels. Marinetti's poems are a study in attempting to both capture and evoke sound.

Sound in Edgar Allan Poe

Poe's stories are not particularly sonorous. In typical romantic style, they depend on visual description and first-person introspection to set the mood. However, this lack of attention to the sonic highlights the moments when Poe decides to include descriptions of sound in his texts. He typically chooses emotionally charged moments, approaching the denouement of the story, to inject sound, in effect heightening the corporeal engagement of the reader. Among his more sonorous stories is "The Masque of the Red Death," a story about Prince Prospero, who tries to escape the plague by sealing himself and a thousand courtiers into a secluded abbey. Under the illusion of safety, the prince and his companions revel. Several months into their stay, Prince Prospero arranges a most unusual ball: a masquerade with seven rooms, each with different color themes. It is at this party that the specter of the plague, the Red Death, appears.

Poe provides ample visual detail of the rooms, the color and texture of the light and upholstery, to draw the reader in. A key detail is that in the final room, decorated in black velvet and blood red light, there is a large ebony clock.

> Its pendulum swing to and fro with a dull, heavy, monotonous clang; and when the minute-hand made the circuit of the face, and the hour was to be stricken, there came from the brazen lungs of the clock a sound which was clear and loud and deep and exceedingly musical but of so peculiar a note and emphasis that, at each lapse of an hour, the musicians of the orchestra were constrained to pause, momentarily, in their performance, to harken to the sound; and thus the waltzers perforce ceased their evolutions; and there was a brief disconcert of the whole gay company; and, while the chimes of the clock yet rang, it was observed that the giddies grew pale. And the more aged and sedate passed their hands over their brows as if in confused reverie or meditation.[10]

At midnight, a masked figure appears.

> Before the last echoes of the last chime had utterly sunk into silence, there were many individuals who had found leisure to become aware of the presence of a masked figure which had arrested the attention of no single individual before. And the rumor of this new presence having spread

itself whisperingly around, there arose at length from the whole company a buzz, a murmur, expressive of disapprobation and surprise – then, finally, of terror, of horror, and of disgust.[11]

"Who dares insult us with this mockery? Seize him and unmask him—that we may know whom we have to hang, at sunrise, from the battlements!"
   It was in the eastern or blue chamber in which stood the Prince Prospero as he uttered these words. They rang throughout the seven rooms loudly and clearly, for the prince was a bold and robust man, and the music had become hushed at the waving of his hand.[12]

In these instances of sound, Poe brings the reader into the horror and mystery of the moment. The scene of the story is set by the extensive visual detailing: from the ravages of the Red Death in the countryside to the decadence of Prince Prospero and his love of the bizarre, the story flows through surreal visuals. However, it is the detail of sound that brings the shiver. The chimes of the clock are masterfully described. The sound from the brazen lungs that is not only clear, loud, deep, and musical but also so unusual that it arrests movement and music—sound that cancels sound. This is a writerly paragraph, requiring the reader to imagine what this sound is. It is notable that Poe does not use "chime," "bell," or "whistle," typical descriptors of the sound that emanates from a grandfather clock. His neutral "sound" leaves the reader to fill in the specifics, based on their own experiences with clocks.

Despite Poe's extensive visual description, this passage is written in a way that requires the reader to create a sound in the mind's ear that defies categorization and suppresses the actions of the revelers in the mind's eye. Word of the ghastly partygoer moves like a wave—buzz to murmur to disapprobation and surprise, and finally to horror. The ripple of the spoken word through a social setting is described perfectly in sound and sentiment. Finally, there is the voice of Prince Prospero, the only quoted speech in the story, issuing from a bold and robust man and ringing through the rooms with clarity. Through Poe's description, the scene is set up visually for sound to move through it in ways that engage the mind's ear through verisimilitude. We have never heard the clock or the voice of Prince Prospero, but we can imagine them through Poe's details of sound and its effects, in congregation with our own experiences.

In "Masque," Poe uses sound at the moments where terror is the most visceral: the foreshadowing of the clock's ringing as a harbinger, the evolving sentiment of the courtiers as they notice the presence of the Red Death, and the only and final words of Prince Prospero, signifying his arrogance and hubris. In this example, Poe's use of sound is both writerly and prone to verisimilitude. His description of the clock is an act of imagination, while the bubbling sounds of shock, terror, and disgust and the robust voice of Prospero ask the reader to graft their auditory library onto the written word.

A slightly different use of sound is apparent in Poe's "The Pit and the Pendulum," which is written in the first person, and based on being imprisoned in the city of Toledo during the Spanish Inquisition. At the outset of the story, Poe invokes the ears in his terror and confusion:

> The sentence—the dreadful sentence of death—was the last of the distinct accentuation which reached my ears. After that, the sound of the inquisitorial voices seemed merged in one dreamy indeterminate hum. It conveyed to my soul the idea of the *revolution*, perhaps from its association in fancy with the burr of a mill wheel. This only for a brief period; for presently I heard no more.[13]

As the horror of his imprisonment in the dark unfolds, the narrator attempts to make sense of his situation:

> Very suddenly there came back to my soul motion and sound—the tumultuous motion of the heart and, in my ears, the sound of its beating. Then a pause in which all is blank. Then again sound, and motion, and touch, a tingling sensation pervading my frame. Then the mere consciousness of existence.[14]

> Groping about the masonry just below the margin, I succeeded in dislodging a small fragment, and then let it fall into the abyss. For many seconds I harkened to its reverberations as it dashed against the sides of the chasm in its descent; at length there was a sudden lunge into water, succeeded by loud echoes. At the same moment there came a sound resembling the quick opening and as rapid closing of a door overhead.[15]

The narrator then finds himself tied to a table with the dreaded pendulum blade descending slowly toward him. It hisses through the air as it passes over.

> I forced myself to ponder upon the sound of the crescent as it should pass across the garment—upon the peculiar thrilling sensation which the friction of cloth produces on the nerves. I pondered upon all this frivolity until my teeth were on edge.[16]

Finally, on the edge of both madness and death,

> There was a discordant hum of human voices! There was a loud blast of as many trumpets! There was a harsh grating as of a thousand thunders!

The fiery walls rushed back! An outstretched arm caught my own as I fell, fainting, into the abyss ... The Inquisition was in the hands of its enemies.[17]

The profundity of this story is translated to the reader through its focus on the senses. Deprived of light for most of the story, the sensations of touch, smell, taste, and sound are used to craft the experiences of the narrator. "The Pit and the Pendulum" is an excellent example of the reality effect, even if the story itself has deep allegorical elements. The senses of confusion, the experience of the heart beating in the ears, and the imagination that sounds trigger have the effect of flattening the mediation of the sign and creating a pure experience between the reader and the text. Sound, in particular, is used sparingly and exclusively in moments of heightened disorientation and terror: the hiss of the blade, the terrible anticipation of waiting to hear the stone reach the bottom of the pit, and the relief at the cacophony of voices, trumpets, and the prying open of gates. This use of sound is less writerly than the narrative of "The Masque of the Red Death," as it does not require the reader to imaginatively fill in the sonic blanks through but rather uses familiar sound to trigger feelings in the reader. This affective writing is a key to understanding the poetry of poet F. T. Marinetti.

Sound Writing

Born in Egypt in 1876, Marinetti was educated by the noises of urban France and Italy in the throes of the Industrial Revolution. His life's literary work, as an author, publisher, editor, and theorist, was a critique of the past, its aesthetics, and institutions. The mind-set for this destruction was freedom—liberation from constraints of taste and the hindrances of cultural gatekeepers. His desired aesthetics ranged from violence and speed to noise and destruction. Those who joined him in his short-lived Italian Futurist movement extolled bold colors, obtuse angles and curved lines, imitation of industrial noises, and a glorification of the machine and industrial culture. Their futurist stance was always confrontational, and their gatherings were known for fistfights and mayhem.

Written in 1912–3, Marinetti's *Words in Freedom* is a collection of poems with topics that range from a love letter to machines, to the body, and the sounds of battle. In 1919, dedicating his publishing house, Peosia, to the project, Marinetti writes:

> Words in freedom are an absolutely free expression of the universe in which prosody and syntax have no part, a new way of seeing and feeling,

a measuring of the universe as a sum of the moving forces. These forces intersect in our conscious and creative self, which records them exactly, using every possible means of expression.

In this way, the free-wordists orchestrate colors, noises, sounds, form evocative combinations out of the material of language and patois, arithmetic and geometric formulas, old words, distorted words and invented words, animal cries and engine noises, etc.[18]

Marinetti's poems from this era represent experiments in capturing sound in text. They use onomatopoeia but move beyond it into spatial dimensions, to capture the movement of sound and its place within its context and the perceptive field. The cover of *Zang Tumb Tumb*, published in 1914, is a depiction of the sound of the siege of Adrianapole in 1912.

Marinetti's text integrates the sounds of warfare, particularly heavy artillery, with variances in font and text size to imitate variances in volume, the silences between sounds, and noises drawing closer and moving further away. The intersection of "Parole in Liberta" (Words in Freedom) and the cascading "TUUUMB" is even designed to resemble a sound cone. Given Marinetti's distaste for syntax and conventional form, it is unclear if the line of "TUUUMB" is meant to be read left to right or right to left. The poems in *Zang Tumb Tumb* show tremendous spatial and font variation, at times reading in portrait orientation and, at others, in landscape. Dramatic use is made of figures like {, +, and =, and some words are written in circular or diagonal formation. Marinetti uses font and spacing to denote the dramatic sounds of war, as well as a host of onomatopoeic words like "BOOM," "buzzzzzzzz," "pik-tok-tom," and "drrrums" to bring the reader into his narrations of war. His writing imitates the sounds and sensations of warfare and integrates them into the experiences of siege, discomfort, hunger, excitement, and the various narratives of his experience.

Marinetti's later innovations would be more dramatic. His works in the 1920s expanded on his physical representations from the cover of *Zang Tumb Tumb*. His poem "After the Marne, Joffre Toured the Front by Car" combines large letters *M* and *S* as symbols for mountains and winding roads with descriptions of the drive, graffiti, hand-written words and signs, phrases like "pneumatic spiral of a spin of the wheel," and a "dynamic verbalization of the road," a section in the lower right-hand corner that contains a series of unusual onomatopoeic words like "fralingaren" and "viamelokranu" as well as phrases like "x x + x" and "= = = = + =." There is no sense of conventional line or space—it is as if the page were a canvas to paint on, where the eye moves freely across the image, rather than a page to print a linear narrative on that implies movement from left to right, top to bottom.[19]

A poem from a similar period, "At Night, Lying in Bed, She Rereads the Letter from her Gunner at the Front," does much the same with text. While treating the page as a canvas, Marinetti intersperses dramatic visual depictions of the sounds of war with bold dashes of black ink and small phrases of neat cursive writing meant to depict Marinetti's letter to his beloved. He writes "I received your book while bombarding Mount Kuk, F.T.M.," and includes a part of her response in her letter, "thanks and best wishes to you and your bold comrades."[20]

Marinetti's poems perform two elements of sound writing that differ from the projects of both Dell Hymes and Dennis Tedlock. Marinetti's works are examples of both sound knowledge and sound writing, theorized recently by Deborah Kapchan. In *Theorizing Sound Writing*, Kapchan defines the two as follows:

> *Sound knowledge*—a nondiscursive form of affective transmission resulting from acts of listening.

> *Sound writing*—a performance in word-sound of such knowledge. Not a representation. Not just an intersemiotic translation. Sound writing is a gong resonating through bodies, sentient and non.[21]

For Kapchan, theorizing through Western and non-Western sonic epistemologies, there are forms of knowledge through sound that cannot be translated or wholly represented in conventional text. This experiential knowledge is difficult to translate into prose or analysis and can only be gained through sonic contact. Sound writing is the effort made to perform this experience, to activate sound knowledge rather than translate it. Kapchan uses the term "resonate" intentionally, as it is a metaphor for both experiencing and being physically impacted by sound. Kapchan conceives of sound writing as a form of induction rather than representation.

Marinetti's poetry is resonant and expressionistic. It takes experiences from the battlefield and translates them into ink but not into prose or poetry in the conventional sense. His dramatic depictions of sound, unlike Tedlock's transcriptions, are not meant to be performed or to reproduce a specific experience when read aloud. Marinetti's later works completely deviate from performable poetry, and indeed, Marinetti writes that "free-wordists distinguish themselves clearly from Homer because we are no longer content to create a narrative sequence, but instead the integral, dynamic, and simultaneous expression of the universe."[22] Homer's long tradition of oral poetry is banished from what Marinetti terms the "typographic revolution and free expressive orthography."[23]

For the futurists, the sounds of modernity were beautiful. Machines, speed, and danger produced the raw materials of the new utopia. These experiences piqued the emotions of the modern soul more effectively than the tired bourgeoise art music of the concert hall, light classical fare, artworks, and literatures of the great masters.[24] The mandate of futurist composers was to utilize these raw materials to compose the new music of the future (see Chapter 6). For futurist painters and poets, this experience became the basis for their antiestablishment aesthetic. Marinetti's poetry is a response to his experience of the present, an attempt to make the reader resonate with industrial modernity; to alter the reader and shake them out of their apathetic, polite slumber; and convince them to wake up, seize life, and live it in reckless fullness. His work is both sound knowledge and sound writing: the soundscapes of industry and warfare helped to create Marinetti's aesthetic, and his writing is not a transcription or semiotic translation that seeks to control sound through incorporating it into a legible discourse. Marinetti's work seeks to change the reader, to affect their behavior and their perception of the world, and to alter their notion of what it means to live life and be alive.

Marinetti, as well as other futurists, made art to change aesthetic perceptions, to have readers and listeners hear the noises of modernity as art. This is partly accomplished through the act of reading sound and being changed by it.[25] Marinetti's visual poetics—breaking the laws of grammar, syntax, and orthography—act as a transformative device, a set of abstract instructions or visceral representations of freedom, rather than transcriptions or translations of sound.

Sound in Graphic Literature

A (relatively) contemporary literary form that simultaneously exhibits a multiplicity of sonic representations is the comic book or graphic novel. As pictorial and textual representations of action in time and space, graphic novelists have tremendous latitude to present sound in different graphic forms. From representations of the voice—volume, accent, tone quality, and pacing—to the sounds of actions and sound as agentive entity, the artistic, literary, and imaginative work of graphic novels allows for dramatic variation in representations of sound on the page. There are myriad ways that sound can be rendered into visual form, and each of these styles and variations is an artistic and aesthetic decision that relates to how writers craft and readers receive the story and its many meanings.

Although comics scholar Scott McCloud rarely mentions sound in his seminal *Understanding Comics: The Invisible Art*, his drawings hold numerous sonic cues. There are few speech bubbles in his entire book that do not exhibit varied texts that imply the many different ways the narrator speaks. His words grow in size, are italicized and bolded in different ways, and are impeccably punctuated to render discernible speech patterns, which are effectively Scott McCloud's different voices: authorial, scholarly, causal, or wistful. McCloud's speech bubbles resemble something akin to Dennis Tedlock's transcriptions, crafted with enough specificity to direct a verbal performance. Even while theoretically ignoring the soundscape of comics, McCloud takes pains to represent the sounds of his speech in his comics (see chapter 3 for more on the voice).

As Eric Wong demonstrates in his brief but informative essay "Breaking the Silence: How Comics Visualize Sound," even the most rudimentary form of sound in a comic—the text bubble—is laden with complexity. For example, the shape of the bubble, circular and symmetrical, resembling an explosion, drawn with dotted lines, or frozen like an icicle, conveys different qualities of the speech contained within. In a nod toward Roland Barthes's critique of verisimilitude, the quality of the speech in the bubbles corresponds to the listener's aural imagination and familiarity. Are the words in the frozen bubble delivered through the chattering of teeth, whispered through a jaw nearly frozen shut, or is their tone emotionally icy? Does the pitch of a voice that is shouting in bold print rise or deepen? These variations create what Scott McCloud terms "closure" where the reader of a comic completes the panel or scene, filling in the missing parts, a writerly, painterly, and sound-designerly text. As comics are only snapshots of action, the reader must imagine parts of the scene that are left out. Sound is one of them.

Wong continues, addressing the color scheme and font, the use of symbols rather than words or onomatopoeia, and the creativity of drawing within sound or placing sound words on top of the illustrations. The speech of different characters can be cued by font or color so that the voice is "recognized" even if the character is not in the frame. Color can also cue the mood of the speaker or focus the connotations of the text. From the standpoint of verbal performance, words can be placed into bold or enlarged text to indicate the character's emphasis on a word, phrase, or syllable. These possibilities allow for representations of speech patterns and expressions that exceed what can be easily accomplished through traditional literary conventions. They offer flexibility to the author/illustrator and also engage the writerly side of readers, allowing readers' minds to fill in the blanks with familiar sounds and personalities (a sonic act, similar to the visual verisimilitude of Barthes's reality effect).

Perhaps the most famous sonic element of the comic or graphic novel is the sound effect. Examples like Irv Norvick's "Whaam!," made famous by pop artist Roy Lichtenstein, to Batman's "Biff!" "Bam!" and "Pow!," the demonic sound of the Joker's "HA HA HA," and Spiderman's "Thwip," show that some times it is the visual representations of these sounds that are most notable. These images have become iconic in pop culture, at times serving as metonyms for the comic or character. In the case of cartoonist Don Martin, his work, which translated the slapstick nature of *Mad Magazine*'s comedy into visual language, became as much a symbol of the franchise as Alfred E. Newman (its cartoon mascot). Fan shirts, hats, and buttons carry these sound pictures as signifiers of fandom.

Beyond the vast possibilities of text, the space made for these sounds within the comic panel exhibits a diversity of approaches. There are times when the sound follows the action, as is the case with Frank Quietly's "BWAKSSSSsssss…" from *Batman and Robin* (quoted in Wong). There are others, as was the case with classic Batman comics, where the sound of the impact, the "Pow!," is drawn at the point of impact, as Batman delivers a hook. However, there are other moments in the comic where Batman is the only person in the frame, surrounded by multicolored "Pow!" "Bam!" and "Biff!" bubbles, indicating Batman taking on a gang of bad guys by himself. The objects of these actions are not drawn, but the sound effects serve as indexes of the narrative action.

Outside of the world of bold actions and their dramatic visual soundscape, comic artists have tremendous leeway to illustrate quotidian sound. The squeak of a rusty bicycle wheel can emanate in a single line, rather than in a bubble, or can float in the air, requiring the reader to make the connection between a squeaky wheel and its movement. The squeak can simply be written as a "squeak" or can be more onomatopoeic "rrreeeeet." Furthering the synesthetic association, the artist can render the squeak in a rust color—a red or brown—and texture and can shape the noise to as a crescendo, decrescendo or rhythmic occurrence.

In other words, comic artists can participate in the reality effect. The inclusion of textual sounds that serve no structural purpose, that define the environment or the everyday detail of a tire crunching gravel and birds singing, accomplishes a pure encounter with the reader. In these instances, the details included by the author set a sense of place and space, injecting the missing dimensions into a supposedly mono-sensory medium.[26]

A comparative example of the uses of sound in a comic is Gareth Hinds's rendering of Edgar Allan Poe's "The Masque of the Red Death" from his book *Poe: Stories and Poems*. The notable sounds from the story—the clock, the murmur of the guests, and Prince Prospero's outrage—are all visually depicted. In a dramatic foreshadowing, the sounds of the ebony clock are drawn in rough brush strokes of bold red. The dull and monotonous "clang!" of the pendulum swinging is rendered in medium size font, larger than the narration but unobtrusive. However, the "TONGGGGGGGG" of its sonorous and peculiar sound stretches across the frame, with the "TO" slightly cut off by the bottom left gutter and the "GGGGG" continuing across to the right gutter. In addition, the musicians in the blue room, whose music is silenced by the sound of the clock, look frightenedly at the sound text as if it were a character in the room.

Left out of Hinds's abridgement and his rendering of the sound is the musicality of the clock. In the original text, Poe also describes the sound as musical. Hinds leaves that description out, allowing him to render the sound of the clock rougher and more foreboding than a reader of Poe's text might conceive it as. When the clock strikes midnight, again the "TONGGGG" fills the space, but this time, the surprised and shocked faces of the revelers as they behold the Red Death are drawn over the sound, as if to indicate that their attention, rather than being solely occupied by the unsettling sound of the clock, has been turned toward the unwanted guest. Prince Prospero's

FIGURE 4 *From Gareth Hinds,* Poe: Stories and Poems. *Somerville, MA: Candlewick Press, 2017*

words of anger, the only speech in Poe's original text, are rendered in neat and orderly type within white speech bubbles, set off against the monochromatic backgrounds and the narrative, which is rendered on a textured light beige, resembling parchment. Prospero's words are not drawn in dramatic style but are presented in a matter-of-fact manner, shifting attention to the drawing of his angry and hateful expression. When he is struck by the red death, there is a small, simple "Aah!" in a spiked bubble, indicating a short scream. In Hinds's adaptation, the clock and its sound serve as the main character and the focal point, and the visual representations of its noises are drawn in a way that makes sound itself an agent in the story.

It is also worth looking at comics in which sound is not overtly written in—there are no onomatopoeic texts—but it is implied. A good example of this is Shaun Tan's *The Arrival*. Drawn in the sepia-toned style of silent film, the book is a story of immigration and acculturation. The story is masterfully drawn in sepia tones without text. However, like silent films, the denotation of sound is everywhere. For example, the opening sequence is a close-up of the protagonist's hands as he packs a family portrait into his suitcase. One cannot help but hear the gentle folding of the cloth around the picture and the closing of the suitcase. When the main character arrives in the port, he is depicted with a quizzical look on his face, then he looks up, and, in the next frame, there are birds flying over the boat. It is implied that as he stands on the bow of the boat, a sound catches his attention. He looks toward it and sees the unusual creatures flying overhead. When he enters customs, there is a painful twelve-picture sequence where he faces an interview, and it is clear that he does not understand the interviewer and vice versa. His body language, cupping his ear, scratching his head, and using his hands, projects both the sounds and the feelings of lost communication and frustration. The book is full of illustrations like this—demonstrating the sonic element of cultural acclimation, from unknown sounds to new music, laughter, and storytelling.

Unlike text-only literature, where the author can only intentionally inject sound through overtly positioning it within the text, graphic novels and comics allow for sound to be implied through the pictures without the aid of text at all. This makes these visual media quintessentially writerly texts. Through the act of closure that is implied in the form itself, readers can inject familiar sounds to bring the text to life and make it meaningful in relation to their own experiences.

Conclusion

Literature and poetry are far from a silent media, even when on the page. From descriptions of sound in novels to poetic expressions, textual and graphic experimentation, and comics, sound is an essential part of textual culture. While experiments in literature continue and multimedia and interactive technology improves, new ways of depicting sound will be utilized. One important point to remember, following Roland Barthes, is that texts are writerly, and this is especially true with sound. Our sound references and sonic memories are strong, and the "Pow!" of Batman or the sound of the ebony clock are not the same for every reader. Sound in literature is often written through verisimilitude, the subjective that tilts the readers mind towards the objective. What we hear when we read is singular and should be cherished. This makes the orchestrating of sound and sonic decisions challenging. This is particularly true when representing the language of others in all its complexities. It is important to remember the care that sociolinguists have shown in representing the speech of others in social context. It is also important to balance that with the creative subjectivity that allows readers to imagine sounds in ways that are uniquely meaningful to themselves.

In-class Exercises

Ask the Class to:

1 Bring a sonorously interesting passage from literature to share with the class.

2 Bring a comic to class. Discuss what kind of sounds/voices/music cues could be used if the comic were to be animated or turned into a live-action skit.

3 Write a sonorous description of your class (this can be combined with other chapters, particularly the "Voice" chapter).

**Project I: Adding Sound to a Comic
(best done as a group project)**

Step 1:
  Choose a three- to five-page section of a graphic novel or comic. Photograph each panel and load them into a movie or slideshow program. Turn this animation into a full multimedia project. Record different voices for each character or narrator, and add sound effects and music (if desired). Write a one-page paper on your aesthetic decisions.
  Work in small groups. It is best done when at least two groups have the same comic or graphic novel section; this allows for comparative work.
Step 2:
  Screen and critique the class projects.
Step 3:
  Compare your projects. What similarities and differences do they have? Are there common sonic references? Do all the sonic decisions make sense, or are some confusing, disorienting, or produce an unintended effect?

> **Project II: Translating Sound into Text
> (best done individually)**
>
> Step 1:
>   The instructor or the class can choose a sonorous scene from a film or TV show.
> Step 2:
>   Using one of the models discussed above (nineteenth-century literature, comic/graphic novel, poem), create a textual representation of the scene.
> Step 3:
>   Share and discuss similarities/differences and interpretations.
>   **Variation:** For larger classes, several scenes can be chosen, and discussion groups can be formed with students who chose the same scene.

Notes

1. It is important to remember that these assignments are arbitrary. There is no correlation between the shapes and the appearances of letters or characters and their sounds.
2. Derrida, *Of Grammatology*.
3. Webster, "'The Validity of Navajo Is in Its Sounds,'" 2.
4. Ibid.
5. Tedlock, 20.
6. https://archive.mpi.nl/tla/elan.
7. Edward Said, in his classic "Orientalism," provides a scathing critique of this form of colonial European literary realism. In the wake of this, myriad others have pursued decolonizing analyses of Euro-American literary representation. Hamdi, "Edward Said and Recent Orientalist Critiques," 130–48.
8. Barthes, *The Rustle of Language*, 148.
9. Ndalianis, *The Horror Sensorium*, 4.
10. Poe, *18 Best Stories by Edgar Allan Poe*, 43.
11. Ibid., 45.
12. Ibid., 46.
13. Ibid., 264 (italics in original).
14. Ibid., 266.
15. Ibid., 270.

16 Ibid., 274.
17 Ibid., 279.
18 Marinetti, *Selected Poems and Related Prose*, 86.
19 Ibid., 119.
20 Ibid., 121.
21 Kapchan, *Theorizing Sound Writing*, 2.
22 Marinetti, *Selected Poems and Related Prose*, 86.
23 Ibid., 89.
24 Russolo, see chap. 2.
25 See Nancy, *Listening*, for theory about resonating with sound.
26 McCloud, 1994.

Bibliography

Apollonio, Umbro. *Futurist Manifestoes*. Boston: MFA Publications, 1970.
Barthes, Roland. *Image-Music-Text*. New York: Hill and Wang, 1977.
Barthes, Roland. *The Rustle of Language*. New York: Hill and Wang, 1986.
Derrida, Jacques. *Of Grammatology*. Baltimore: Johns Hopkins University Press, 1997.
Hamdi, Tahrir K. "Edward Said and Recent Orientalist Critiques." *Arab Studies Quarterly* 35, no. 2 (2013): 130–48.
Hinds, Gareth. *Poe: Stories and Poems*. Somerville, MA: Candlewick Press, 2017.
Hoijer, Harry. "The Sapir-Whorf Hypothesis." In *Language, Culture, and Society*, edited by Benjamin Blount, 219–31. Winthrop, 1974.
Hymes, Dell. "Helen Sekaquaptewa's 'Coyote and the Birds': Rhetorical Analysis of a Hopi Coyote Story." *Anthropological Linguistics* 34, no. 1 (1992): 45–72.
Kapchan, Deborah. *Theorizing Sound Writing*. Middletown: Wesleyan University Press, 2017.
Marinetti, F. T. *Selected Poems and Related Prose*. New Haven, CT: Yale University Press, 2002.
McCloud, Scott. *Understanding Comics: The Invisible Art*. New York: William Morrow Paperbacks, 1994.
Ndalianis, Angela. *The Horror Sensorium: Media and the Senses*. Jefferson, NC: McFarland, 2012.
Poe, Edgar Allan. *18 Best Stories by Edgar Allan Poe*, edited by Vincent Price and Chandler Brossard. New York: Dell Publishing, 1965.
Tan, Shaun. *The Arrival*. New York: Arthur A. Levine Books, 2006.
Tedlock, Dennis. *The Spoken Word and the Work of Interpretation*. Philadelphia: University of Pennsylvania Press, 1983.
Webster, Anthony K. " 'The Validity of Navajo Is in Its Sounds': On Hymes, Navajo Poetry, Punning, and the Recognition of Voice." In *The Legacy of Dell Hymes: Ethnopeotics, Narrative Inequality, and Voice*, edited by Paul

V. Kroskrity and Anthony K. Webster. Bloomington: Indiana University Press, 2015.

Wiesner, David. *Mr. Wuffles!* Boston: Clarion Books, 2013.

Wong, Eric. "Breaking the Silence: How Comics Visualize Sound." December 31, 2014. *Sequart.org*.

Recommended Further Reading

Barry, Lynda. *Syllabus*. Montreal: Drawn and Quarterly, 2014.

Chute, Hillary. *Graphic Women: Life Narrative and Contemporary Comics*. New York: Columbia University Press, 2010.

Chute, Hillary and Patrick Jagoda. "Comics and Media." *Critical Inquiry* 40, no. 3 (Spring 2014): 1–10.

Dolar, Mladen. "The Burrow of Sound." *Differences* 22, nos. 2 and 3 (2011): 112–39.

Kroskrity, Paul V., and Anthony K. Webster. *The Legacy of Dell Hymes: Ethnopoetics, Narrative Inequality and Voice*. Bloomington: Indiana University Press, 2015.

Madden, Matt. *99 Ways to Tell a Story: Exercises in Style*. New York: Penguin, 2005.

Nancy, Jean-Luc. *Listening*. New York: Fordham University Press, 2007.

Sammons, Kay, and Joel Sherzer. *Translating Native Latin American Verbal Art: Ethnopoetics And Ethnography of Speaking*. Washington, DC: Smithsonian Institution Press, 2000.

Sherzer, Joel. *Speech Play and Verbal Art*. Austin: University of Texas Press, 2002.

Szendy, Peter. *Listen: A History of Our Ears*. New York: Fordham University Press, 2008.

5

Sound Design/Designing Sounds: Intentionally Crafted Sonic Worlds

Key concepts: audiovisual contract, consumption, intentional design, skeuomorphism, synchresis

Orientation: Three Sound Designs

I. In São Paulo and Rio de Janeiro, Brazil, the central event of *carnaval* is a multiday competition among large samba "schools" that parade the length of a specially built avenue (the *sambódromo*) outfitted with permanent concrete bleachers capable of seating approximately 100,000 spectators. Each school is allotted roughly an hour to traverse the avenue and will have thousands of people participating in its parade.[1] For many North Americans and Europeans, Brazil's *carnaval* evokes the twin concepts of excess and transgression: highly sexualized and extravagantly revealing costumes; elaborate floats; an assumption of gluttony (whether in terms of sexual activity or alcohol consumption); and associations with a kind of sanctioned debauchery.

Many Brazilians, of course, understand *carnaval* quite differently. One reason for this is that Portuguese is not typically a "destination language" (if we may coin a term) in the way that Mandarin, Spanish, or even its romance-language sisters French and Italian are. As a result, non-Portuguese speakers are typically unable to decode the meanings of *samba enredos*, the songs whose music is central to the parade, and whose lyrics are often geared to addressing themes of national relevance (and therefore are emotionally resonant with samba school performers). In other words, non-Portuguese speakers, often already immersed in a culture that skews heavily to the visual, are left reducing *carnaval* to a largely visual experience; this is in addition to the fact that Brazil has long carried associations in Western popular culture with (female) sexualization (e.g., the enduring popularity of "The Girl from Ipanema," who is "Tall and tan and young and lovely" and makes the men who pass her go, "Ahhhhh!") and (male) sex tourism. But samba school participants speak in ways that bear little relationship to this: they instead foreground the preparations for *carnaval* (selecting the particular *samba enredo* that it will perform, building the floats, rehearsing the musical parts, and choreography for the avenue) in language that evokes engagement, belonging, excitement, and community.[2]

As each school travels the length of the *sambódromo* during the parade, the sound is both extremely loud[3] and densely layered. Some of this is due to the nature of samba musical arrangement and instrumentation, which consist of highly syncopated and interlocking rhythmic lines. Harmonic accompaniment is provided by various stringed instruments (*cavaquinho*, as well as amplified guitars). Most noticeable is the massive percussion ensemble (*bateria*) composed of bass drums (*surdos*), high-pitched aluminum drums (*repiques*), snare drums (*caixas*), frame drums with heavy metal disks (*pandeiros*), cymbal-less tambourines played with plastic rods (*tamborim*), friction drums (*cuícas*), shakers (*ganzás*), cowbells (*agogô*), and metal scrapers (*reco-recos*). All these melodic and percussive sources accompany the samba's lead singer (*puxador*), who is coordinating all the group singing by the hundreds or thousands of the school's costumed singers and dancers from the top of a moving "sound car" *and* keeping this in sync with the *bateria* in front of the car.[4] All these sound sources are amplified as they travel down a narrow street (a mere 39 feet wide in Rio de Janeiro, 46 feet in São Paulo), with concrete bleachers rising several stories above the avenue, filled with roughly 100,000 shouting, cheering spectators. The *sambódromo*'s *soundscape* is ripe for sonic muddiness, cacophony, and utter auditory unintelligibility (Schafer's ultimate lo-fi nightmare: see Chapter 1). For both spectators in the *sambódromo* and television viewers watching the parades, it matters that these sonic outcomes are avoided.

Eduardo Lemos, owner of the sound production company Transasom, which produced the sound for the first parade to take place in Rio's current *sambódromo* in 1984, said of its acoustics, "The architect did not think about it." Lemos and the sound engineers who worked on the 1984 sound production were reportedly "horrified" by the sonic "mess" that resulted from sound bouncing off the *sambódromo*'s all-concrete surfaces in ways that caused a deeply muddy, flat sound through both the avenue's public address (PA) system and on television.⁵ Lemos and his team spent the next nine years creating a theoretical approach via acoustic engineering and technological innovations that could enact solutions.

Transasom developed a series of systems to address the specific challenges of the parade and the *sambódromo*. For example, because the amplified sound on the top of the sound car that coordinates the singing and percussion travels more slowly through air than it travels electrically to the public address system the audience is listening to, the live audience would hear the "same" music at fractionally different times (sooner through the PA system, slightly later through the air). To address this, Lemos and his engineers created a software-based delay system to slow down the PA in order to synchronize its audibility with the sounds coming from the car; accomplishing this necessitated obtaining GPS data to monitor the location of the sound car as it moves down the avenue within an accuracy of 1 meter. However, the speed with which sound moves through air is contingent upon temperature and, though to a lesser extent, humidity. As a result, the software also had to be able to take into account current weather conditions. Lastly, a crucial element of sound for the crowd on the avenue was its positionality (i.e., the verisimilitude) of the amplified sound coming from the street compared to the sound coming from the public address system. If the sound car or the *bateria* had passed one's location, one should not have heard it the same through the public address speakers as when it was approaching the listening location: the sound would be softer, and the sound color would be different. To address this, further means of independently controlling the signal feed to the public address speakers was programmed into the system.⁶

One can think of two layers of sound design with respect to *carnaval* and the *sambódromo*. The first is the sound design of the physical space itself: a long, narrow, vertically contained corridor that would be highly amplificatory, and highly reflective, of any sounds created within it. Given the density of musical sound that characterizes *samba enredo* and the sheer number of sound-emitting people that each samba school brings to the avenue, the fit between the architecture and what happens within it is not optimal. But the second way to think about sound design is to take this complicated fit and examine how the active design of its sound could make it more suitable to the activities it hosts. Lemos and his team are social actors utilizing technologies to create acoustic spaces that both reflect and help create the experiences that people have in them. In this view, sound design is active and intentional, seeking to create added value.

II. All-inclusive vacation resorts are a staple of European and North American travel to the Caribbean and a lynchpin of many Caribbean nations' economies.

All-inclusive resorts make an economic argument to tourists: stay at a location that, for a (largely) fixed fee, will provide one with access to "all" of the "best" that the locale has to offer: recreational activities such as snorkeling, scuba diving, or visiting cultural heritage sites; local cuisine (and alcoholic drinks); "indigenous" entertainment such as music and dance. No matter the truth (or not) of this economic logic, all-inclusive tourism additionally sells an ironic promise: that the most authentic and enjoyable experience of the locale is attained *by not needing to venture deeply into it.* The ideal version of the island is—through careful curation—contained within the resort's walls or, if one is going off-site, most richly encountered when chaperoned by its employees. At least two questions follow from this: (1) Who is doing the curating? The (usually) multinational corporations that own these resorts, or local residents of the island? And, (2) to what extent are such resorts in fact designed to shield tourists from encounters with the realities of economic deprivation, and racial and class tensions, that much of the Caribbean inherited from its deep history of colonial subjugation and that continues to define the lives of many of the resorts' employees?[7] As Johnny Rotten of the 1970s British punk band Sex Pistols snarled derisively at the opening of the band's song, "Holidays in the Sun," "A cheap holiday ... in other people's misery."

Vacation is often conceived of and marketed as a time and experience in which negativity disappears, in which the surroundings facilitate leaving the cares of the world behind. Accomplishing this often requires that the labor conditions of those who work at resorts (such as in minimal wage service jobs disproportionately occupied by the most racially and economically marginalized members of society) remain invisible so as not to impede the tourists' pleasure or de-emphasizing the histories of colonial relations that paved the road to those contemporary labor relations to facilitate the vacationer's relaxation and physical, spiritual, or emotional renewal. As Jocelyne Guilbault and Timothy Rommen argue in a provocative collection of studies of all-inclusive resorts in the Caribbean, "The creation of an island of leisure and pleasure within a physical island can ... only exist at the expense of erasing the insurgent and noisy sounds of that locale's past."[8]

Sound and music are key in this endeavor of erasure, of forgetting, and of overlooking local histories of inequity and exploitation while simultaneously evoking a sense of localness that links how tourists think a place should sound to how it in fact sounds.[9] To put it cynically, all-inclusive Caribbean resorts design their sonic environments to match both tourists' stereotypes of what the Caribbean sounds like (ocean waves, steel pan drums, reggae, employees' local accents[10]) and replicating fantasies of what an ideal vacation is. Such sonic design is a matter of policy made by the resorts and their management teams as well as the work done by laborers ranging from musicians to front-desk staff, all under the constraints imposed by corporate decisions about which tourists a given resort is being marketed to (Older or younger? Families or singles/couples without kids? Upper-class or middle-class clientele?). Such decisions are, of course, offered with the goal of maximizing resorts' profits but are designed to extract that profit through a careful calibration of how to engage vacationers' emotional experiences ranging from excitement to serenity to deep satisfaction.[11] They also rely upon deep financial commitments to the sonic environment of the resort: whom it hires, what music is played in common spaces, who is hired to provide live music, and what efforts are made to sonically isolate the resort from the larger island soundscape it is embedded in.

If Lemos's work on the sound design of Rio de Janeiro's *sambódromo* reads as the solution to a problem created by architectural space, all-inclusive Caribbean resorts suggest sound design as a more proactive construction of sonic space and one more deeply rooted in maximizing profit potential. Given the cultural and social importance of *carnaval* in Brazil, the sound design of the avenue would likely not give people pause about attending or watching the parades on television (though it would change the quality of that experience), but a Caribbean resort with the wrong sound design might very well lose clientele if its sound failed to meet expectations of what it should sound like to be at the beach, of what local music is thought to be, or of the intelligibility of the accents of hotel staff. Once again, sound design needs to be understood as intentional and active, geared to accomplishing specific goals.

III. What does a car sound like? How much of what a car sounds like is simply about the unavoidable mechanics of the vehicle, and how much has been deliberately engineered beyond those mechanics? Consider, for example: does a particular car's turn signal sound more like a *pocka-pocka*, a *deeka-deeka*, or a syncopated *cliiiick-clack-cliiiick-clack*? Does it intrude loudly into your experience of driving when activated or largely sit unobtrusively within the car's soundscape? Or is it noticeable enough to alert you to having forgotten to disengage the signal after you changed lanes in a way that didn't activate the car's automatic turn signal shut-off system (if your car has this feature)? Do you like different signal sounds equally, or are some more or less pleasant than others?

Automobile manufacturers invest huge amounts of money in crafting how their cars will sound. We tend to think of this mostly in terms of cars' audio systems and of which audio companies have signed exclusive partnerships with which automobile manufacturers: Bang & Olafsen with Audi, Aston Martin, and Ford; Bose with Mazda, Cadillac, Infiniti, Kia, and Fiat; Panasonic with Acura; Harmon Kardon with BMW; and so on. But imagine for a moment the first time you open a specific car's door, close it behind you as you settle into the driver's seat, and later close it from the outside when you've arrived at your destination. Is the door sound a *click*? A *thunk*? A *thud*? Does it sound different if you are inside the car or outside of it? Does the door sound evoke sensations of the car's cheapness or sturdiness?

Because automobile makers know that customers deeply associate sonic properties with perceptions of quality, safety, and luxury (or not), virtually every aspect of car sound is deliberately designed by teams of acousticians, audio engineers, and sound artists, and in turn is deeply woven into the brand images (not unlike what was discussed concerning Victoria's Secret in Chapter 1). This is especially true of high-end brands. Audi, for example, utilized a large team of haptic and acoustic engineers to design a particular "click" sound that is incorporated into all cars and SUVs in its fleet and that unifies drivers' experiences of everything from opening and closing climate control vents to moving between apps on the vehicles' touch screen panels.[12] Mercedes has focused on the sound of its door handles, turn signals, and an integrated approach to make all sonic design elements within one of its vehicles "harmonious."[13] These are but two of many examples: extensive use of focus groups and other means of market research are common among all automakers as they seek to develop a better understanding of how consumers react to car sounds and design cars that will appeal to their target market segment.[14]

When the turn signal was introduced as a standard feature in Buick's 1939 automobile line as a novel safety element, drivers were hearing a mechanically produced sound resulting from a thermocouple device that moved a bimetallic spring between contacts in order to close and open an electrical circuit, which lit and unlit the turning lamps.[15] Subsequent turn signal designs involved a solenoid-like switch that used electromagnetic current to move a small plate of metal, again to open and close electrical flow to the lights. Modern cars, however, use computer-controlled solid state relays that make no noise whatsoever; that we still hear the sound of a turn signal in cars has nothing to do with how the signals work.[16] One can speculate about the reasons to "keep" turn signals audible—perhaps to serve as potential reminder that they are on for a forgetful driver, or to reassure drivers that they are engaging in safe driving practices—but the main reason is likely skeuomorphism: retaining features that were unavoidable in their original medium but that are currently incorporated simply as design elements.[17] That there is still a turn signal sound itself is skeuomorphic; that turn signals still largely sound like the earlier mechanisms and are engineered to play at relatively the same loudness as their mechanical forebears is doubly so. In principle, *any* sound imaginable could now accompany the blinking of the turning lights (a doorbell chime, finger snaps, alternating notes of a musical fifth, dog barks), and one could be allowed to download one's own preferred "blinker-tone." Just as easily, drivers could be given the ability to adjust the volume of the turn signal sound, so that it could still be heard when playing music more loudly, or as one's hearing starts to decrease with age. But the fact that this has not happened (yet) speaks to conservatism in sound design for cars based on market research that suggests buyers' hesitancy to radically reconceptualize what a turn signal should sound like.

Defining "Sound Design"

The term "sound design" is most often associated with film and video game soundtracks and used to refer to the total sonic artifact, often comprising music, voices, and sound effects, that accompanies images. In our view, this is an unnecessarily restrictive usage of the term, which overlooks the extent to which sound is (and has historically been) designed in and for multiple dimensions of people's lives, often in the pursuit of selling goods and services in ways that maximize profit and are deeply implicated in the workings of consumer capitalism. Further, we wish to stress that "sound design" is just as much an activity or a process as it is the sounded object. To return to *carnaval*, "sound design" is not just what attendees and television viewers heard as the outcome of Lemos's work, but it is the very work that Lemos and Transasom did in arriving at both a conceptualization of the desired *sambódromo* sonic experience and realizing it technologically. This definition of sound design, therefore, also stresses intentionality. That is, any given sound design seeks to achieve specific outcomes: to render the *samba enredo* less muddy, or to craft a sonic experience of the Caribbean to be deployed in the consumer capitalism of tourism, for example.

In *The Soundscape*, R. Murray Schafer argued for the importance and increased use of "acoustic design," which he defined as "an interdiscipline in which musicians, acousticians, psychologists, sociologists and others would study the world soundscape together in order to make intelligent recommendations for its improvement."[18] It was discussed in the "Soundscape" chapter of this book that Schafer's work assumed a world rapidly declining into a lo-fi soundscape, a world in need of acoustic, ecological intervention to return it to a romanticized, "healthier," hi-fi state. Perhaps because he was principally a composer, Schafer likened acoustic design to musical composition and orchestration: "The acoustic designer may incline society to listen again to models of beautifully modulated and balanced soundscapes such as we have in great musical compositions."[19] Schafer writes of learning how to arrange sounds in the environment so that they may be turned into positive advantages for the soundscape. While this prescriptive and ideologically driven concept of acoustic design has largely been discredited for the reasons outlined in the "Soundscape" chapter, it is worth noting that Schafer's conception, however flawed, shares the dimensions of intentionality and active construction of sound that we suggest should be foregrounded in the definition of "sound design."

The remainder of this chapter describes three areas of cultural production in which intentional sound design is central: cinema; sound recording; and restaurant interiors.

Sound Design in Cinema

Our suggestion that a definition of sound design limited to film and video game production is too narrow does not change that the term does carries a specific weight and set of relevancies in those fields. Intentionally creating the fit among all the possible sonic elements of a film scene—dialogue, music, sound effects, ambient sound—is the task of the sound designer, and it is a crucial, if a sometimes underappreciated, role. For narrative cinema, it has long been argued that sounds both lend meaning to the images on screen and work perhaps even more effectively than images in creating viewers' emotional states that result from what they see. A classic case study involves remixing the opening credits of Stanley Kubrick's *The Shining*,[20] replacing the slow-tempo, French Horn-defined, foreboding dirge, with "happy" music. One of the authors of this book uses a student-created version in class that pairs the original mix against one using John Denver's performance of the song, "Rocky Mountain High," an up-tempo, celebratory exaltation of life in the Colorado Rockies. Asked how they "see" the camera work and the images during the credits differently, students almost unanimously experience the credits as shorter and the images as moving more quickly in the John Denver version; indicate that the balance between sun and shadow is inverted; and note that the "this is not going to end well" premonition that the original soundtrack creates dissolves into an assumption that this is going to be a film about a good summer road trip.

Film scholar and composer Michel Chion argues that describing film sound as "lending" meaning to the images is, in fact, too simple a conception of their relationship. Sounded film, in fact, creates a new, indivisible form of perception—a joint seeing/hearing, a trans-sensory audio-viewing. In his book *Audio-Vision: Sound on Screen*,[21] Chion argues that sound and image do not "naturally" correlate to one another but rather that when watching films, audiences create an "audio-visual contract" in which sound and image become a single entity. As a result, sounds show us an image differently than the images show on their own, and images make us hear sound differently than if it had no visual accompaniment. This reciprocal and mutually constituted meaning creates "added value" from the relationship forged between what one hears and what one sees in the film at any given point in time (synchresis). Chion writes, "With the term *audio-vision*, I designate the type of perception that is peculiar to film and television, in which the image is the focus of conscious attention, but where sound at every moment brings about a number of effects, sensations, and significations that, thanks to the phenomenon of projection ... are credited to the framed image and appear to emanate naturally from [it]."[22] As Chion points out, it is reductive to say that one is going to "watch" a movie tonight (and he notes that the very phrase betrays a long Western history of privileging sight over the other senses);[23] rather, one is going to "listenwatch."

Much, if not most, of what one hears in a film is created after the filming is complete, in what is called "post-production." For projects with large budgets, post-production work is often handled by teams of people working on different aspects of the film's overall sound. For example, dialog editors will take recorded sound from the film set—most often dialog—and work to clean it up: evening out fluctuations in the loudness of voices; removing wind or mouth noise; smoothing out the ambient sound behind the voices. Inevitably, some dialog will be unsalvageable, so a separate team works with actors in a process called Automatic Dialog Replacement (termed ADR) to re-record their lines and to sync the new recordings to the images of filmed speech. Common, everyday sounds such footsteps, doorknobs, swallowing, and so forth may be created by so-called Foley artists (named after an early practitioner, Jack Foley), who often perform the sounds in real time while watching the visual footage, so as to sync the sounds to on-camera action. A composer may be hired to write original music for the film; when this occurs, directors often work quite closely with them on the overall atmosphere they want the music to create. A music supervisor's role is to generate ideas about what existing music to include (e.g., pop songs) and to secure the rights to use them in the film. Sound designers are often tasked with one (or both) of two things: creating sounds for entities that don't exist in the sonic world contemporary humans inhabit (e.g., aliens, dinosaurs, orcs, light sabers[24]) and envisioning at a macro level how all these sounds will weave together in the final mix.[25] It bears repeating that depending on the film's budget, this work may be distributed more broadly across a smaller number of people, but accomplishing this set of tasks and the ways in which all that work combines to create the overall soundtrack of a film are standard features of creating film sound.[26]

The first person credited as a "Sound Designer" in a Hollywood film was Walter Murch for his work on Francis Ford Coppola's Vietnam War film, *Apocalypse Now*, released in 1979, for which Murch won an Oscar for sound. The term, in fact, came from Murch himself, who described his work on the film's sound as "not that different from interior design. You are given an architectural space, and you put things in it and you make it look good. I did the same thing with sound, so 'sound design' came out of what I had done."[27] *Apocalypse Now* represented a significant moment in film sound history for a number of reasons, but Murch cites primarily that it was the first dramatic film to use quadraphonic sound. Prior iterations of surround sound could create the impression in theaters of sounds in front of and behind listeners, but it wasn't until quadraphonic sound that one could steer a sound through or around a 360-degree spectrum. Thus, Murch created detailed mappings of sound effects, music, and dialog before the final mix was created so that there was a plan for which sounds at any given moment would be in mono, in simple stereo, or would use full quadraphonic sound.[28]

Murch's sound mixes wonderfully illustrate Chion's discussion of the audiovisual contract and synchresis. In the opening sequence of *Apocalypse Now*,[29] for example, one hears two predominant sound sources: the pulsing sound of helicopter rotors and Jim Morrison and The Doors' recording of "The End." The song is forward in the mix, occupying the entire soundstage. Spatially, the helicopter drifts more quietly and unpredictably through quadraphonic space: it starts in the right back, moves to the left back, then to the left front, followed eventually by the right front. The listener is, therefore, figuratively ensnared within a sonic lasso of the war machine that, more than any other, signified the American fighting tactics of the Vietnam War. But the helicopter sound also moves between a more realistic sonic representation and a more abstract one. For example, one first hears a rhythmically regular, repeated "scritching" sound, while the image on the screen is simply of a stand of palm trees. The source of the sound can't be determined with any certainty, both because nothing in the visual frame could emit it (it is a so-called acousmatic sound),[30] and because as a sound, it does not attach to any easily determinable real-world objects. Twenty-eight seconds into the opening, a (partially seen) helicopter flies across the space between the camera and the palm trees, and in this moment, the sound and the object it represents become locked as one into the viewer's mind. In that split second, the helicopter sound takes on a more representational quality. Murch moved between using "helicopter-ish" sounds created on synthesizers and using recordings made of real helicopters, linking his choice at any given moment to the narrative context in which the helicopter sound was happening. It is ultimately unknowable whether that more representational impression at 0:28 into the film is because Murch mixed in more "real" helicopter sound (and a noticeable doppler effect) or because the audiovisual contract has done its work of trans-sensorial representation.

Many of these sound design issues gloss unproblematically onto video game sound design, but there is one major exception: for action role-playing games, the gamer has an active presence in the audiovisual field of the game itself. In cinema, audiences are witnesses to the audio-visual presentation of the narrative.[31] In RPG settings, however, gamers actively participate in and create those audiovisual narratives; they are agents in, not witnesses to, the unfolding of the game. Thus, game sound designers must, in addition to considering dialog, music, background sound, and sound effects, create sounds that adhere to the gamer themselves. Such sounds may be linked in a very literal way to the player's movements through and actions upon the game (e.g., the sound of footsteps as the gamer runs, a shriek of pain made when wounding or killing one's combatant). They may also be linked to the action but in a more abstract way, such as when the fading of one's own life in a game is represented by a gradually intensifying audio evocation of tinnitus, such as was the case in the *Drake's Fortune* series (2007–16).[32]

Sound Design in Audio Recordings

Arguably, to make a sound recording is inescapably to engage in sound design, if we keep in mind that sound design is intentional action designed to realize a goal related to the world of sound. This claim is often met with the objection, "What about documentary sound, or ethnographic field recordings?" While one might justifiably posit a meaningful distinction between *sound art* as highly designed and compositional compared to more "naturalistic" recordings, that distinction is more one of degree than of kind, for two principal reasons. First, microphones and ears are not identical devices for intaking sound, even though they share some design features: both, for example, use a membrane (the microphone's diaphragm, the ear's tympanum or eardrum) to convert acoustic energy into electrical impulses. Ears have particular properties of sensitivity to sound (it takes much more energy for a low-frequency sound to be perceived as being as loud as a higher-frequency one), for one; some mics pick up sound in a 360-degree field around them (as the ear does), but many do not, and when they don't, sounds that originate on the boundaries of their "pick-up pattern" may be "colored" in ways the human ear doesn't do. So even the act of selecting which microphone to record a sound with is, in effect, to start to "design" what the recorded sound will sound like. Second, and more important, microphones are not attached to brains that take the total sonic input being received through the ear and selectively focus on specific portions of it. Colloquially known as the "cocktail party effect," this capacity to concentrate on extracting particular sounds from the total sonic environment in which they are embedded has no parallel in the world of microphones. Even the simple act of holding a stereo microphone in front of oneself to capture the sound around one requires making decisions that will impact the recorded sound; mixing in a studio setting only ups the ante. Recording, then, is sound design by default.

Perhaps the most important element of sound design in recording relates to perceived spatialization within a mix. There are two principal types of spatialization to consider. First, for music that does not originate entirely electronically or is not assembled from previously recorded material, part of the recording process inevitably involves capturing sound that is occurring in some physical space. As a result, one kind space "in" the recording itself is (potentially) that of the space in which the sound occurs and how that space "colors" the sound itself. For example, if the sound is being made in a room with a fair amount of echo, is that echoic property left audible in the recording, or is it dampened?[33] Another kind of space that can be "in" the recording itself is a constructed representation of an imaginary space that the sound is presented as having been sounded in. Through the addition of reverberation, for example, one can make a sound appear to have originated in a space quite different from the one it was actually recorded in. And perhaps the most significant kind of spatialization that is "in" the recording itself is how sounds are spatialized with respect to one another as heard in a stereo or surround-sound mix, where sounds can be (and always are) placed at a particular point (or points) in a three-dimensional "sound stage," in which the x-axis represents lateral location, the y-axis represents a sense of height (largely due to psychoacoustics of hearing that locate higher pitches higher in audio space), and the z-axis represents distance from the listener (due both to volume and sonic cues provided by reflected sound or reverberation).[34]

Much has been written about the Beatles'—and more specifically, their producer George Martin's—use of the studio as a compositional tool,[35] so while any stereo mix of any genre of music could be analyzed for its spatialization, "Hey

Jude" (1968) and "Let It Be" (1970) will serve as useful illustrations here. The two songs are similar in several respects, especially in terms of instrumentation, tempo, and their initial juxtaposition of two musical lines (piano and voice) before gradually adding other layers. The first 1:30 of "Hey Jude" consists of seven vocal and instrumental elements: Paul McCartney's lead voice; piano; strummed electric guitar; tambourine; harmonized backing vocals; drum kit;[36] and electric bass. "Let It Be" has nine in its first 2:00: piano; Paul McCartney's lead vocal; harmony background vocals; hi-hat; electric bass; full drum kit; electric organ; electric guitar; and finally a solo electric guitar. Yet despite their musical similarities, these two songs are remarkably different from each other sonically.

If you can, play the first two minutes of each before reading further; write a few adjectives that describe the sound quality of each as you experience it, and try to explain those differences by comparing and contrasting what you hear in each song. You may wish to listen to each a few times, and "Let It Be," especially, may require very close listening. To help guide your comparing and contrasting, you may wish to focus on the following:

- Where is the piano located in three-dimensional space? How much of the piano is "direct" sound, and how much is reverberated, decaying sound?

- Where is the lead vocal located in three-dimensional space? How much of the lead vocal is "direct" sound, and how much is reverberated, decaying sound?

- How do the background vocals differ between the two songs, especially in terms of placement and movement within three-dimensional space?

But do not feel limited only to these aspects of the sound if others strike you as significant.

****

One might roughly describe the sound design of the two songs as follows.

"Hey Jude" opens with a piano located almost entirely on the right side of the mix, and with the voice located nearly dead-center, there is a resulting left/right spatial imbalance through the first verse. At 0:27 when the second verse starts, an acoustic guitar enters, followed quickly by a tambourine located dead-center in lateral space; the guitar is panned left, which now creates a spatial symmetry with the right-side piano, though, as the piano is mixed more loudly, the imbalance does not fully disappear. When harmony vocals enter at 0:40, they too are situated at the center of the mix but occupy a wider portion of the stereo field than the tambourine. Suddenly, the soundstage that began as imbalanced and relatively sparse, is both fuller and more fully balanced. At 0:50, drums enter from the left and—contrary to most mixing practices in which drum kits occupy the full width of the soundstage—stay almost entirely to the left; particularly noticeable in this regard are the ride cymbal and the toms. By 0:55, the start of the so-called middle-8 section, the song's first bass lines are sounded. The lowest-pitched information in the track, the bass is located across the width of the stereo field, providing a metaphorical platform above which the more precisely spatialized pitch information of the guitar, drums, and piano rests throughout the remainder of the section. At 1:33, when the third verse begins, a shaker sounding an 8th-note pattern, and mixed quite prominently, is added to the center of the stereo field. The fastest-moving rhythmic element, the shaker, also occupies the highest pitch space of any instrument in the mix. Throughout this verse, then, the highest (shaker) and lowest (bass) pitches occupy the widest and most central positions of the mix, bringing a newfound balance.

"Let It Be" similarly opens with piano and lead vocal. Here the piano is panned slightly to the left but nowhere near as off-center as the hard-right piano panning in "Hey Jude." At 0:39, harmony vocals enter at the start of the first chorus. Hovering higher in pitch space and recorded quite dryly, they emerge gently from left-of-center in the mix, and as their pitch contour moves downward along with the chord progression, the voices travel in coordinated fashion from left to center and finally to the right side of the mix, eventually exiting "out the wings" as McCartney moves into the second verse. As with "Hey Jude," the next verse and chorus progression of "Let It Be" are largely defined by a filling in of the soundstage, both in terms of the stereo field and the pitch space. At 0:53, at the start of the second verse, the high-hat figure enters slightly right-of-center but with reverb that is heard mostly to the left. At 1:03, the bass enters for the second half of the verse, once again spread across the stereo field and in the lowest pitch space in the mix, providing a platform for all that occurs above it. A build-up coalesces at the start of the second chorus at 1:18; this can be heard as a crescendo—a loudening of the music—and in part it is. But just as importantly, it is a densification of the mix, as several things happen simultaneously. First, the harmony vocals re-enter, but unlike their first appearance in which they occupied a very specific spatial point in the mix (to the left, before their eastward journey), this time they are panned far more broadly (and arguably appear as distinctly separate sounds in the right and left channels). Second, the organ enters with sustained chords that mimic and add density to the vocal harmonies. Third, the high-hat figure changes from sounding only on the third beat of each measure to playing an every-beat (quarter-note) pattern, which occurs simultaneously with the first full use of the snare and toms of the drum kit.

Two specific elements of the songs' mixes that make them very different sonically are how the voices and the pianos are treated with respect to reverberation. In "Hey Jude," McCartney's voice is very "flat" and upfront, with absolutely no reverberation present. This can be heard clearly if one focuses on the end of the word that ends each phrase in the first verse: "Jude," "bad," "better," "remember," "heart," "start," "better." The sound of his voice immediately and abruptly drops off as soon as he finishes articulating the final consonant of each word. There is no sense of his voice bouncing off a studio wall or of being sounded in a real space; it is as if the microphone is inches from his mouth, and when his voice stops, all sound dies with it. The piano has a little more reverberation than McCartney's voice but not much.

"Let It Be" is starkly different, washed in reverberation. Listening to its phrase-final words—"trouble," "me," "be," "standing," "me," "wisdom," "be"—each decays into what feels like a large space, in most cases taking almost a half-second to die away fully. Whether this results from sound reflecting off the walls of the real room McCartney was singing in, or from the addition of artificial reverberation that mimics the sonic properties of singing in a large room, this "wet" treatment of McCartney's voice creates a very different spatialization than heard in "Hey Jude," one in which the voice encompasses far more territory in the stereo field. This is combined with a similar effect on the piano, which, though panned slightly left in the stereo field, has the deep reverberation not only of a sustain pedal but also of a piano being played with a sustain pedal in a reverberant room.

Many rock bands in the late 1960s and early 1970s started to see the recording studio as a compositional space offering great freedom to create albums that were equal parts music and explorations of sonic possibility.[37] And as recording and mixing technology moved into the digital realm during the 1980s and 1990s, with ever greater abilities to control, craft, and modify sound, the possibilities of sonic design in recordings have only increased over time, to the point where disentangling, in many genres, musical recordings from sound design is not only difficult but also nonsensical.

Sound Design in Restaurants

In the United States, multiple surveys performed since 2010 of diners' top complaints about eating at restaurants repeatedly concern excessive loudness (competing principally with perceived poor service).[38] Restaurants can be loud for many reasons, some of which reflect deliberate choices and others of which can be linked to economic realities and constraints in the restaurant industry, especially since the Great Recession. Deliberate choices range from interior design and choice of construction materials (carpeting, drapery, cloth upholstered chairs and banquettes, the use of tablecloths), to decisions about the sound system (placement and volume), to whether there is an open or a closed kitchen (or a mix of the two), to the placement of the bar (if any) in relation to dining areas.[39] Economic constraints include rental cost per square foot (which, of course, impacts the affordability of space and thus how large a dining area can be and how densely packed its tables may be), to the relative profit margins of food as opposed to alcohol sales, to the costs of acoustical treatment of indoor spaces. Active choices and economic constraints have dovetailed since the late 1990s (especially in restaurants in urban areas) such that smaller and louder restaurants have become more common.[40]

Many food writers locate the start of the deliberately loud restaurant trend with New York City's *Babbo Ristorante e Enoteca* during the tenure of now-disgraced chef Mario Battali, who in 2017 and 2018 was accused by several women of harassment and sexual assault, and who subsequently sold his ownership stakes in multiple restaurants and culinary holding companies, as chefs came under scrutiny alongside Hollywood figures in the #MeToo movement.[41] Asked in an interview shortly before the accusations became public what Battali would tell people who complained specifically about loud music in his restaurants, he responded:

> It's loud and vibrant because when you walk into one of my restaurants you know you are not anywhere else; you are in New York City and the vibe and energy is palpable and impressive.
>
> We have evaluated every single detail from how the door is painted to the way the floor feels when you walk in to the lighting to the fabric on the chairs to the kind of plates we have to the olive oil to the salt to the kind of coffee we have to the kind of milk we use to the way we say hello to the way we say goodnight. So you think we are not thinking about the music, too? It's a curated experience, and it is what we want. Every critic writes about it but there are a lot of people out there who are not critics.[42]

Note the reference to the "vibe and energy" of New York City and its reflection in the deliberately constructed (i.e., "curated") sound of the restaurant's dining room: sound is, of course, a vital component of a restaurant's atmosphere and the experience it generates for diners.

Yet it is also the case that deliberate decisions about diners' aesthetic tastes, and research about what kinds of interior design currently lure those most willing to spend on eating out, extend far beyond Battali's comments about loud music. Wood or tile floors have largely replaced carpeting; heavy tablecloths, drapes, and upholstered banquettes that signified wealth and dining-among-the-stars for much of the 1950s, 1960s, and 1970s have largely disappeared, so less sound that is made in service or hospitality, or even by conversation, is absorbed in their absence.[43] Just as drivers have come to associate certain car sounds with safety, quality, and luxury, so too have loud, reverberant restaurant spaces come to be associated for restauranteurs and many (especially younger) diners with the positive valence of conviviality, excitement, community, and abundant energy. Bucking the trend of restaurant critics bemoaning loud dining rooms, Pete Wells notes, "A noisy restaurant is the end product of a business that helps us have a good time, just as purring is the end product of scratching a cat's chin the right way."[44] Restaurants are places to come together with family and friends, and the better that coming together is, the louder people are likely to be, he argues. Even if there are very specific cultural assumptions about conviviality embedded in his account, Wells is not wrong that celebration and sound-making often go hand-in-hand.

It is worth, though, remembering that complaints about restaurant loudness are abundant. Critics of loud restaurants often suggest that sound is overlooked in dining room design or that money that might be spent on acoustics is too often value-engineered out of construction and design budgets.[45] To an extent, this is true: to hire an acoustic engineer adds an additional layer of cost, and acoustic materials (such as sound-absorbing ceiling tiles or wall coverings) are often quite expensive—and even more so when they are also asked to serve as further enhancements to the overall visual aesthetic of an interior space. Restauranteurs rarely work on a large budget before opening a new restaurant, so decisions that are perceived to have the highest impact on the dining experience are prioritized: visual design (e.g., artwork, table settings, seating and table choices) and kitchen equipment tend to supersede the seemingly less tangible domain of auditory concerns.

The harshest critiques of loud restaurant sound design focus on public health concerns for restaurant employees subject to long-term exposure to high levels of sound, long thought to be associated with higher levels of stress and greater risk of hypertension and heart disease, not to mention hearing loss over time. It is not uncommon for restaurants adopting the aesthetics described here to reach loudness levels continuously at or above 90 decibels during peak times, equivalent to being close to a power mower or a motorcycle. The US Occupational Health and Safety Administration (OSHA) requires that workers who are exposed to 90 or more decibels during an eight-hour work shift wear hearing protection and that employers who expose workers to more than 85 decibels should provide hearing tests. But restaurant front-of-house (FOH) workers such as waitstaff and hosts cannot wear hearing protection as their work relies heavily on communication with patrons. This, combined with the lack of a union structure to advocate for restaurant workers' rights, leaves FOH staff with little recourse to mitigate the potential health consequences of long-term exposure to high levels of sound.[46]

No one wants to eat at a restaurant that is uncomfortably quiet, as if the food is being served in a funeral home, or where one has to be concerned that no conversation is private, or that one might have to overhear other diners talking about things one would rather not have to know or think about. Equally, it may be off-putting to eat in dining room where the most common word in the conversation is "What?" directed to your dining companion. Restaurants, therefore, walk a fine line in crafting a designed sonic space conducive to customers' experiences and restaurant economics. The deliberate, meticulous control over sound design that can be undertaken in sound design in cinema or in a sound recording mix is neither common nor particularly possible in the world of restaurants; nonetheless, the acoustics of restaurant spaces still result from processes of design, some related to sound and others not.

Conclusion

This chapter has suggested that with a broad definition of sound design—one that can encompass all forms of deliberately created (and of deliberately creating) sonic environments—it is possible to analyze physical or filmic or musical or video game spaces through an approach that focuses on intentional efforts put into crafting sonic experience. It suggests that such design is generally goal-driven: automobile manufacturers want to sell more cars or to create distinction from their competitors; Caribbean resorts want to attract more tourists, which may necessitate backgrounding elements of the Caribbeans' colonial history; restaurants want to sell more food and drink; films seek to create emotional resonances that capture the imagination of their audiences. Often, these goals are deeply linked to consumer capitalism, to the maximization of profit, and to creating brand identity. They may not be entirely divorced from aesthetics, but they make clear that the aesthetics of sound design are deeply entwined with sales, profit, and capital.

SOUND DESIGN/DESIGNING SOUNDS

Project I

Working in groups, choose a short scene from a film and create two alternate soundtracks, informed by anticipating how audience reception will differ. Show the two different versions in class, and lead focus group discussions. Compile and analyze your findings; do they conform to your anticipated outcomes?

Project II

Select a 1:30–2:00-minute-long excerpt from a contemporary music recording, and write a descriptive analysis of its sound design, similar to how "Hey Jude" and "Let It Be" were discussed in this chapter. Imagine how you might utilize a different sound design to give the selection a different mood, meaning, or emotional resonances.

Project III

Choose a short scene from a film or video game that you think has interesting sound design, and write a descriptive analysis similar to how the *Apocalypse Now* opening scene was described in this chapter. Describe all the sonic elements that are present and how they work together to create emotional resonance, set a mood, propel the narrative, and relate to the images on the screen.

Notes

1. For Rio de Janeiro, see Moehn, " 'The Disc Is Not the Avenue,' " 47–83. For a description of samba schools in São Paulo, see Brunet, *Carnaval, Samba Schools and the Negotiation of Gendered Identites in São Paulo, Brazil.*
2. Brunet, *Carnaval, Samba Schools and the Negotiation of Gendered Identites in São Paulo, Brazil.*
3. Street-level volume is approximately 112dB (Moehn, " 'The Disc Is Not the Avenue,' " 47–83).
4. Brunet, *Carnaval, Samba Schools and the Negotiation of Gendered Identites in São Paulo, Brazil.*

5   Quoted in Moehn, "'The Disc Is Not the Avenue,'" 47–83. The architect was Oscar Niemeyer, who designed Brazil's capital city of Brasilia. Niemeyer also designed São Paulo's *sambódromo*.
6   Moehn, "'The Disc Is Not the Avenue,'" 47–83.
7   Harewood, "Listening for Noise," 107–33.
8   Guilbault and Rommen, "Introduction," 9–39.
9   This is true far beyond the Caribbean, of course. In the United States, so-called dude ranches in Western states sell a romanticized "cowboy" experience that is, in part, defined by singing songs with simple acoustic guitar accompaniment around the evening campfire.
10 Guadeloupe and Halfman, "All-Inclusive Resorts in Sint Maarten and Our Common Decolonial State," 134–60.
11 Guilbault, "Sound Management," 161–92.
12 See: https://www.youtube.com/watch?v=u3T0nVsvaJk.
13 See: https://www.youtube.com/watch?v=d53zBUjCwNI.
14 Bi, Reid, and Davies, "Characterization of Next-generation Car Sounds," 1517–26.
15 Tracy, "Here's Why Your Turn Signals Make That Clicking Noise."
16 What drivers hear now is most often emitted through the car's audio system.
17 Digital representations of objects and actions in the physical or analog world are often skeuomorphic: there is no physical shutter mechanism in an iPhone camera, but a shutter-like click sound still accompanies taking a picture with one; deleted digital files are dragged into icons that look like wastebaskets or trash cans, and so forth. For a fascinating account of how the Moog synthesizer interface came to take the same form as keyboards from the analog world, see Pinch and Trocco, "The Social Construction of the Early Electronic Synthesizer," 9–31.
18 Schafer, *The Soundscape*, 4.
19 Ibid., 5.
20 https://www.youtube.com/watch?v=LjLip2FZLuA.
21 Chion, *Audio-Vision*, 237.
22 Chion, *Sound*, 150–1. One might well question whether what he calls "peculiar" to film and televion is replicated—whether exactly or in modified form—in first-person video games.
23 Chion leaves deaf cinematic experiences unaddressed in his work.
24 See: https://www.youtube.com/watch?v=tZj1mYLC7h0 for sound designer Ben Burtt's recounting of how he conceptualized and created the light saber sound for *Star Wars*.
25 This is not an exhaustive list of job titles for audio post-production, just representative of the most common.
26 For a fascinating history of and interviews with key figures in film sound design, see the documentary, *Making Waves: The Art of Cinematic Sound* (Costin). And older but still fascinating work is Vincent LoBrutto's (*Sound*

SOUND DESIGN/DESIGNING SOUNDS

on Film) book of interviews with sound designers, from which much of the discussion of Walter Murch's work is drawn.

27 LoBrutto, Interview with Walter Murch, 1994.
28 Ibid.
29 https://www.youtube.com/watch?v=E-QefTioe3I.
30 Sounds that are heard without the ability to see what causes them are typically referred to as "acousmatic," following terminology popularized by *musique concrète* composer Pierre Schaffer. For more on acousmatic sound, see Chion, *Guide to Sound Objects*; Kane, *Sound Unseen*; and Schaffer, *Treatise on Musical Objects*.
31 Narrative films can, of course, invite audiences to inhabit the point of view of particular characters or be positioned as first-person voyeurs to what is transpiring onscreen. But this does not give agency to participate in or shape the narratives of the film.
32 For a deeper dive into video game sound design, see Collins, *Game Sound*; Grimshaw, *Game Sound Technology and Player Interaction*; Sinclair, *Principles of Game Audio and Sound Design*; and Collins, Kapralos, and Tessler, *The Oxford Handbook of Interactive Audio*.
33 For an example of this in relation to recording and mixing drum kits, see Porcello, "Music Mediated as Live in Austin," 103–17.
34 Sound engineer David Gibson's *The Art of Mixing: A Visual Guide to Recording, Engineering, and Production* provides a template for how to visually render all the sonic elements present in the three-dimensional sound space of a mix and goes so far as to suggest that different genres or styles of music can often be associated with particular spatial arrangements of instruments. A two-and-a-half-hour video demonstration by Morton can be found at https://www.youtube.com/watch?v=TEjOdqZFvhY. A shorter video that applies his approach to Michael Jackson's "Thriller" can be found at https://www.youtube.com/watch?v=HZ_0vca-jFg.
35 See, e.g., Emerick and Massey, *Here, There, and Everywhere*; Lewisohn, *The Beatles Recording Sessions*; Martin and Hornsby, *All You Need Is Ears*; Ryan and Kehew, *Recording the Beatles*, among others.
36 Although composed of several sound sources—the individual components of the kit as well as the individual microphones used to record them—the kit is treated here as a single sonic element in the music.
37 In many cases, in fact, being able to perform live what one could construct in the studio posed significant challenges to touring and of being able to reproduce in concert what fans heard on records and wanted to hear in live performance.
38 See, e.g., Consumer Reports, "Top Restaurant Complaints and Worst Offenders."

39 For broad and historical accounts of the relationship among built space, sound, and architecture, see Thompson, *The Soundscape of Modernity*, and Blesser and Salter, *Spaces Speak*.
40 One notable exception to this trend includes high-end sushi restaurants, which have generally remained quite quiet.
41 Battali also figures deeply in the rise of the "celebrity chef," particularly through his eight-year affiliation with The Food Network on several of its shows and later as a co-host on ABC's *The Chew*, from which he was forced to resign in 2017.
42 Subramanian, "For Mario Battali, Good Food and Loud Music Lead to a Curated Experience."
43 McLaughlin, "Pass the Salt … and a Megaphone."
44 Wells, "Is Restaurant Noise a Crime?"
45 "Value engineering" is a term used in design and construction, which refers to the creation of formulas by which the added value of spending money on a particular design or construction decision can be measured against its functional return. Value, here, is defined as the ratio of function to cost; elements with a low ratio are usually considered better candidates for elimination when budgetary constraints require changing project scopes.
46 This stands in contrast to how flight attendants were instrumental in banning smoking on planes in the US airline industry. The Association of Flight Attendants, now part of the Communications Workers of America (CWA), argued before Congress about the long-term health risks and consequences for on-board airline employees, especially those working in the cabins. For a detailed discussion of their influence, see Pan, Barbeau, and Levenstein, "Smoke-Free Airlines and the Role of Organized Labor," 398–404.

Bibliography

Bi, Youyi, Tahira Reid, and Patricia Davies. "Characterization of Next-generation Car Sounds." *INTER-NOISE and NOISE-CON Congress and Conference Proceedings*, 1517–26. Institute of Noise Control Engineering, 2016.

Blesser, Barry, and Linda-Ruth Salter. *Spaces Speak: Are You Listening?* Cambridge: MIT Press, 2009.

Brunet, Carla. *Carnaval, Samba Schools and the Negotiation of Gendered Identites in São Paulo, Brazil*. Berkeley: UC Berkeley Electronic Theses and Dissertations, 2012.

Chion, Michel. *Audio-Vision: Sound on Screen*. New York: Columbia University Press, 1994.

Chion, Michel. *Guide to Sound Objects*. Translated by John Dack and Christine North. ElectroAcoustic Research Site, 2009.

Chion, Michel. *Sound: An Acoulogical Treatise*. Translated by James A. Steintrager. Durham, NC: Duke University Press, 2016.

Collins, Karen. *Game Sound: An Introduction to the History, Theory, and Practice of Video Game Music and Sound Design.* Cambridge: MIT Press, 2008.

Collins, Karen, Bill Kapralos, and Holly Tessler. *The Oxford Handbook of Interactive Audio.* Oxford: Oxford University Press, 2014.

Consumer Reports. "Top Restaurant Complaints and Worst Offenders." September 20, 2016. *Consumer Reports.* https://www.consumerreports.org/restaurants/top-restaurant-complaints-and-worst-offenders/ (accessed March 13, 2021).

Emerick, Geoff, and Howard Massey. *Here, There, and Everywhere: My Life Recording the Music of The Beatles.* New York: Penguin, 2006.

Gibson, David. *The Art of Mixing: A Visual Guide to Recording, Mixing, and Production.* 2nd ed. Nashville, TN: Artistpro, 2005.

Grimshaw, Mark, ed. *Game Sound Technology and Player Interaction: Concepts and Developments.* Hershey, PA: IGI Global, 2011.

Guadeloupe, Francio, and Jordi Halfman. "All-Inclusive Resorts in Sint Maarten and Our Common Decolonial State: On Butterflies That Are Caterpillars Still in Chrysalis." In *Sounds of Vacation: Political Economies of Caribbean Tourism,* edited by Jocelyne Guilbault and Timothy Rommen, 134–60. Durham, NC: Duke University Press, 2019.

Guilbault, Jocelyne. "Sound Management: Listening to Sandals Halcyon in Saint Lucia." In *Sounds of Vacation: Political Economies of Caribbean Tourism,* edited by Jocelyne Guilbault and Timothy Rommen, 161–92. Durham, NC: Duke University Press, 2019.

Guilbault, Jocelyne, and Timothy Rommen. "Introduction: The Political Economy of Music and Sound." In *Sounds of Vacation: Political Economies of Caribbean Tourism,* edited by Jocelyne Guilbault and Timothy Rommen, 9–39. Durham, NC: Duke Univeristy Press, 2019.

Harewood, Susan. "Listening for Noise: Seeking Disturbing Sounds in Tourist Spaces." In *Sounds of Vacation: Political Economies of Caribbean Tourism,* edited by Jocelyne Guilbault and Timothy Rommen, 107–33. Durham, NC: Duke University Press, 2019.

Kane, Brian. *Sound Unseen: Acousmatic Sound.* Oxford: Oxford University Press, 2014.

Lewisohn, Mark. *The Beatles Recording Sessions.* New York: Harmony Books, 1988.

LoBrutto, Vincent. "Interview with Walter Murch." In *Sound-on-Film: Interviews with Creators of Film Sound.* Westport, CT: Praeger, 1994.

LoBrutto, Vincent. *Sound on Film: Interviews with Creators of Film Sound.* Westport, CT: Praeger, 1994.

Making Waves: The Art of Cinematic Sound. Dir. Midge Costin. Ain't Heard Nothin' Yet. 2020.

Martin, George, and Jeremy Hornsby. *All You Need Is Ears: The Inside Personal Story of the Genius Who Created The Beatles.* New York: St. Martin's Press, 1979.

McLaughlin, Katy. "Pass the Salt ... and a Megaphone." February 10, 2010. *Wall Street Journal.* https://www.wsj.com/articles/SB10001424052748704022804575041060813407740 (accessed March 13, 2021).

Moehn, Frederick. " 'The Disc Is Not the Avenue': Schismogenic Mimesis in Samba Recording." In *Wired for Sound: Engineering and Technologies in Sonic Cultures*, edited by Paul D. Greene and Thomas G. Porcello, 47–83. Middletown: Wesleyan University Press, 2005.

Pan, Jocelyne, Elizabeth M. Barbeau, Charles Levenstein, and Edith D. Balbach. "Smoke-Free Airlines and the Role of Organized Labor: A Case Study." *American Journal of Public Health* 95, no. 3 (2005): 398–404.

Pinch, Trevor, and Frank Trocco. "The Social Construction of the Early Electronic Synthesizer." *Icon* 4 (1998): 9–31.

Porcello, Thomas. "Music Mediated as Live in Austin: Sound, Technology, and Recording Practice." In *Wired for Sound: Engineering and Technologies in Sonic Cultures*, edited by Paul D. Greene and Thomas G. Porcello, 103–17. Middletown: Wesleyan University Press, 2005.

Ryan, Kevin, and Brian Kehew. *Recording the Beatles: The Studio Equipment and Techniques Used to Create Their Classic Albums*. Houston, TX: Curvebender, 2006.

Schafer, R. Murray. *The Soundscape: Our Sonic Environment and the Tuning of the World*. Rochester: Destiny Books, 1994 [1977].

Schaffer, Pierre. *Treatise on Musical Objects: An Essay across Disciplines*. Translated by Christine North and John Dack. Berkeley: University of California Press, 2017.

Sinclair, Jean-Luc. *Principles of Game Audio and Sound Design: Sound Design and Audio Implementation for Interactive and Immersive Media*. Waltham, MA: Focal Press, 2020.

Subramanian, Arthi. "For Mario Battali, Good Food and Loud Music Lead to a Curated Experience." April 11, 2017. *Pittsburgh Post-Gazette*. https://www.post-gazette.com/life/food/2017/04/12/mario-batali-chef-restaurant-author-music-review-orange/stories/201704120019 (accessed March 13, 2021).

Thompson, Emily. *The Soundscape of Modernity: Architectural Acoustics and the Culture of Listening in America, 1900-1933*. Cambridge: MIT Press, 2004.

Tracy, David. "Here's Why Your Turn Signals Make That Clicking Noise." March 17, 2017. *Jalopnik*. https://jalopnik.com/heres-why-your-turn-signals-make-that-clicking-noise-1793380845 (accessed December 12, 2020).

Wells, Peter. "Is Restaurant Noise a Crime? Our Critic Mounts a Ringing Defense." January 21, 2020. *New York Times*. https://www.nytimes.com/2020/01/21/dining/restaurant-noise-level-loud.html (accessed March 13, 2021).

6

Sound Art: What Is Sound Art? Debates and Examples

Key concepts: musique concrete, soundscape, multimedia, site-specific, Deep Listening, biophony

Exhibit 1

In 1966, the first iteration of "Dream House" was installed in the New York apartment of visual artist Marian Zazeela and composer La Monte Young. "Dream House" was the product of decades of experimental music that sought to create new sounds and experiences that differed from the conventional repertoire of the concert hall. Zazeela had trained as a painter but developed her reputation through her innovative light shows that accompanied performances by the Theater of Eternal Music group (of which she and Young were part). Young, one of the early minimalist composers in the New York scene and a veteran of the Fluxus movement, was turning away from the stilted formalism of high modernism, enticed by artistic concepts of indeterminacy and subjective experience that were animating other avant-garde composers and artists.

Dream House's concept is relatively simple: each room in the house (or apartment, as was the case in its first installation) is illuminated in a single color, accompanied by a sine wave oscillating at a fixed, constant tone and volume. The sound is intended to be loud enough that the vibrations are both a visceral and an auditory experience. An ideal encounter in the Dream House (which was relocated to lower Manhattan and now houses Theater of Eternal

Music as well as a number of musical ensembles and rotating exhibitions) is multisensory—auditory, visual, tactile—and self-guided, as observers move through at their own pace. The experience of sound and light, even in the exhibit's monochromatic and monotone rooms, differs by spatial positioning, time, and movement. "Dream House," first installed as a 24/7 addition to the collaborator's living quarters, was meant to bring art into a state of permanence, inextricable from daily life, even in sleep.

The Significance of "Dream House"

The installation was part of several larger artistic innovations in the postwar era. The first was that artists sought to disrupt conventional means of perception and interpretation, using art as a technique to alter how audiences experienced and acted in daily life. Many cultural critics in the postwar era were wary of the increasing speed, sensory overload, and consumerism of modern life. They thought of art as an act of resistance and a pedagogical exercise, confronting the circuits of both consumer and high culture in the postwar era. Consumerism was centered on shopping malls and retail stores, and high culture on bourgeois art institutions. For these avant-garde artists, including the early "sound artists," art had the power to change perception, alter awareness, and bring individuals into confrontation with their own socially ingrained practices. Zazeela and Young, along with their colleagues in Fluxus and composers like John Cage and Pauline Oliveros, aimed to push musical awareness away from decoding the concepts and forms of music in structural listening and toward altering perceptions of sound and cultivating critical awareness of social life and everyday experience. This included a reimagining of power relationships and questioning the role of the individual in society.[1] The concept and design of "Dream House" employ the notion of sound (and the arts) as a critical intervention into modernity, inviting experiencers to linger on single colors and sounds rather than indulging in the frantic experiences of modernity.

The second movement that "Dream House" participated in is site-specific artworks, also referred to as installations. As a circumvention of the museum establishment and a tool for expanded creativity and criticism, artists used open air spaces, empty storefronts, or their own private residences as locations to construct and display art.[2] These exhibits enabled experimentations in performance art, sound art, and other multimodal artistic practices (as well as facilitating extremely large sculptures). Getting outside of the sterile and uniform spaces of the museum also created a different audience experience, as these works introduced elements of interactivity and flexibility into the art encounter. "Dream House" was innovative in its placement—an exhibit that takes up an entire apartment—as well as being constant, defying even the logic of a typical concert program, festival, or exhibit. The installation made a bold statement by blurring the lines between art spaces and the space of quotidian life.

Third, Zazeela and Young's installation was part of intellectual movements that sought to better understand audience encounters with sound and to use those insights to heighten consciousness and awareness. These works often harnessed a total approach to subjective experience, combining sound and emotion with haptic sensation, vision, and, in some cases, olfaction and gustation. Those who experimented with sound used instruments in unusual ways (John Cage's works for common kitchen appliances or transistor radios), built their own instruments (Harry Partch), or composed pieces that were meant to alter the audience's relationship to the act of listening itself (John Cage's 4'33" or Pauline Oliveros's *Sonic Meditations* and site-specific "Deep Listening" performances). Artists of different media (composers, performers, sculptors, recording engineers) worked to transform the art experience, using new means, methods, sounds, and spaces. Some of these experiments were so radical in their departure from the sounds and protocols of the concert/composition tradition that they were termed "sound art" because their presentation was too far afield to be labeled "music" or "theater" for many critics and curators.

Much of the brief history of sound art also takes flight from critiques of museums and concert halls, their relationship to elite audiences, and allegiance to a narrow set of aesthetic principles. As music, art, dance, and theater responded to postwar and postcolonial conditions, artists sought to move the art experience out of confining and proscribed spaces and to engage new audiences on their own terms. They also looked to actively alter the physical and cognitive behavior of those who encountered their works (more on this later). "Dream House" was one experiment early in the genre of sound art that looked to impact both the waking and the sleeping environments of the artists (and also the audience, but on a different level).

Exhibit 2

In 2014, the Peabody Essex Museum hosted the exhibit "From Here to Ear," an installation by composer Celeste Boursier-Mougenot. The exhibit involved a large room, transformed into an aviary, complete with three tons of sand on the floor, hanging bird houses, and ten electrified instruments.

In this case, the instruments were six iconic Gibson "Les Paul" guitars and four Gibson "Thunderbird" basses, mounted horizontally with the strings facing upward. The instruments were tuned to chords commonly heard in rock and blues music. Their amplifiers were positioned to high-gain, low-volume settings, making them sensitive to the small birds alighting on their strings and producing a flurry of sound when the small creatures took flight. The amplifiers also utilized onboard digital sound effects, reverb and delay, which prolong the sounds made by the birds and add artificial depth. The relatively low volume of the electrified instruments also made auditory space for the chirping of the birds and, after a short period of acclimation, ceased to frighten them. In addition to the setup of the installation, traffic in and out of the exhibit was controlled and limited to twenty people at a time so that the birds, easily habituated to human presence, would not be disturbed by excessive noise or motion. This also ensured that visitors could move through at a slower pace and have simultaneous vantage of several instruments. When sounds occur, locating the point of origin is easily facilitated without crowding, allowing the participant to link action and sound and provide an immersive experience.

A Different Approach to Installation

Boursier-Mougenot's work adds a different dimension to the immersive sound art world of "Dream House" and similar sound installations. While spontaneity and aleatoric aspects were part of earlier works of sound art, the artificial inclusion of birds in the interior of the museum space presents different auditory and visual elements. The composer cannot choreograph birds chirping any more than they can predict their flight patterns. The design of "From Hear to Ear" includes spontaneous creations of sight and sound over which the composer has little control. The first is the sound of the birds, which varies by time of day, the social activities of the colony, and the place of the listener within the exhibit. The second is the zebra finches themselves. The visual experience of the birds is also dependent on time of day, and the specific space that the experiencer inhabits as well as the room in which it is installed.[3] The third is the sound of the instruments, which are played by birds going through their daily activities and are by design irregular and subject to fluctuations in tuning over the course of a day. With ten instruments, a patron might be looking at birds on one instrument while hearing sounds from several other instruments that are out of sight or only peripherally visible. The listener knows that the sounds they are hearing are generated by birds but may or may not witness the act of creation. The final factor is the birds' adaptation to their new surroundings. Most of the instruments end up with hay or grass in their strings, as the birds build a new habitat to suit themselves within the exhibition. This alters the sounds emanating from the instruments. These four factors come together to provide a unique experience, or set of experiences depending on the viewer's interpretation, on each visit. The sounds of the exhibit become layered, as a viewer focuses on one instrument and the activities on and around it but is aware of bird calls from above and the rustlings of other instruments in the room.

Unlike "Dream House," which sought a space outside of established museums and which currently inhabits a multi-art space, "From Hear to Ear" inhabited a traditional museum space, with adjoining galleries that showcase plastic arts from around the world.[4] The contrast between the exhibit and the rest of the galleries at the Peabody Essex Museum were a stark contrast, because of the sonic and biological elements (the installation has been displayed in many galleries since its inception in 2010), which differed from both the collection and the other special exhibits at the museum. "From Hear to Ear" confronts the quiet of museum space, as well as the permanence of its artworks, by utilizing a nonhuman performative dimension, letting the beauty and unpredictability of a zebra finch colony make art in real time, while also slyly referencing popular music through the instruments, their tuning, and the amplification.

Boursier-Mougenot's conception further differs from "Dream House" in that a commercial recording of the sound from the Peabody Essex Museum on May 23, 2014, was made. Produced as two 23-minute sides, the recording was released by Cassauna Records, a boutique affiliate of Important Records. Cassauna produces limited edition releases on cassette tape, vinyl and digital, the former two formats featuring letter-pressed notes and silk-screened artwork. The small label's catalog contains a number of experimental and ambient releases by Pauline Oliveros and Michael T. Bullock, Sarah Davachi, the Overtone Ensemble, and Caterina Barbieri.[5] The combination of mediums—a cassette in 2014, boutique artistic design, and a company that specializes in less commercially viable genres—places the recording of "From Hear to Ear" into a realm of "art music," distanced from more commercial and commodified popular music but in the form of a souvenir, a commodity that is familiar to museum goers.

Despite these theoretical and practical differences, both "Dream House" and "From Hear to Ear" are classified as sound art. This raises questions about the efficacy of the term, its application and appropriateness to different works, and its relationship to criticism, music, art, and institutions.

What Is Sound Art?

These two contrasting works demonstrate the range of works that fall under the leaky umbrella term "sound art" and the difficulties inherent in the terminology. While the "Dream House" installation is not the first work classified as sound art, its position in the pantheon raises interesting questions about the genre itself. Is "Dream House" sound art, or is it a work of architecture and design? Is "Dream House" in its complete incarnation not a sound work but rather an articulation of interdisciplinary arts (since sound is only one component, making the label "sound art" insufficient and incomplete)? What is the nature of "From Hear to Ear": is it the experience of walking through a room filled with auditory, visual, olfactory, and tactile information? Can it be classified as "sound art" if the experience is one that piques multiple senses? What part of the work is captured by the cassette release, which is sound and artwork that are not immediate to the exhibit, limited by technologies that foreclose variation, subjective gaze, and the layered listening inherent in the live experience? Or is the recording a separate entity apart from the installation? If so, how does a cassette recording of less than an hour of unique recorded sounds, that are unlikely to ever be repeated during a visit to the installation, relate to a typical exhibition catalog that features photographs, which are at least partial representations of the works on display?

Existential and aesthetic questions like these continue to hang heavy over sound art, even as auditory installations and exhibits become more common in museums, galleries, public spaces, and the internet. Can any work that emits or alters sound in a gallery be considered "sound art"? Are works that make use of everyday sound—bits of conversation, electronic oscillations, amplifications of insects, or contact microphones placed on household surfaces—automatically classified as "sound art" rather than music? Is a walking and listening tour of a city or a sonorous natural location an example of "sound art"? What about the practice of displaying musical instruments accompanied by recordings of music played on them? Are there secondary parameters that trim this massive field of possibility into something structurally coherent and available to criticism and creativity? What forms of criticism can help decode the meaning and purpose of establishing sound as a field in the realm of the fine arts apart from established forms of concert music, score, and accompaniment?

Rather than answer these elusive questions, this chapter looks at a handful of major works within the dynamic world of sound art, offering a sketch of the many different paths that sound art walks. The variety of methods, approaches, and articulations is impressive for a field that is young and rapidly developing.

The Futurists and Varese

The field of sound art, as represented in writings that attempt to capture its histories and variances, is a postwar phenomenon, with roots in the early twentieth century (although McCormack places "resonant statuary" at a much earlier date). The postwar boom in technology—from magnetic tape to multitrack recording, stereo and quadrophonic sound, sophisticated amplification, and digital recording—has aided in the development of sound as a malleable auditory medium apart from the voice and traditional instruments. Experiments like those of John Cage, who sought to make the audience hear every sound encountered with the concentration and attention they afford to music, the nature soundscape recordings of Steven Feld, Annea Lockwood, and Bernie Krause (which are subject to manipulation in post-production), and intentional confrontations like that of Boursier-Mougenot, are aided by technology and architecture. This relationship between sound art and technology ties various projects in the postwar years to European futurists, who were arguably the first sound artists.

As noted earlier (See Chapters 2 and 4), European (and Russian) Futurists' aesthetics were influenced by industrial technology and sought to transform this energy and ontology into forms of expressive culture. These experimental works range from the visual poetry of F. T. Marinetti to the metaphysical paintings of Carlo Carra, the noise machines of Luigi Russolo, and the extreme deployment of factory sirens by Avraamov, which could be heard across Azerbaijan in performance.[6] Futurists sought to challenge the art establishment and create works that communicated directly with modern industrial society. In many of these pursuits, sound became a model for the new art aesthetic: it is temporal, active, and emotive; it eludes the clean lines, formal structures, and precise angles of European high art. In sound's lack of restraint and possibilities for becoming tactile and visceral, sound transforms into an organizing principle and a point of confrontation (see chapter 2 for a discussion of sound at high volumes).

Futurist manifestoes advocated replacing existing artworks and modes of production with futurist aesthetics and approaches.[7] These included an oppositional approach to art, the art establishment, and conventional notions of topic, virtuosity, beauty, and meaning. They criticized the veneration of old masters, the canon and its aesthetics, the conservatory, and established institutions like museums, concert halls, and theaters. Futurists' critiques helped pave the way for the intellectual and conceptual work that undergirded sound art in the postwar years.[8] Some of their ideas, like expanding the palette of orchestral sounds by adding unconventional sound producers and departing from the established strictures of melody, harmony, and form, became hallmarks of twentieth-century music.

Notable among these early experiments were interwar works by French composer Edgar Varese, who used sirens and magnetic tape in his compositional practices and composed the first concert works for percussion ensemble. His *Ameriques* (1921/1926) for orchestra challenges earlier ideas of form and development, unwinding through timbre and sonority rather than melody and harmony, and includes a large percussion battery, including a siren. The work is a vivid representation of New York City, where Varese lived. Later he composed *Ionisation* (1931), the first Western concert work for percussion ensemble (percussion ensembles have long been part of some African and Asian court traditions). In the postwar years, his composition *Poem Electronique* was installed in the Philips Pavilion at the 1958 World's Fair. The building, designed by architect Le Corbusier (with aid from composer Iannis Xenakis), played *Poem Electronique* to accompany a film of black-and-white photographs curated by Le Corbusier. The work, for three-track tape, contains "pure electronic sounds, machine noises, bells, solo and choral voices, piano and percussion, all with or without modification."[9] The sound was played back on a complex system of several hundred speakers divided into groups of twelve that could be independently controlled, creating a spatialized listening experience.

Poem Electronique foreshadowed sound art installations in several ways. First, it is multimedia, as it was paired with a visual element as a necessary part of the experience. Second, it is site-specific, installed in a unique space (which has since been demolished) with a specialized audio playback system that altered the experience of sound in space. Third, it is all electronic, employing no acoustic or traditional instruments in live performance. Finally, it takes place outside of conventional concert space. *Poem Electronique*, *Ionisation*, and *Ameriques* were visionary works that fused early twentieth-century critiques of art with postwar innovations.

4'33" and the Big Umbrella of Sound Art

The postwar years were a time of divergent experimentation in Western concert halls as artists sought to innovate in ways that broke with tradition. Among the underlying critiques that animated artists were a desire to move art outside the rarified air of institutions, a valorization of everyday life (and its constituent sounds, motions, and objects), communication with the body (rather than just the mind), and movement away from the total control of the composer/artist. These criticisms led to experiments in improvisation, early computer music, collective composition, chance operations, and public arts.

One of the experiments that helped to shape the development of sound art was John Cage's 4'33" (1952). First performed by pianist David Tutor at the Maverick Concert Hall in Woodstock, New York, the piece is notorious for being a composition without music, where the pianist sits at the piano but does not play. Part of the design of the piece was the location of its premiere. Nestled within the Hudson Valley woods, Maverick Concert Hall has no sophisticated sound proofing and allows for natural light and sound to enter from windows and open doors at the rear of the theater. According to composer Kyle Gann, during the first 30-second "movement" of 4'33", the audience heard the wind rustling through the trees. During longer the second movement (2:23), the patter of rain on the roof became audible. For the third and final movement of 40 seconds, the audience began to fidget and grumble.[10] Cage considered this a success, despite one of the audience members saying, "Good people of Woodstock, let's drive these people out of town!" in the post-concert discussion.[11]

In 4'33", Cage moves toward extracting the will of the composer from the composition, something that he had also attempted through works that incorporated transistor radios or used processes from the *I-Ching* to determine musical elements. Instead of the composer using more and more abstract procedures to remove themselves from a composition, Cage shifted his focus to the act of listening. By asking the concert hall audience, who are culturally conditioned to be hyper-attentive to sound, to simply listen to their surroundings, Cage was making a statement about the music of everyday life and the politics of listening. He believed that any sound could be listened to with the same intensity that concert music is and that this act would heighten our awareness and our sense of interconnectedness (Cage was also profoundly influenced by Zen philosophy and environmentalism). Cage also viewed the hierarchy of composer-performer-audience as problematic and sought ways to undercut situations that reinforced it.

Templates for a New Field

In 4'33" Cage brought together various currents that would shape sound art. The first is the conceptual mechanism that makes the articulation of the art itself, the experiential product, less important than the animating idea or ideas. The specific aesthetics of the "composition" and "performance" of 4'33" are less important than designing a work that makes an audience listen to everyday sounds with the same attention that they give to concert music. The second is site-specific design. While 4'33" has been performed in a number of different venues, the premier was at a specific location that reflected and enacted Cage's aesthetics and ideologies.[12] The venue itself (as well as its geographic and institutional location) was an important part of the concept and the experience. Modern concert halls, with their sound engineering and architecture, are perhaps less effective in executing the composition or translating the ethical and environmental parts of Cage's concept. Finally, Cage aimed the experience of sound to be transformative rather than strictly contemplative. Where art aesthetics tended toward contemplation or realization, Cage and others in the postwar moment were seeking a new aesthetic of art, one that also aimed to transform the actions and perceptions of individuals and society. These three generative currents—conceptual, site-specific, and transformative—provide unifying themes to the vast and disparate field of sound art. When combined with innovations in technology and its uses, we can begin to grasp the threads that loosely connect works in the field of sound art.

In a different critical attempt to define the field's loose parameters, David Toop cites an interface with the visual and a work that is either context or site-specific.[13] Labelle, in a simultaneously abstract and grounded definition, acknowledges sound art as both a thing and a reflection of a thing, giving it two components, as opposed to traditional plastic arts—painting, sculpture, or concert music—which are singular in presentation. Sexton's key to sound art, as definition and fulcrum for criticism, is that (1) sound art invites an audience to pay attention to sound as a material presence in new ways and (2) that sound interacts with space(s)[14]. He also points to works of sound art that offer audiences tools to hear the world differently and generative works that move away from control by the artist.[15]

But even these broad definitions fail to include other forms of sound art, particularly Pierre Schaeffer and Pierre Henry's musique concrete and soundscape recordings by Bernie Krause, Steven Feld, or Annea Lockwood (see Chapter 1 for more about soundscape recordings). Pioneered by Pierre Schaeffer in the immediate postwar years, musique concrete made use of magnetic tape as both the means to capture sound and, through basic editing processes, recombine and manipulate these found sounds into an original composition. In keeping with the different traditions that sought to stretch the definition of music and expand the palette of sounds could be considered music, early examples of musique concrete from the 1940s, like "Etude aux Chemin de Fer" (1948), use a mix of sounds that are readily identifiable and others that are less obvious. In the case of "Etude," all the sounds come from trains and bear the marks of Futurist fascination with machinery, but are subjectively mixed and altered by

Schaeffer. Later works, like Pierre Henry's "Orphée 53" (1953), mix the sounds of the concert hall with spoken words and sounds rendered mysterious without context or through analog manipulation. In Pierre Henry's later works, pieces of sound are assembled as a multitrack tape with the individual sounds brought to the forefront or muted by the composer in performance on a mixing board.[16] Schaeffer and Henry's tape works followed in the pathway of the futurists, Varese and Cage, in expanding notions of what is considered appropriate sound for the concert hall. Musique concrete corresponds to Labelle's definition, but slips through both Toop and Sexton's.

For environmental soundscape artists like Krause and Feld, both of whom attach their artistic practice to environmental research and justice, their works attempt to represent the sounds of particular places, especially those endangered by human activity. Ideologically, their work has more in common with Romantic-era landscape painters or the protectionist environmentalist poetics of photographer Ansel Adams. Krause and Feld would like their works to engender a sense that these places, people, and spaces are important and endangered, without inspiring touristic desire. Their works are a catalyst for political action, the sounds they capture and edit a proxy for fragile life composed by using vérité techniques.[17] These works, more than musique concrete, fit the varied definitions of Toop, Labelle, and Sexton.

Critiques of Sound Art

One of the chief critical issues with sound art is the openness of the term. If sound art is defined like painting—by its medium of sound—what differentiates sound art from experimental music, performance art that makes use of sound components, or avant-garde spoken poetry that uses nonlinguistic sound? Douglas Kahn sees the term itself as flawed because the umbrella is simply too broad. It admits a diversity of practices, and often nonsonic features, that weaken the field by eliminating relationships and commonalities. Alan Licht questions the term itself, pointing to a long history of association between the plastic arts and sound. Theoretically, Ryan McCormack critiques sound art for its focus on positioning new multimodal art within old aesthetic conversations that reinforce existing hierarchies, discouraging new identities for art and restraining daring interpretations of older works.

Artist Max Neuhaus has critiqued the term "sound art" as a cover for modern experimental music that takes place in museums or other institutional art spaces. In Neuhaus's view, sound art is more often a collection of sounds that defy expectations or are more diverse than typical uses of sound in curation.

In his estimation, much of modern sound art has limited relationships to either art or sound.[18] Neuhaus rejected the term "sound artist" and said of his own work, "I am not interested in making music exclusively for musically initiated audiences. I am interested in making music for the people."[19] Many of Neuhaus's installations are aimed at audiences outside of the concert hall and other art institutions, observers uninitiated into conventional understandings of how musical pieces function in the high art traditions. His installation *Times Square* (1977) creates a subtle resonance that emanates from a subway grate between 45th and 46th Streets in New York City. During rush hour or other busy times, it is almost unnoticed, blending into the city's soundscape. But afterhours, the hum is clearly audible, lending an ethereal quality to the outdoor space.

Times Square accomplishes a political and conceptual move that expanded and enacted Cage's notions of the politics of art (critiques of art's elitism were common in the postwar years). Cage looked to dismantle and challenge the hierarchy of composer-performer-audience that is cemented in the Western concert hall, museum, and gallery. However, many of Cage's works still found their audiences in concert halls and similar venues. Neuhaus met this challenge by not requiring the level of attention (on par with a designation that a work is "art") that Cage's works, like 4'33", demanded. *Times Square* often sits unnoticed and becomes meaningful when a pedestrian locates the unusual sound. It also does not dictate the terms of engagement, allowing the listener to determine their own experience by choosing to stop and take a deep listen, listen casually while walking by, or not listen at all.

Neuhaus also integrated audience sound in a more active manner. His work *Public Supply I* (1966) called upon citizens to provide sonic content. By designing a system that allowed callers to submit live sounds to a sound board controlled by Neuhaus. Although Neuhaus was the conductor and had a certain amount of artistic control over the sounds that were played over the air, the content itself was determined by listeners who called in to talk, sing, and offer homemade or environmental sounds. *Public Supply I* not only asks the listener to attend to unusual sound assemblages, as musique concrete and "From Hear to Ear" do, but also makes them active in the sound gathering process, something that 4'33" only does surreptitiously.

The Natural World and the Unheard Made Audible

The umbrella of sound art has also broadened into representations of location-specific works that contain few or no human-made sounds. These include a range of works, like the environmental recordings of Bernie Krause, Annea Lockwood, and Steven Feld, and works made using sounds that cannot be heard with the naked ear. The latter include early works that utilized phonograph needles and contact microphones to amplify the sounds of breaking wood, twisting metal, and mechanical vibration. Innovations in sound capture have also enabled artists to record animal sounds, radio waves from the cosmos, and the earth's tremors and integrate these sounds into installations and recordings. The final addition to the sound art arsenal is new technology that allows sounds to be made with varying degrees of experience or training. Like an extension of Neuhaus's *Public Supply I*, artists have challenged themselves to design interfaces for music making that are radically inclusive and make use of real-time interaction, at times facilitating cooperation across long distances.

Using new sound capture technologies, early sound recordists began documenting the sounds of the outdoors, focused primarily on wildlife. Ludwig Koch, whose extensive recordings are held in the British Library, recorded wildlife for several decades. Some recordings capture the sound of single creatures, like the American bullfrog or the Skylark, or produce audio comparisons of two species, like the Malayan and Brazilian Tapir. The holdings in the British Library also include two soundscapes, labeled "Afrotropical Atmosphere," split into "day" and "night." These are among his longest, at three and a half minutes apiece, and feature the sounds of running water along with numerous animal sounds. These sounds are not explained or specified in the liner notes, apart from the nebulous and problematic caption "Compilation of African wildlife sounds heard during the day" or night. These two recordings are different in that they are not as specifically documentary as most of Koch's others. Although there is little information available on them, it seems that they are edited together rather than being a single three-minute moment, a kind of highlight reel of atmospheric sounds. That specific locations within a vast and diverse African continent are not offered in the track description or liner notes points to an imaginative component, one that invites the listener to picture a moment in an imaginary (colonized) Africa.[20] As problematic as this is, the gesture is reminiscent of a pastoral or landscape painting: it is an invitation to be in the presence of ideal forms of the animals, landscapes or moments that are depicted (there is also a resonance with Roland Barthes's notion of the "reality effect" from Chapter 4 that is translated into this new medium).

Koch also pioneered the sound book, something that would evolve with multimedia technology. His sound books, done in collaboration with German and British zoologists, were illustrated guides to birdsongs that paired pictures and photographs with attached gramophone records that provided audio samples. His work led him to be featured on the BBC and, after his retirement, to a four-part retrospective entitled "Ludwig Koch and the Music of Nature."[21] The title itself gives the listener a ready-made interpretation: that animal sounds are music, to be listened to as such. However, his recordings also point to something that captures the specificity of space (if not always of time) and contains a conservationist politics of appreciation for and knowledge of the natural world that pervades much of the sub-genre of sound art that deals in natural soundscapes.

Acoustic Ecology and Soundwalks

Acoustic ecologist Bernie Krause has used his sound recordings as both art and advocacy for environmental conservation. In 2002, he published a book and CD entitled *Wild Soundscapes* and, in 2012, followed it up with *The Great Animal Orchestra*. Both of these multimedia publications, which include pedagogical components, are aimed at a mainstream audience and encourage a DIY approach to recording and learning about natural sound. Krause's arguments involve ethics, and his aesthetic choices are pedagogical. His work is connected to the transformative aspects of sound art: it builds upon critiques of our listening practices and seeks to make listeners aware of their natural surroundings and the importance of conservation.

In both the text and the online component of *The Great Animal Orchestra*, Krause makes overt comparisons between the biophony (his term for the totality of natural and undomesticated sound in a given area) of the natural soundscape and the quintessential ensemble of Western art music: the orchestra. In explaining the soundscape of Gonarezhou, Zimbabwe, he depicts the animal sounds in a circular field divided by both sound quality (high, mid-range, and low pitches) and animal (insect, bird, mammal). He explains and arranges sounds in a way that is organizationally similar to an orchestra and points out the evolutionary and practical purposes of sounds that occur in particular pitch bands. In a subtle nod in the direction of progressive politics, he states that often when animals use similar pitch ranges, they wait for one animal to finish singing before beginning their own song. The recordings included in *The Great Animal Orchestra* are far more specific than those of Ludwig Koch, containing both location and approximate time—dawn, midday, sunset, midnight—and, by his own admission, editing of many hours of recording into biophonic musique concrete.[22]

By comparing the sounds of the natural world with the orchestra, Krause is making a case for his recordings (which are meticulously edited and mixed), and their natural counterparts (the ecosystem), to be classified as art (or art music). This implies a drive for environmental preservation, similar to the way that concert music is put into a canon (and enshrined in institutions called "conservatories"). Like the works of Cage or Oliveros (discussed later), Krause's work is aimed at affecting the listener's awareness and behavior. Krause's book *Wild Soundscapes* is a handbook on recording, identifying, editing, cataloging, and archiving natural sounds, a DIY soundscape manual. *The Great Animal Orchestra* is also pedagogical but in a way that is reminiscent of Leonard Bernstein's "Young Person's Guide to the Orchestra." In the online component, Krause explains groups of sounds and how they fit together. The online component also has identification exercises to sharpen the participant's ear. Both texts and their additional multimedia components are ultimately aimed at training the ear and the mind and, by extension, crafting a different relationship between the listener and the natural world.

In contrast to the preindustrial sonic purity sought by Krause (also see Chapter 1 for more on *soundscapes*), Hildegard Westerkamp's works thoughtfully engage industrial and natural sound, along with oscillators and sophisticated sound processing. Her soundscape works contrast urban and rural sounds, creating sonic journeys that at times mirror the experience of walking through spaces and at others offer a composer's transparent assemblage of captured sounds. Her "Kits Beach Soundwalk" and "A Walk through the City," from her album *Transformations* (1989), offer insight into her methods. "A Walk through the City" is an aural study of Vancouver, Canada. It begins with undistinguishable ambient and electronic sounds that bleed into automobile sounds and then to human voices, expressing the conditions of living in the city in different sonic modalities. The piece travels from the outskirts of the city to the Skid Row area, narrated by the voice of poet Norbert Reubsaat, whose poem of the same name inspired the piece. The piece is a combination of musique concrete, utilizing sounds from the World Soundscape Project, Ruebsaat's spoken performance that the composer assembles and manipulates, and Westerkamp's own electronic composition, that she adds to the mix. "Walk" provides the listener with a multi-layered aural sense of place by utilizing city sounds (similar to Barthes "Reality Effect") combined with Ruebsaat's textual commentary and Westerkamp's compositional rhetoric that adds emphasis and ambience and controls the pacing.

"Kits Beach Soundwalk" uses similar methods, but, like Krause's *Great Animal Orchestra*, it is pedagogical. The composer's narrative of her experience on "Kits Beach," from the day, time, and weather to her dreams, is clear and placed over recorded sounds, in the style of an audiobook or narrative. Westerkamp recounts her stories of the beach into the listener's ears, going so far as to mix the ambient sound of the city at different levels, to detail how the beauty of the beach scenery changes her perception of the noise. In the narrative, she explains how she lowers the sounds of the city in the studio to emphasize the sounds of nature, but when she tries to listen for the sounds of the barnacles the sounds of the city intrude. In contrast to "Walk," "Kits Beach" is a soundscape, a work of musique concrete (unlike "Walk," there is no added musical composition), and an audio narrative, a meditation that starts with a specific place and moves into the imagination in a fanciful but transparent way, creating an evocative, expressionistic work. As Westerkamp writes about "Kits Beach," "In this soundwalk composition we leave the city behind eventually and explore instead the tiny acoustic realm of barnacles, the world of high frequencies, inner space and dreams."[23]

Deep Listening

Composer Pauline Oliveros coined the term "Deep Listening" in 1989 to accompany a recording of her improvisations with fellow musicians Panaiotis and Stewart Dempster. In this improvisational practice, the musicians brought instruments into exceptionally resonant spaces and collectively improvised. The success of the recording led to a composer's manifesto of the same name and eventually an institute in upstate New York. However, Oliveros's engagement with the practices of deep listening began much earlier.

Oliveros's work straddles "music" and "sound art" in that her compositions are a vehicle for personal transformation and an enactment of an inclusive, aware consciousness. Her *Sonic Meditations* (1971) are not geared toward a concert audience but instead utilize sound making and improvising as transformative community practices apart from the stage. In the brief "Introduction I" to *Sonic Meditations*, she states:

> With continuous work some of the following becomes possible with Sonic Meditations: heightened states of awareness or expanded consciousness, changes in physiology and psychology from known and unknown tensions to relaxations which gradually become permanent. These changes may represent a tuning of mind and body. The group may develop positive energy which can influence others who are less experienced. Members of the Group may achieve greater awareness and sensitivity to each other. Music is a welcome by-product of this activity.[24]

The composition, consisting of twenty-five modular exercises (the last of which is a writing exercise), is designed with healing and community building as outcomes, not music. In this case, making sound is a vehicle for creating new social and spiritual relationships and relationships within the individual. *Sonic Meditations* are an attempt to "return the control of sound to the individual alone, and within groups, especially for humanitarian purposes; specifically healing." Oliveros also writes that, "[a]ll that is required is a *willing commitment to given conditions*" (emphasis in the original).[25] Her work sought to enact a critique of consumer society and the hierarchies within modernity, including the relationships between composition-performance and performer-audience. Her works encourage any participant to make music and improvise and also to listen and feel more attentively, removing the need for an audience and making any participant (regardless of skill or training) both performer and audience.

In crafting these transformational spaces, works like *Sonic Meditations* and her composer's manifesto/manual, *Deep Listening: A Composer's Sound Practice* (2005), used sonic and kinetic practices from across the globe as inspiration (she studied Buddhism, Taoism, and Yoga for inspiration). *Deep Listening* is a compendium of exercises to alter awareness and consciousness, explanations of ways of listening and thinking, and a series of compositions that use these practices. The compositions range from group practices of listening and sharing to reminders for the individual to be aware of the art that is innate in their everyday lives. In her work, Oliveros takes calls from the 1960s to recognize the beauty in the everyday and systematically crafts a radically inclusive practice that can engage anyone in both recognizing and participating in art and community through sound.

Natural and Supernatural Sounds

Composer Annea Lockwood has taken a similar methodological approach as Krause (extensive field recording followed by painstaking editing) to documenting the natural world in several of her sound installations. In contrast to Bernie Krause or Steven Feld, several of her works center on moving bodies of water (rather than on animal sound), a common theme in her work, and the interaction of the river sounds with wildlife and human sound. Her recordings of the Danube River, running from the Bregquelle in southwest Germany east to the Black Sea, and the Hudson and Housatonic Rivers in the United States, trace the flow of the rivers from their source to the sea, aurally chronicling changes in the speed, terrain, animal life, and human sound. Each installation features an elevated four-speaker system, which gives the listener a 360-degree auditory experience, and a map of the river that shows the locations for the different sections of the recordings with data on the time and date of the recordings and corresponding time stamp in the work.

Lockwood's river installations and corresponding recordings (of the Danube and Hudson) walk a fine line among documentary, ethnography, and art. Like earlier conceptual sound art, the projects begin with a design that corresponds to both a politics and an object for investigation. While the scope of the project belongs to the composer—in the design, editing, and presentation—the sounds that are captured are unpredictable and shape the work. The installation of the projects seems to consciously avoid picturesque representations (all three of Lockwood's locations have been the subject of many painters and photographers). Photographs from the Danube installation show a bare gallery room with white walls, a bench in the center of the room and speakers installed on high columns at the four corners. The bench is situated to face a wall with a map of the Danube beneath which is a felt strip on the floor covered with rocks collected from the journey. An installation of "Sound Map of the Housatonic River" at Vassar College featured only a map of the river and recording locations with no other artifacts or visuals. This mode of centering aural experience and encouraging listeners to form their own interpretation based on sound and experiential design aligns with some of the larger goals of art criticism in the twentieth century: it crafts a sonic experience that is accessible to a wide range of audiences (it does not require knowledge of form, structure, harmony, etc.) and encourages all sounds to be listened to as "music" or at least with similar attention and concentration.

"Wild Energy," an outdoor installation by Lockwood and Bob Bielecki, exhibits a combination of approaches to gathering its sonic materials: it utilizes natural sounds from the ultra and infra spectra, too low or too high to be heard by the human ear. Installed at the Caramoor Art Center's "Garden of Sonic Delights" (2014), Lockwood and Bielecki took inspiration from the surrounding wooded area and its life cycle. By either speeding up very low-frequency (VLF) sounds or slowing down radio waves into the human auditory spectrum, they craft a sonic representation of the many energies that make life. Their sound samples range from solar oscillations (sped up 42,000 times), Whistlers (VLF magnetic waves caused by lightening), and the subsonic rumbles of earthquakes, to ultrasounds from the interiors of trees, sonar signals from bats, the calls of the endangered Sei whale, and auroral kilometric radiation (responsible for the northern lights). By piecing these sounds together into a fifty-minute loop played through speakers situated in a wooded area, "Wild Energy" invites the listener into a sound world that is otherwise inaudible.[26] Along with the scientific virtuosity and ingenuity exhibited by the numerous researchers who gave Lockwood and Bielecki permission to use their recordings, the work assembles an aural journey through interconnected life on earth. The sounds of the sun begin a journey through time and space leading to the earth's Van Allen Belt, the upper atmosphere, plant and animal life, and down to the earth's core. The artists invite experiencers, who on a good day are surrounded by sunshine, flora, and fauna, to experience life as a process that begins eight light minutes away and continues nearly 2,000 miles below the surface.

By utilizing modern technology, "Wild Energy" renders selections from the world of inaudible vibration into a piece of sound art that offers the experiencer not only a perspective on the picturesque grounds of the Caramoor Art Center but also a novel way of engaging with sunlight, plant and animal life, and the ground on which they tread. In doing this, "Wild Energy" expands on ideas of transforming the consciousness of experiencers that animated 4'33", *Times Square*, and *The Great Animal Orchestra*. Lockwood and Bielecki also engage in an updated version of *musique concrete*, editing found sounds together into an artistic assemblage.

Crafting New Tools for Listening

Christina Kubisch's "Electrical Walks," which began in 2004, are based on a personal hearing technology developed from years of experimentation. Taking advantage of the many electromagnetic waves present in industrial society, Kubisch designed a pair of headphones that interact with electromagnetic waves from everyday sources like ATMs, lighting systems, wireless internet, cell phones, surveillance systems, and so forth. By wearing these headphones, experiencers hear the spaces they traverse differently. Everyday sights are recoded into sounds that shift as wearer walks. Although a general map of the city with points of sonic interest is provided for each city, the wearer's own movements are free, and Kubisch points out that each participant becomes a co-composer through motion.[27] By creating unique listening technologies, Kubisch gives listeners a new way of experiencing space: enabling them to hear a variety of constantly present but inaudible manmade sounds that are connected to technologies that we often think of as silent. Kubisch's works also remind us of the vast and ubiquitous technologies that surround us and impact our lives, often without our explicit consent.

Music from Outer Space

New and more sensitive technologies enable sound artists to seek more and more distant vibrational sources and inaudible vibration as raw material.

When combined with advanced algorithms, these tools take ideas that began in the 1960s and push them into new territories. A compelling contemporary example is *VLBI Music* (2013) by Norwegian composer Oyvind Brandtsegg. In a complex set of computational processes, *VLBI Music* (standing for Very Long Baseline Interferometry) is a process used in intricate mapping processes that allow for satellite and global positioning systems to function accurately. Using pairs of telescopes, radio noise from two telescopes aimed at the same distant quasar (approximately a billion light years away) is compared and filtered (the noise to signal ratio is 1000:1) to make precise measurements of distance. Shared data from global radio telescopes is then sent to the Max Planck Institute for Radio Astronomy in Bonn, Germany, for processing.[28]

Using the data from Bonn, Brandtsegg designed a computer program using Csound and Python to turn the signal data into audible sound. The programs mapped frequencies onto pitches and used telescope location to situate pitches within the auditory field. He also designed a clock feature, which syncs different signals, making them speed up to slow down depending on the signal. *VLBI Music* was designed as a continuous signal, as the information gathered at Max Planck is continuous.[29] This can be heard on either the web page livestream or app.[30] The app also features a visual display that uses the generated sounds as data.

The installation of the physical work was done in the offices of the Norwegian Mapping Authority. The building contains a glassed-in walkway that connects the larger main building to a smaller building. The sound is connected to a twelve-channel system that transmits vibration onto individual glass panes on either side of the walkway, turning the architecture itself into speakers that project sound both into the walkway and out into the exterior. This gives the composition a sense of space, separating sounds and making the clocking function more obvious, as well as integrating the installation into the architecture. Movement through the space, either the walkway or the courtyard below, also changes the experience of the sounds.

In his 2014 TEDx talk, Brandtsegg makes an interesting observation about his work and how he interprets its meaning and message. He frames *VLBI Music* as a way of gaining new perspective.[31] This follows a long trajectory of auditory theory: R. Murray Schafer's advocacy for a more distinct understanding of the sonic environment, John Cage's desire for his audiences to learn to hear everyday sound in a new way, Bernie Krause and Annea Lockwood's environmental hearings, Hildegard Westerkamp's soundwalks, Christina Kubisch's electrical walks, and others. The politics of embodiment and sustained alteration in perception have been an undercurrent in sound art, and in the arts in general. Brandtsegg's *VLBI Music* offers an update to this, locating the human experience within the massive expanse of the cosmos and within unfathomable stretches of time and space. If Max Neuhaus advocated for his works to let listeners locate themselves in their own time, *VLBI Music* locates listeners in cosmic time, a concept so vast that it begs us to rethink our existence.

Conclusion

As we can see from these few diverse examples from the field of sound art, there are conceptual, material, and aesthetic threads that tie some works together, but there are just as many divergences as there are similarities. As important to grasping some of the larger debates about sound art is understanding its criticisms and limitations—that the term is too broad, that it is simply a cover for contemporary music or performance art, or that the pairing of the sonic and plastic arts has a history that dates back millennia rather than being a recent genre. Some of the critical ideas that animated sound art's rise to an established canon in the postwar years—accessibility, audience, critique of everyday life, transparency of process, cultivation of awareness, and environmentalism—are still relevant to the present. Just like other arts, sound art has been profoundly transformed by innovation: new sound-capture and playback technology, new architecture, new building and sounding techniques, and new critiques. While contemporary artists continue to grapple with the possibilities of making art that is meaningful in light of contemporary political and aesthetic issues, it is intriguing to consider how multimedia arts can continue to challenge assumptions, make aesthetic experience relevant to a broadening and more diverse audience, or can bring newer and more nuanced critiques into the sphere or art, art making, and social life.

In-class Exercises

1 Discuss with the class or in small groups what sounds (music or otherwise) have transformed your perception or your senses of time, space, and place? How or why?

2 What artistic hierarchies exist at your institution, in your neighborhood, or in places where you have lived? How do they affect your concept of art, appropriateness, place, and space?

3   Do a 4'33" listening practice before class—go to a place on campus or near home and sit quietly for 4'33", observing the sounds that you hear. Document your experience. Come to class and discuss the exercise, how were each of your experiences similar and different?

Project I: (group)

Prompt: In small groups, design a sonic installation that is meant to be experienced by a single individual. The project can be executed on one or more laptops, tablets, or cell phones and can contain visual information or not (the option for a "hidden" sound source is valid, or the use of wireless earphones connected by Bluetooth).
The experience should be at least 1:00 in length, not more than 5:00.
Your experience can also contain other sensory material (visual, tactile, olfactory) but must be able to be installed in a classroom (or other available space).
For this experience, you can create new sound, capture, manipulate, loop, and edit new sounds. The same is applied for visual materials.
Write a one- to two-page curatorial statement on the genesis of the project, the process of creating it, and your purpose in creating it; that is, what do you want an observer to gain from this project?
Have a class installation and discussion about the projects.

Project II: (group/individual)

Prompt: Using Pauline Oliveros's *Sonic Meditations*, or *Deep Listening*, gather in a small group and go through several of the exercises. Document your experiences doing this.
Step 2: Design your own sonic meditation or Deep Listening exercise. Include the experience you want the practitioner to have.
Step 3: Walk the class, or a small group from the class, through your exercise. Have them talk about what they experienced. Compare their experiences to what you hoped they would have. How do they compare?
Step 4: Write a short paper about the experience.

Project III: (individual)

Prompt: Choose an existing work of art (or interesting public display) that is local.

Step 2: Design a sonic element of three to ten minutes to accompany the display, but add a new dimension to the meaning of the work (option: write curatorial notes). This display can be designed for speakers or for private listening (as is the case with guided tours in many museums).

Step 3: Display your work, and have members of your class experience your work.

Step 4: Discuss with the class your intentions and their interpretations.

Notes

1. LaBelle, *Background Noise*, Ch. 5.
2. See Vivian Van Saanze, *Installation Art and the Museum*, 17–21.
3. Photos show that the rooms in which the exhibit was installed vary substantially.
4. Since its inception, "From Hear to Ear" has been installed in a number of spaces, the vast majority of them art spaces, such as Copenhagen Contemporary, Musée des Beaux-Arts de Montréal, Palais de Tokyo in Paris, the Barbican Art Gallery in London, Yverdon-Les-Baines Center D'Art Contemporain in Switzerland, and the Venice Biennale.
5. Listen to the IMPREC podcast, episode 6, "The Cassauna Episode," for a sampler of Cassauna's oeuvre. https://soundcloud.com/importantrecords/podcassauna-mixdown.
6. Dennis and Powell, "Futurism."
7. Apollonio, *Futurist Manifestoes*; Black.
8. The figure of Luigi Russolo hangs heavy over John Cage; however, other futurist notions, like turning the academy into a corporate space, which reflected their veneration of the factory and industrial models, and an embrace of fascism, were directly opposed to the ideas of postwar artists following fascism's destruction of Europe and Asia.
9. Paul Griffiths, "Edgard Varese." *Grove Music Online*. 2001. https://doi-org.libproxy.vassar.edu/10.1093/gmo/9781561592630.article.29042.
10. https://maverickconcerts.org/history/.
11. Hermes, "The Story of 4'33"."
12. https://maverickconcerts.org/history/.
13. Quoted in Sexton, *Music, Sound and Multimedia*.
14. Labelle, 88.

15 Ibid., 91, 97.
16 Mallet and Darmon, 2006.
17 Feld and Brenneis, "Doing Anthropology in Sound," 461–74; Krause, *The Great Animal Orchestra*. Also see, Hillman, "Nature's Orchestra: Sounds of Our Changing Planet."
18 Neuhaus, in Kelly, 2011.
19 Quoted in LaBelle, *Background Noise*, 147.
20 British Library; Colin Schultz.
21 Science Museum Group.
22 Krause, *The Great Animal Orchestra*; Krause, *Wild Soundscapes*.
23 Westerkamp, "Kits Beach Soundwalk (1989)."
24 Oliveros, *Sonic Meditations*. Smith Publications, 1971, 1.
25 Ibid., 2.
26 gardenofsonicdelights.org.
27 https://vimeo.com/54846163.
28 https://www.researchcatalogue.net/view/55360/55361.
29 Ibid.
30 http://85.252.0.77:8000/stream/1/.
31 https://www.youtube.com/watch?v=aBEGnLtVk64.

Bibliography

Apollonio, Umbro. *Futurist Manifestoes*. Boston: MFA Publications, 1973.
Brandtsegg, Øyvind. "VLBI Music." *Research Catalogue* (2020). https://www.researchcatalogue.net/view/55360/55361/0/0 (accessed August 15, 2020).
Cage, John. *Silence*. Middletown, CT: Wesleyan University Press, 1973.
Darmon, Eric and Franck Mallet. *Pierre Henry: The Art of Sounds*. Memoire Magnetique, 2006.
Dennis, Flora, and Jonathan Powell. "Futurism." *Grove Music Online*, edited by Deane Root. www-oxfordmusiconline-com (accessed October 2, 2021).
Elwes, Catherine. *Installation and the Moving Image*. New York: Columbia University Press, 2015.
Feld, Steven, and Donald Brenneis. "Doing Anthropology in Sound." *American Ethnologist* 31, no. 4 (2004): 461–74.
Hermes, Will. "The Story of 4'33"." May 8, 2000. *NPR.org*. https://www.npr.org/2000/05/08/1073885/4-33.
Hillman, Robert. "Nature's Orchestra: Sounds of Our Changing Planet." The Video Project, 2015.
Kahn, Douglas. "The Arts of Sound Art and Music." *Iowa Review* 8, no. 1 (2006): 1–11.

Kahn, Douglas. *Noise Water Meat: A History of Sound in the Arts.* Cambridge: MIT Press, 1999.

Kassabian, Anahid. *Ubiquitous Listening: Affect, Attention and Distributed Subjectivity.* Berkeley: University of California Press, 2013.

Kelly, Caleb, ed. *Sound: Documents of Contemporary Art.* Cambridge: MIT Press, 2011.

Kostelanetz, Richard, ed. *John Cage, Writer: Selected Texts.* New York: Cooper Square Press, 2000.

Krause, Bernie. *The Great Animal Orchestra: Finding the Origins of Music in the World's Wild Places.* Boston: Little, Brown, 2012.

Krause, Bernie. *Wild Soundscapes: Discovering the Voice of the Natural World.* Berkeley: Wilderness Press, 2002.

Labelle, Brandon. *Background Noise: Perspectives on Sound Art.* 2nd ed. New York: Bloomsbury, 2015.

Licht, Alan. "Sound Art: Origins, Development and Ambiguities." *Organised Sound* 14, no. 1 (2009): 3–10.

McCormack, Ryan. *The Sculpted Ear: Aurality and Statuary in the West.* College Park: Penn State Press, 2020.

Moore, Stephan. *In the Garden of Sonic Delights: Exhibition Catalogue.* Katonah, NY: Caramoor Center for Music and the Arts, 2014.

Russolo, L., and F. Pratella. *The Art of Noise: Destruction of Music by Futurist Machines.* Edited by Candice Black. Sun Vision Press, 2012.

Schaefer, R. Murray. *The Soundscape: Our Sonic Environment and the Tuning of the World.* Rochester, VT: Destiny Books, 1994.

Schultz, Colin. "Let Wildlife Recordings from the 1930s Take You Back to Nature." Smithsonianmag.com. (accessed December 4, 2014)

Sexton, Jamie. *Music, Sound and Multimedia: From the Live to the Virtual.* Edinburgh: Edinburgh University Press, 2007.

Westerkamp, Hildegard. "Kits Beach Soundwalk (1989)." *On Transformations. Empreintes Digitales, IMED* 9631 (1996).

Recommended Further Reading

Chion, Michael. *Film: A Sound Art.* New York: Columbia University Press, 2009.

Cox, Christoph. *Sonic Flux: Sound, Art, and Metaphysics.* Chicago: University of Chicago Press, 2018.

Duhautpas, Frédérick, and Makis Solomos. "Hildegard Westerkamp and the Ecology of Sound as Experience. Notes on Beneath the Forest Floor." *Soundscape: The Journal of Acoustic Ecology* 13 (2014): 3–10.

Eidsheim, Nina S. *Sensing Sound: Singing and Listening as Vibrational Practice.* Durham, NC: Duke University Press, 2015.

Gilmurray, Jonathan. "Ecological Sound Art: Steps towards a New Field." *Organised Sound* 22, no. 1 (2017): 32.

Graham, Stephen. *Sounds of the Underground: A Cultural, Political and Aesthetic Mapping of Underground and Fringe Music.* Ann Arbor: University of Michigan Press, 2017.

Kelly, Caleb. *Gallery Sound.* New York: Bloomsbury, 2011.

Masaoka, Miya, and Miki Kaneda. "Listening Histories: Miya Masaoka in Conversation with Miki Kaneda." *ASAP Journal* 4, no. 1 (2019): 58–70.
Nakagawa, Katsushi, and Tomotaro Kaneko. "A Documentation of Sound Art in Japan: Sound Garden (1987–1994) and the Sound Art Exhibitions of 1980s Japan." *Leonardo Music Journal* 27 (2017): 82–6.
Oliveros, Pauline. *Sonic Meditations*. Sharon, VT.: Smith Publications, 1971.
Robinson, Dylan. *Hungry Listening: Resonant Theory for Indigenous Sound Studies*. Minneapolis: University of Minnesota Press, 2020.
Van Saanze, Vivian. *Installation Art and the Museum: Presentation and Conservation of Changing Artworks*. Amsterdam: Amsterdam University Press, 2013.
Wells, Karen, and Ain Bailey. "Sound Art and the Making of Public Space." *Social & Cultural Geography* 21, no. 8 (2020): 1083–102.
Westerkamp, Hildegard. "Linking Soundscape Composition and Acoustic Ecology." *Organised Sound* 7, no. 1 (2002): 51–6.

Concluding Project: Putting the Pieces Together through Audio Narratives

This short journey into sound studies illustrates only a fraction of the numerous questions, topics of investigation, and experimental techniques that sound studies engages. There are many other fields and methods that examine sound and its effects, histories, philosophies, and materiality. These involve everything from philosophical investigations to empirical studies that use sophisticated radio telescopes and other hypersensitive electronic equipment, to medical and healing practices. We encourage you to continue your studies of sound in its many forms however you encounter it. As a way of engaging the previous exercises holistically, your final exercise will be to create an audio narrative that makes use of the critical and technical skills honed through earlier chapters.

Concluding Exercise: Putting the Pieces Together through Audio Narrative

Audio narratives are having a renaissance in the digital age through podcasts of every variety. The form has roots in radio plays, narrative records, and books on tape and is facilitated by improved audio recording and processing technology and digital distribution. The audio narrative as a form employs all the different parts of sound that this text has investigated: sound design, soundscape, the voice, sound art, use of nonmusical sound, audio production or sound engineering, and the translation of text, idea, and emotion into sound. This exercise is a blank auditory canvas: as a genuinely new endeavor, nothing is pre-arranged, and each sound is an aesthetic and a pragmatic decision by its creators. Anything can be a topic, and sounds can be added, subtracted, edited, or modified as the creator or creators desire. For this exercise, be hyper-conscious of the decisions that you are making and why—every choice has an effect on the following sounds and alters how the listener will perceive your work.

Prompt

Step 1. Create a three- to four-minute audio narrative, complete with sonic scoring, that uses more than one voice (or vocal texture).

Step 2. Write a short essay about your creative process, outlining the choices made in selection of topic, choice of narrator, quality of the voice, and use of sounds as creative and informative tools. For clarity, include time stamps and a bibliography that indicates where sounds are from, any musical selections (pre-existing or new), and the roles that each participant played (voices, director, engineer, producer, editor).

Steps

Select a Topic for an Audio Narrative

This can take many forms: a monologue or exchange from a stage play, a short story (e.g., a short story from *Brevity*), a parable, a character piece, an interview (with a real or fictitious character), a new scripted dialogue, or a short piece of audio journalism. Make sure that your choice has a distinct narrative arc that allows for development. Remember that even thirty-second advertisements have narrative arcs that are augmented and clarified through sound.

Think of yourself as a producer: ask, who is my audience, why am I choosing this narrative, and what do I want my audience to get out of this experience? What story do you feel passionate about telling, and why? What would your audience gain from hearing this? Which narrators would your audience respond to (including nonhuman narrators, real or imagined)? What are your audience's basic audio references, and how can these be utilized in your audio assemblages?

Once you have answered these fundamental questions, start to systematically assemble the pieces.

Each of these narrative possibilities has different audio conventions and variations. For example, adaptations of stage plays typically use an audio mix that gives a sense of physical space in the voices rather than employing the breathy intimacy more typical of contemporary first-person podcasts, or the varying sonic depths of investigative journalism, which often uses voiceover to contrast the in-the-field sound of interviews.

After settling on your chosen narrative, listen to similar examples from related genres, and note which sonic conventions work and which you find to be less effective. Consider how much you want to challenge your listener. If you chose a well-known piece, like a Shakespeare soliloquy or a familiar poem, that would allow you to experiment with interpretation and meaning. For example, using an unexpected or varying vocal texture, a vocoder, or creating a dialogue out of a monologue is more creatively effective with a text that has deep pre-existing associations. If you are introducing your audience to a new work, there are different decisions in terms of setting the space, choosing the narrator, and creating an auditory world that best matches your idea and concept.

Sound and soundscapes are often employed to create a sense of time and place, to help the listener orient to the setting of the story, or to reorient them when the location of the story changes. This sound palette can range from diegetic sounds, like a cityscape, the ocean, a busy office, or cooking in a kitchen, to music that is readily identified with a time period, event or geography, and sounds that are evocative of imaginary spaces like outer space, the future, or prehistoric times. Easy examples include swing jazz for the United States in the 1920s, Conjunto or banda music for the US-Mexico borderlands, samba for *carnival* in Rio de Janeiro, or clicks and pops bathed in deep reverb and echo for outer space. Keep in mind that auditory memory is flexible and that connotations are not universal. Some uses of music to set a sense of time and space might need clarification to be fully understood. Carefully think through your interplay of narrative, music, and desired effect. You can also allow for this experience to be experimental, as we saw with some sound artworks. For example, the addition of a low drone underneath a narrative may have different effects for listeners; this may be desirable and create different experiences rather than aiming for a fixed interpretation.

Auditory effects can help to move narratives along and give additional meaning to characters and actions. They can also be used in lieu of text, to keep the narration focused.

For example, if a character travels, the sound of an airplane, car, or train can provide additional information or can streamline the text. Auditory effects can also heighten the listener's engagement. Adding footfalls, snoring, or dogs barking underneath a narrative brings the listener into the story; just be careful not to overload the listener and to balance narrative and sound effect. This goes for the use of music as well. We are drawn to and habituated to music score underneath advertising, film, television, and podcasts. Be aware that music is information that carries connotations and associations that may run counter to your narrative for some listeners. Music is also an auditory distraction when it is too active or too forward in the mix. Be aware of the space in your mix and of how different sounds take precedent with listeners. This is something to think about with the stereo field: where sound comes from adds to the narrative. Moving sounds in space can have a powerful effect on the listener.

Finally, consider how you will collect your auditory information. Who will your narrators, actors, or interviewees be? Why? How will you capture and edit their voices? How will their voices be mixed, EQ'd, and processed? How will you make use of the stereo field? Do you want the voices to sound natural or manipulated, close or distant? Will the voices be consistent, or will they change over the course of your narrative? Are you informing or taking your audience on a journey?

Think through these different questions before proceeding, and be free to revisit them as you begin assembling and editing your narrative.

Make an Auditory Plan

Beginning with the script on the page, carefully plan your soundscape. Consider: What sense of time and space do you want to give the listener? How long will this take to be established? Will you open with voice, sound, music, or a combination? The first few seconds are important in setting the tone. Does the listener need to be reoriented at any time in your piece, or is it set in one time/space/place? If you need to reorient, how will that transition take place? What diegetic sounds will enter and when? Will they be spaced before, during, or after the narrative? What is the nature of the interplay between your

CONCLUDING PROJECT

voices and added sounds? Are the sounds characters or added to color the text?

An effective way to do this is by mapping sound onto a printed copy of your script (think about this as similar to a stage play with staging directions in it). This can also be done with graph paper in a way that helps to visualize time as well as sound on the page. This approach can also help narrators to think about the pacing of their voice and to put pauses in places that accommodate added sound, making the sound editing less difficult. This is important to consider if sound effects like echo and reverb, which lengthen the duration of the sound, are to be added in post-production.

Record and Edit

Using hardware and a software program that you are comfortable with, record the sounds one at a time. Begin with the narrative. If you are making an interview-like podcast or doing audio journalism, record more material than just three minutes. While strategies vary, a simple equation is that every one minute of sound represents a minimum of eight to ten minutes of recording. A short piece needs to be concise, and often interviews take time to unfold, which will require a lot of recording before the meaningful and interesting pieces are captured. Voiceovers, monologues, or dialogues should be recorded several times in their entirety and compared for nuance, precision, and feel. Remember to record several seconds of ambient "room sound" wherever you record and keep it catalogued for use in your editing process—you can later insert it into conversational or sonic breaks to maintain auditory continuity in the editing process.

Experiment with microphone distances and recording apps (if you are using a cell phone as your primary hardware). Each speaker uses their voice differently, so there are different ideal microphone distances. If you are using a phone, start with the phone's microphone positioned 4–6 inches below the chin and 6–8 inches away. Have them speak the same sentence several times, and experiment with moving the phone further away or closer to accommodate louder, softer, higher, or lower pitch voices. When testing for different audio samples, bring headphones to listen to playback. If possible, be conscious of your space, and record in rooms where the sound matches the ambience that you desire. Avoid recording in large rooms with hard surfaces, unless you want a lot of natural reverb. Scout your recording locations, and make short recordings to compare sound quality, reverb, and background noise.

In the editing process, start with more auditory space and edit the spaces out as desired. It is easier to edit out space than it is to insert space to change the pacing. This will also give you more space to work with auditory manipulation and adding sound effects and music cues. It may take some time to make dialogue or voiceovers that are edited together feel natural.

Post-Production

Add the necessary sound effects, balance and EQ voice, music, and sound effects; add effects like compression and reverb; and finalize your use of the stereo field. This is best done with headphones so that you experience the immediacy of your work without interference from the noises in your workspace. Make sure that your levels are consistent and that your sounds are balanced in volume and across the stereo dimensions.

Processing the voice is the most difficult task, since this is a centerpiece of a narrative. As we saw with sound design, sounds can be subtly layered to augment the meaning of the voice. For example, adding white noise or distortion to your voice signal can artificially age your sound, or give a sense of dread and foreboding. If you roll off the low end through EQ or a high pass filter, your voice can sound like an old AM broadcast. Reverb and echo can be used to give a sense of space or to give an ethereal quality to voiceover. Be sure to choose an aesthetic that fits with your narrative and the character you wish to portray. These can also change as your narration demands. However, always start with a good, clean, clear voice recording before processing it.

In assigning your sounds within the stereo field, decide where your narration starts from, and build out from there. Placing the voice in the center of the listener's ear is quite different from the voice starting off to one side, or a voice migrating (like an actor giving a monologue while crossing the stage). Moving the voice can be deployed to masterful effect, but too much movement can be disorienting. The same principle applies to sound effects. If they are meant to shift or alter auditory awareness, like the sound of a door opening or footsteps, these sounds can be augmented by utilizing space in the stereo field. If you are doing audio journalism with a generally static field, make sure to position your sounds so that there is a space for each one.

Optional Step

Provide a curatorial note for your work. In cases of sound art, as with the work of Hildegard Westerkamp, notes are part of the presentation. While not necessary, feel free to provide guidance to your listeners as needed. If you choose to provide curation, be succinct, your audio work is your centerpiece, and your curation is a modest guide to the listening experience.

Final Paper

Write a narrative about your artistic process, from your deliberations when choosing a topic to the finishing post-production touches that make your project sound unique. Be aware and transparent about your aesthetic choices, why and how you made them, and why your sonic models were your inspiration (either for or against particular choices). See how all the different parts of sound production, from conception to post-production, connect and interact in your work.

Author Biographies

Thomas Porcello is Professor of Anthropology at Vassar College and has held visiting teaching and research positions in the music departments at UC Berkeley, Duke University, Columbia University, and New York University. He is the co-editor of *Wired for Sound: Engineering and Technologies in Sonic Cultures* (2005), which was awarded the Klaus P. Wachsmann book prize by the Society for Ethnomusicology.

Justin Patch is Assistant Professor of Music at Vassar College. His work focuses on sound and US political campaigns. His most recent book, *Discordant Democracy: Noise, Affect, Populism and the Presidential Campaign* (2019), examines the sounds of the Obama and Trump presidential campaigns.

Index

A Star Is Born 10, 74–5, 82
acoustemology 8, 28–9, 37n.17, 69
acoustic ecolog, 158
Anderson, Benedict, 4
Apocalypse Now 11, 130
audiovisual contract 130–1

Barthes, Roland, 10, 95, 102–3, 111–12, 115, 157–9
Bijsterveld, Karin, 45, 48–9
biophony 158–9
Blacking, John 55–7
Bourdieu, Pierre 32, 37n.25, 38n.26
Brandtsegg, Oyvind 12, 164–5

Cage, John 12, 55–6, 146–7, 151–6, 159, 164
Carlyle, Thomas 41–2, 45–6
carnaval 11, 121–3, 125, 127
Chion, Michel 11, 128–30
consumer culture 8, 29
consumption 31–4, 37n.25
COVID-19 1–3, 29, 37n.16, 66

deep listening 147, 160–1
Derrida, Jacques 96
"Dream House" 145–50
Dreiser, Theodore 19–21, 23–4, 29–30

echo 19, 30–1, 132
Eidsheim, Nina Sun 67–9, 71, 74, 84n.9
Embodiment 99–100, 103, 164
ethnopoetics 10, 96–7

Feld, Steven 12, 23, 69
  on acoustemology 8, 28–9

soundscape recordings 151, 154–5, 157, 161
Voices in the Rainforest, 20–1
"From Hear to Ear" 148–50, 156, 167n.4
futurism
  aesthetics of noise 51–2, 55–6
  depicting sound in text 103, 107, 110–11
  technology as sound art 151, 154–5

Goodman, Steve 49

hearing loss 2, 9, 49, 137
"Hey Jude" 11, 133
Hymes, Dell 10, 96–100, 109

I-Ching, 153
intentional design 123, 125, 127–8, 131

Kapchan, Deborah 109–10
keynote sounds 25
Koch, Ludwig 157–8
Koch, Robert 46
Krause, Bernie 12, 151, 154–5, 157–9, 161, 164
Kubisch, Christina 163–4

language
  acoustemology and 8
  digital technology and 100–2
  evidenciality and 36n.11
  ideologies of 73, 85n.25, 121–2
  Kaluli use of 20, 29
  mediation and 27
  noise and 42
  orthography and 91–2

reality effect and 103
transcription as sound 95–100, 115
voice and 69–70, 83
"Let It Be" 11, 133–5
listening
  aesthetics of noise 53, 57
  audio-vision and film 11
  communities 96, 99
  during soundwalks 12, 158, 163
  gendered 66
  epistemological issues 28–9
  perception and 4
  "secondary object" and, 55
  to soundscapes 8, 21, 25–7, 35
  to sound art 147, 150, 152–3
  sound knowledge and 109
  structural 146
  technologically designed 123
Lockwood, Annea 12, 56, 151, 154, 157, 161–4
LRAD 9, 50–1

malls 8, 29–33, 37 n.16, 146
Marinetti, Filippo Tomaso 10–11, 51, 103–4, 107–11, 151
mediation 27–8, 107
metadiscourse 42–4
metaphor
  instrumental mix as 134
  noise as 43–4, 47
  reality effect and 102
  sound as 20, 53
  in sound writing 110
  voice and 75, 82
modernity 44–5, 47, 110–11, 146, 161
musique concrete 52, 55, 154–6, 158–60, 163
Muzak 31, 34, 37n.21

Neuhaus, Max 12, 155–7, 165
noise
  abatement of 23–4, 45–8
  anthropogenic 1
  automobiles and 126
  concept of 5, 9
  cosmic 164
  definitions of 43–4
  desirable 48–52

  in Japanese art music 53–4
  as metadiscourse 42
  philosophy of music and 54–7
  as pollution 23–4
  relation to soundscape 20, 29–30
  risks of exposure 2–3, 8
  sound systems and 53
  sound writing and 107–11
  urban experience of 41–2
  weaponization of 49–50

Ochoa Gautier, Ana Maria 6–7
Oliveros, Pauline 146–7, 149, 159–61
onomatopoeia
  birdsong and 29
  linguistic 70, 85n.18
  in sonic expression, 103, 108–9, 112–14
  writing and 96
orthography 10, 91, 96, 99, 110–11

Peirce, Charles Sanders 9, 70–1, 73
Poe, Edgar Allan 10, 103–6, 113–14

reality effect 10, 95, 102–3, 107, 112–13, 157–9
resonance 66, 71, 78, 156
Rice, Julia Barnett 45–6
Russolo, Luigi 51–2, 56, 151, 167n.8

sawari 53–4
Schafer, R. Murray
  on acoustic design 127–8
  on listening 8, 164
  noise ideal and 48, 122
  on soundscape 23–6, 28–9, 34–5
Schaffer, Pierre 52, 141n30
Schwartz, Hillel 42–3
Scott, James Victor 67–9, 84n9
Scruton, Roger 55–6, 61n48
senses 28, 103–4, 107, 129, 150
skeuomorphism 126–7
signal 26
signal-to-noise ratio 8, 24, 36n.7
somatic knowledge 27–8
soundmarks 25–6, 36n.10
soundscape
  acoustic designing of 127–8

consumerism and 29–34, 125
  definitions of 8, 23–6
  indoor constructions of 22–3
  Kaluli concept of 28–9
  literary creations of 95, 111–13
  lo-fi vs. hi-fi 24
  nature recordings as 157–60
  sambódromo and 122–3
  sound art and 151, 154–5
  urban vs. natural 19–21
soundwalks 158–60
sound art
  approaches to 145–9
  cosmic sources for 163–5
  critiques of 155–6
  deep listening and 160–1
  definition of 5, 11–12, 150
  futurist depictions of 151
  musical experiments with 152–5
  recordings as 131
  utilizing natural sounds 157–60, 161–2
  verbal transcription as 99
sound design
  audio recordings and 131–5
  automobiles and 125–7
  carnaval 121–3
  cinema and, 79, 128–31
  definition of 5, 11, 127–8
  resorts and 123–5
  restaurants and 135–8
  semiotics of 70
  soundscapes and 22
  video games and 131
  visual depictions using 111–15
sound studies
  discipline of ix–x, 4–8
  key concepts in 8–9
  resources in 11–13
  soundscape and 23–6, 35
  study of voice in 83

sound writing
  alphabetic 95
  definition of 110
  digital technology and 100–2
  issues of representation 20
  poetics of transcription and 97–100
  reality effect and 102
  reproduction of speech 96
  sound as presented in 107–11
Sterne, Jonathan 6, 8, 14, 31–3, 35
synchresis 11, 129–30

Takemitsu, Toru 54
Tedlock, Dennis 10–11, 98–100, 109–11

Varese, Edgar 52, 56, 151–2, 155
vibration 163
Victoria's Secret 8, 32–4, 126
voice
  agency and 69, 76, 78, 81
  artificial intelligence and 71–2, 78–82
  definition of 69–70
  in film 74–8, 86 n.34
  as gendered marker 65–8, 79
  graphical depictions of 111–12
  linguistic profiling and 72–3
  materialism and 70
  semiotics and 70–1
  social identity and 73–4
  soundscape and 19–20
  sound design of 129, 134–5
  textual representations of 95–6, 105–7
  timbre of 68–9, 84n.6
  utilization of concept 5, 9–10

Westerkamp, Hildegard 159–60, 164

Zang Tumb Tumb 11, 108–9